DEMOCRATIC INNOVATIONS

Can we design institutions that increase and deepen citizen participation in the political decision-making process? At a time when there is growing disillusionment with the institutions of advanced industrial democracies, there is also increasing interest in new ways of involving citizens in the political decisions that affect their lives. This book draws together evidence from a variety of democratic innovations from around the world, including participatory budgeting in Brazil, Citizens' Assemblies on Electoral Reform in Canada, direct legislation in California and Switzerland and emerging experiments in e-democracy. The book offers a rare systematic analysis of this diverse range of democratic innovations, drawing lessons for the future development of both democratic theory and practice.

GRAHAM SMITH is Professor of Politics in the Centre for Citizenship, Globalisation and Governance at the University of Southampton.

D0723525

THEORIES OF INSTITUTIONAL DESIGN

Series Editor
Robert E. Goodin
Research School of Social Sciences
Australian National University

Advisory Editors
Brian Barry, Russell Hardin, Carole Pateman, Barry Weingast
Stephen Elkin, Claus Offe, Susan Rose-Ackerman

Social scientists have rediscovered institutions. They have been increasingly concerned with the myriad ways in which social and political institutions shape the patterns of individual interactions which produce social phenomena. They are equally concerned with the ways in which those institutions emerge from such interactions.

This series is devoted to the exploration of the more normative aspects of these issues. What makes one set of institutions better than another? How, if at all, might we move from the less desirable set of institutions to a more desirable set? Alongside the questions of what institutions we would design, if we were designing them afresh, are pragmatic questions of how we can best get from here to there: from our present institutions to new revitalised ones.

Theories of institutional design is insistently multidisciplinary and interdisciplinary, both in the institutions on which it focuses, and in the methodologies used to study them. There are interesting sociological questions to be asked about legal institutions, interesting legal questions to be asked about economic institutions, and interesting social, economic, and legal questions to be asked about political institutions. By juxtaposing these approaches in print, this series aims to enrich normative discourse surrounding important issues of designing and redesigning, shaping and reshaping the social, political, and economic institutions of contemporary society.

Other books in the series

Brent Fisse and John Braithwaite, *Corporations, Crime and Accountability*
Robert E. Goodin (editor), *The Theory of Institutional Design*
Itai Sened, *The Political Institution of Private Property*
Mark Bovens, *The Quest for Responsibility: Accountability and Citizenship in Complex Organisations*
Bo Rothstein, *Just Institutions Matter: The Moral and Political Logic of the Universal Welfare State*
Jon Elster, Claus Offe, and Ulrich K. Preuss, *Institutional Design in Post-Communist Societies: Rebuilding the Ship at Sea*
Adrienne Héritier, *Policy-Making and Diversity in Europe: Escape from Deadlock*
Geoffrey Brennan and Alan Hamlin, *Democratic Devices and Desires*
Eric M. Patashnik, *Putting Trust in the US Budget: Federal Trust Funds and the Politics of Commitment*
Benjamin Reilly, *Democracy in Divided Societies: Electoral Engineering for Conflict Management*
John S. Dryzek and Leslie Templeman Holmes, *Post-Communist Democratization: Political Discourses Across Thirteen Countries*
Huib Pellikaan and Robert J. van der Veen, *Environmental Dilemmas and Policy Design*
Maarten A. Hajer and Hendrik Wagenaar (editors), *Deliberative Policy Analysis: Understanding Governance in the Network Society*
Jürg Steiner, André Bächtiger, Markus Spörndli and Marco R. Steenbergen, *Deliberative Politics in Action: Analyzing Parliamentary Discourse*
Bo Rothstein, *Social Traps and the Problem of Trust*
Jonathan G. S. Koppell, *The Politics of Quasi-Government: Hybrid Organizations and the Dynamics of Bureaucratic Control*
Mark E. Warren and Hilary Pearse (editors), *Designing Deliberative Democracy: The British Columbia Citizens Assembly*

DEMOCRATIC INNOVATIONS

Designing institutions for citizen participation

GRAHAM SMITH

Professor of Politics
University of Southampton

CAMBRIDGE
UNIVERSITY PRESS

CAMBRIDGE UNIVERSITY PRESS

Cambridge, New York, Melbourne, Madrid, Cape Town, Singapore, São Paulo, Delhi

Cambridge University Press
The Edinburgh Building, Cambridge CB2 8RU, UK

Published in the United States of America by Cambridge University Press, New York

www.cambridge.org
Information on this title: www.cambridge.org/9780521514774

First published 2009

Printed in the United Kingdom at the University Press, Cambridge

A catalogue record for this publication is available from the British Library

Library of Congress Cataloguing in Publication data
Smith, Graham, 1966–
    Democratic innovations : designing institutions for citizen participation / Graham Smith.
      p.   cm. – (Theories of institutional design)
    Includes bibliographical references and index.
    ISBN 978-0-521-51477-4 (hardback) – ISBN 978-0-521-73070-9 (pbk.)
    1. Political participation.   2. Direct democracy.   3. Legislation–Citizen participation.
    4. Budget–Citizen participation.   5. Internet–Political aspects.   I. Title.   II. Series.
    JF799.G653 2009
    323'.042–dc22   2009016996

ISBN 978-0-521-51477-4 hardback
ISBN 978-0-521-73070-9 paperback

To my parents

Contents

Acknowledgments

This book would probably not exist if Adam Lent had not commissioned me to write a report on democratic innovations for the Power Inquiry. His perceptive promptings and suggestions helped shape the content of *Beyond the Ballot*. The report seemed to catch academic and policy-makers' imagination and the response convinced me that a more considered reflection on democratic innovations was timely.

My ideas have been shaped by discussions with numerous colleagues and students over the past few years, too numerous to thank. I would, however, like to express my gratitude to those individuals who have been willing to read and comment on one or more of the chapters: Chris Armstrong, Ken Carty, Archon Fung, Andrew Mason, David Owen, John Parkinson, Ben Saunders, Mike Saward, Susan Stephenson, Julien Talpin, Corinne Wales, Mark Warren and the anonymous readers from Cambridge University Press.

I wish to express my warmest thanks to Susan Stephenson and David Owen. Susan and I have shared our lives for almost two decades now and her passion – emotional, spiritual and intellectual – has been a source of great joy in my life. David is a rare colleague. He has read all of the chapters at least once – as well as chapters that were eventually ditched – and I thank him for his friendship, generosity and belief in my work.

I would like to thank my supportive department at the University of Southampton for the sabbatical that allowed me to start writing this book and the Arts and Humanities Research Council for granting me a Research Leave Award which provided a further semester of study leave. I would also like to thank Sarum College for generously providing a quiet place to hide away to write when needed and John Haslam at Cambridge

University Press for being a great editor and supporting the right football team.

Finally, I would like to dedicate this book to my parents, Alan and Olive Smith. During the writing of this book they were both taken seriously ill. I was fortunate to be on sabbatical and able to spend valuable time with them and the rest of my family during their recoveries. Thankfully they are now well again. Their health is more important to me than any manuscript.

Introduction

Since 1989, ever-increasing numbers of citizens have taken part in budgetary decision-making in the Brazilian city of Porto Alegre. By 2001 an impressive 16,600 citizens were participating in the annual popular assemblies held across the city. Their initial participation eventually culminated in decisions about the distribution of a significant element of the municipal budget, with a substantial proportion destined for investments in poor neighbourhoods. The following year, the process began again. At the other end of the Americas, in December 2004 after 11 months of deliberation, an assembly of 160 randomly selected citizens delivered a report recommending changes to British Columbia's electoral system. The following year, their recommendation was put to a binding popular vote. And, again in 2004, citizens in 37 states across the United States voted on 162 propositions, almost a half of which were proposals that originated from within civil society rather than the legislature or executive. Some 68 per cent of these propositions were approved by citizens and have or will become law.

Participatory budgeting, the Citizens' Assembly on Electoral Reform and direct legislation are three examples of what we will term 'democratic innovations': *institutions that have been specifically designed to increase and deepen citizen participation in the political decision-making process.* They are democratic innovations in the sense that they represent a departure from the traditional institutional architecture that we normally attribute to advanced industrial democracies. They take us beyond familiar institutionalised forms of citizen participation such as competitive elections and consultation mechanisms such as community meetings, opinion polling and focus groups. Some innovations have a long heritage and have become

1

established institutions in a small number of polities – for example direct legislation in Switzerland and some states in the United States. Others, such as the Citizens' Assembly and participatory budgeting, are more recent developments. All of them are representative of a growing and widespread interest in finding new ways of engaging citizens in the political decision-making process, and it is the aim of this book to offer an evaluation of the democratic potential of these different institutional designs.

In defining 'democratic innovations', we need to stress two aspects of their design. First, these institutions directly engage *citizens*. Many participatory mechanisms are designed to engage individuals who represent organised groups within society – such institutions include stakeholder and corporatist designs. Organised groups and their representatives play a significant role in democratic polities, but we are interested here in whether institutions can be designed to directly engage what have been termed 'lay' or 'non-partisan' citizens, as opposed to experts and partisan campaigners. This difference is not watertight. Experts and partisans are also citizens. However, there is a compelling analytical distinction in operation here. We are interested in democratic institutions that engage citizens because they are citizens, rather than because they claim expert authority or are the representatives of an organised group within society. But even then, there is further ambiguity with the term 'citizen'. Not all individuals who are affected by a particular issue or who have the right to participate in a democratic innovation will necessarily be citizens in the legal sense: this will depend upon the design of the innovation (in particular its selection mechanism). For simplicity's sake we will use the term 'citizen participation' in our discussions of democratic innovations, while recognising the limits of this particular formulation.

Second, we are interested in *institutionalised* forms of participation in political decision-making at strategic levels – democratic devices that provide citizens with a formal role in policy, legislative or constitutional decision-making. It is important to state this clearly and unambiguously for three reasons. First, our interest is primarily in participation in decision-making *beyond* the local level. Arguments for radical decentralisation of power aside, most formal political decision-making power continues to be exercised across larger scales of political organisation. As such, we are concerned with the degree to which citizen participation can be institutionalised at the level of the city, the nation or the transnational/global. Second, democratic innovations aim to take us beyond traditional modes of institutionalised engagement, namely competitive elections and consultation exercises. We are interested in the extent to which participation can have direct influence on political decisions. Third, much of the work on participation in democratic theory tends to refer to more informal forms of citizen engagement in civil society and in confrontational and antagonistic relations with public authorities. Ricardo Blaug (2002), for example, draws a distinction between what he terms 'incumbent democracy' and 'critical democracy'. For Blaug, incumbent democracy 'seeks to improve, though at the same time to control, participatory input, by channelling, simplifying and rationalizing it through institutionalized conduits'. In comparison, critical democracy 'occurs within local and peripheral sites and involves resistance to elite governance. It is characterized by increased participation and empowerment, often on the part of people normally excluded from political activity' (Blaug 2002: 105–6).

> Incumbent democracy is primarily motivated to preserve and improve existing institutions by maximizing and managing orderly participation. Critical democracy seeks, instead, to resist such management and to empower excluded voices in such a way as to directly challenge existing institutions. (Blaug 2002: 107)

There are (at least) three comments to make on Blaug's observations that are pertinent to this study. First, whilst this book focuses on institutionalised forms of citizen participation, it does not argue that such democratic innovations are the only legitimate mode of political activity. A thriving democratic polity will entail a range of different modes of citizen engagement, from formal, institutionalised channels through to informal, independent forms of confrontational activity – incumbent and critical democracy. Second, rather than 'preserve and improve institutions', the innovations discussed in this book can challenge the existing institutional order, potentially weakening more established institutions of advanced industrial democracies. Third, Blaug's distinction is too stark in its representation of democratic practice and theorising. His definition of critical democracy embraces a politics that seeks to 'resist' the management tendencies of incumbent democracy and 'to empower excluded voices in such a way as to directly challenge existing institutions'. This assumes that such resistance and empowerment of the excluded is not possible within democratic innovations. As we shall see, many innovations are designed with such empowerment in mind. Blaug's distinction appears to close the door on the possibility that the type of innovations that we are investigating in this book might have critical impact. It will be an empirical question as to whether such 'managed' forms of participation are able to empower citizens, particularly citizens who are systematically disengaged from the political process.

Whatever the particular institutional form, democratic innovations in principle redraw the traditional division of political labour within representative systems, in particular by providing citizens with more influence in the political decision-making process. The aim of this book, then, is to investigate the way in which different innovations recast the nature of the relationship between citizens and political authorities and to explore the implications and consequences for democratic politics.

Why study democratic innovations?

There is growing evidence of public disillusionment with the institutions of advanced industrial democracies. The decline in electoral turnout, low levels of trust in politicians and political institutions and decline in membership of traditional mobilising organisations such as political parties and trade unions are just three expressions of the growing disconnection between citizens and decision-makers – the difference and distance between the subjectivity, motives and intentions of citizens and those who make decisions in their name (Barber 1984; Offe and Preuss 1991; Phillips 1995). Russell Dalton, a leading authority on political attitudes and behaviour, argues: 'By almost any measure, public confidence and trust in, and support for, politicians, political parties, and political institutions has eroded over the past generation' (Dalton 2004: 191).

This could be taken as a counsel of despair – a growing disillusionment with the 'democratic project'. However, analysts such as Dalton argue that there is evidence that behind these trends there remains a strong and significant commitment to democratic norms and values.

> Even though contemporary publics express decreasing confidence in democratic politicians, parties, and parliaments, these sentiments have not carried over to the democratic principles and goals of these regimes. Most people remain committed to the democratic ideal; if anything, these sentiments have apparently strengthened as satisfaction with the actuality of democratic politics has decreased. (Dalton 2004: 47)[1]

Embedding democratic innovations that increase and deepen citizen participation in political decision-making could thus be perceived as one strategy (amongst others) for re-engaging a disillusioned and disenchanted citizenry. As Dalton concludes:

> The public's democratic expectations place a priority on reforms that move beyond the traditional forms of representative democracy. Stronger parties, fairer elections, more representative electoral systems will improve the democratic process, but these reforms do not address expectations that the

---

[1] Matt Henn and his colleagues offer similar evidence of support for democracy but disenchantment with its current institutional expression amongst young people (Henn *et al.* 2005).

democratic process will expand to provide new opportunities for citizen input and control. (Dalton 2004: 204)

This emphasis on increasing participation is also a consistent theme within contemporary democratic theory. Over recent years a range of theoretical perspectives have emerged that emphasise increasing and deepening citizen participation in political decision-making. Examples include participatory democracy (Pateman 1970), deliberative democracy (Bohman 1998), direct democracy (Saward 1998), difference democracy (Young 1990) and cosmopolitan democracy (Held 1995). There are important differences in emphasis and, on occasion, substance between these different theoretical streams. Participatory democrats such as Carole Pateman tend to emphasise the intrinsic value of participation – its educative and developmental effect on citizens. Participation is a beneficial activity in its own right, increasing citizens' political efficacy and understanding of their own interests and political responsibilities (Parry 1972: 26–31). As Pateman famously argues:

> The major function of participation in the theory of participatory democracy is…an educative one, educative in the very widest sense, including both the psychological aspect and the gaining of practice of democratic skills and procedures…Participation develops and fosters the very qualities necessary for it; the more individuals participate the better able they become to do so. (Pateman 1970: 42–3)

Whilst the intrinsic value of participation remains an important consideration, contemporary theorists tend to focus more attention on instrumental arguments for increased citizen participation (Parry 1972: 19–26). The instrumental value of participation can rest on a range of arguments (often combined by theorists), for example: participation as the most effective defence against arbitrary power; the individual as the best judge of their own interests; the generation of better-informed decisions; or increased legitimacy and trustworthiness of political decisions. As the name suggests, deliberative democrats pay particular attention to the process by which decisions are made. For example, Amy Gutmann argues: 'the legitimate exercise of political authority requires justification to those people who are bound by it, and decision-making by deliberation among free and equal citizens is the most defensible justification anyone has to offer for provisionally settling controversial issues' (Gutmann 1996a: 344). In contrast, direct democrats emphasise the moment of decision: political legitimacy rests on the idea that 'all citizens have equal effective inputs into collective decision-making' (Saward 1998: 43). The particular contribution of difference democrats has been in drawing attention to the way which disadvantaged and oppressed social groups are marginalised or excluded from the political process. As Anne Phillips argues: 'when policies are worked out *for* rather than *with* a politically excluded constituency, they are unlikely to engage all relevant concerns' (Phillips 1995: 13). Thus judgements of political legitimacy rest on whether distinct voices and perspectives of these social groups are recognised and represented in political decision-making processes. Finally, cosmopolitan democracy is unashamedly global in its pretensions, questioning the degree to which the decisions of transnational political authorities can be deemed legitimate without the active consent and participation of affected populations.

While there are differences in emphasis, arguably the dominant current within contemporary democratic theory is one that places a premium on increasing and deepening citizen participation. We will have more to say about the continuities and discontinuities of democratic theories as the analysis in this book progresses. Much of the debate operates at a high level of abstraction. As such, this study of actually existing democratic innovations will provide a valuable occasion to investigate the extent to which the normative commitments of different democratic theories can be institutionalised. To what extent can different designs express theorists' democratic hopes and expectations?

Overview of the book

To develop an effective and systematic comparative analysis of democratic innovations with quite different design features, much rests on the analytical framework. Chapter 1 argues that the unfortunate disengagement between political science and democratic theory means that there is relatively little guidance on how to engage in theoretically informed analysis of innovative democratic practices. Rather than follow the deductive approach that tends to be favoured by those few democratic theorists who do engage in debates about institutional design, we instead offer an approach where innovations are evaluated according to the extent to which they realise goods of democratic institutions. The chapter offers a defence of the choice of six goods: inclusiveness, popular control, considered judgement, transparency, efficiency and transferability. The extent to which these goods are realised enables us to judge the democratic legitimacy and practical feasibility of innovations. The chapter ends by distinguishing four categories of innovations that are to be evaluated using this analytical framework.

Chapter 2 focuses on innovations that are based on open or popular assemblies. While there are a number of small-scale designs that are worthy of analysis – we focus particularly on New England town meetings and Chicago Community Policing – much of the chapter is devoted to the analysis of participatory budgeting as practised in Porto Alegre,

Brazil. In this innovation, large popular assemblies are integrated with representative bodies in a process where decisions are made about the distribution of significant elements of the city's budget.

Chapter 3 takes as its subject mini-publics: forums that are constituted by (near-) randomly selected citizens. While interest in the use of mini-publics has been growing over recent decades – for example, citizens' juries, consensus conferences and deliberative polling – a step-change in practice was witnessed by the establishment of the Citizens' Assembly on Electoral Reform that sat over eleven months in British Columbia. The 160-strong Assembly was charged with reviewing the province's electoral system.

Chapter 4 turns our attention to direct legislation: an institutional design with a long heritage in a limited number of advanced industrial democracies. Legislative referendum, popular referendum and the initiative differ from other forms of referendum because their decisions are binding rather than simply advisory. Popular referendum and the initiative also provide a mechanism for citizens to place propositions on the ballot.

The fourth empirical chapter, Chapter 5, takes a different tack, reviewing participatory developments in information and communication technology (ICT). Developments in e-democracy are still in their infancy and so the chapter draws lessons from a range of designs, including 21st Century Town Meetings, internet discussion forums, online deliberative polling and ICT-enabled direct legislation.

Chapter 6 and the Conclusion assess what can be learnt from a comparative analysis of these different types of democratic innovation. In what ways and to what degree do different designs realise the six institutional goods that form our analytical framework? What are the implications of the different combinations and weightings of goods? This comparative analysis will also offer insights into the sustainability of various claims of democratic theorists. In what sense can their ideas be realised in practice? To what extent can institutions be designed that create effective opportunities for citizen engagement?

1

Studying democratic innovations: an analytical framework

Until fairly recently, relatively little attention has been paid to the systematic evaluation of democratic innovations, and there is thus a dearth of systematic comparisons.[1] Why is this? Democratic theorists have proved to be strong on arguing the case for citizen participation, but, with a few notable exceptions, discussions have remained at a high level of abstraction – there has been a failure to systematically engage in the 'messy' and detailed task of institutional design. Perhaps our expectations of democratic theorists are too high and we need to recognise the division of labour within the discipline of politics: there are other scholars who (should) pick up this task of studying innovations. There is, for example, a formidable community of political scientists – such as Russell Dalton, whose work was discussed briefly in the Introduction – who study citizens' democratic attitudes and behaviour. However, they tend to focus on elections and other more familiar modes of political activity: democratic innovations are relatively marginal forms of democratic practice and typically fall below political scientists' radar.[2] As with democratic theorists, their studies often point towards the need to consider alternative modes of political engagement, but generally take us no further.

There would thus appear to be a gap in the discipline – a lack of concerted attention to theoretically informed, comparative studies of democratic innovations. This has exercised a number of democratic theorists. David

---

[1] One of the few attempts to compare different innovations is a survey article by Archon Fung (2003b).

[2] To be fair, Dalton has been involved in discussions of expanding opportunities for citizen participation, although there has been relatively little work on the type of developments evaluated in this book (see for example Cain *et al.* 2003).

Beetham goes as far as to suggest that this kind of gap can be explained by 'the disciplinary divorce within the academic study of politics, between normative theory and empirical political analysis, which has encouraged the separation of institutional accounts of democracy from any analysis of democracy's underlying principles, as if they belong to quite different worlds' (Beetham 1999: 29). Similarly, Ian Shapiro argues that there is an uncomfortable gap between normative theories 'that seek to justify democracy as a system of government' and explanatory theories 'that try to account for the dynamics of democratic systems'.

> Normative and explanatory theories of democracy grow out of literatures that proceed, for the most part, on separate tracks, largely uninformed by one another. This is unfortunate, partly because speculation about what ought to be is likely to be more useful when informed by relevant knowledge of what is feasible, and partly because explanatory theory too easily becomes banal and method-driven when isolated from the pressing normative concerns that have fuelled worldwide interest in democracy in recent decades. (Shapiro 2003: 2)

Finally, Archon Fung starkly contends: 'This division of labour has become a segregation of thought that now poses a fundamental obstacle to progress in democratic theory' (Fung 2007: 443). Democratic theorists may offer compelling explanations of the limits of existing democratic practice and strident arguments for increased and deepened citizen participation. But if we wish to evaluate the potential of different types of democratic innovations what approach should we take?

Whilst evaluations of democratic innovations tend to be rather patchy, there is a small but significant body of democratic theorists who have turned their attention to more detailed discussions of institutional design. There is one approach that tends to dominate this work, namely a search for institutions that best 'fit' or express the basic principles of a particular theoretical model of democracy. Examples include the defence of the citizen initiative and referendum as the expression of political equality and responsive rule amongst direct democrats (Budge 1996; Saward 1998); citizens' juries and deliberative opinion polls as the institutional realisation of the principles of deliberative democracy (Fishkin 1997; Smith and Wales 2000); gender quotas or group representation as a way of enacting the politics of presence/difference (Phillips 1995; Young 1990).

These examples reflect what Michael Saward takes to be the dominant *deductive* approach to institutional questions within democratic theory: democratic principles can be 'deduced from a deeper religious (or contractarian) foundation, and in turn institutions and practices can be deduced from the principle' (Saward 1998: 162). This deductive approach to institutional design is symptomatic of a 'common approach in political theory' that attempts 'to stipulate a *literal* or proper meaning for a political principle. Behind this strategy is the assumption, normally unspoken, that there is one, correct, interpretation of a given principle' (Saward 1998: 165). Institutional analysis tends to be situated within debates between competing democratic theories or 'models', be they deliberative, direct, cosmopolitan, liberal, aggregative, ecological, communicative, difference, agonistic, etc., that rest on competing political principles.

This type of deductive approach to the analysis of democratic innovations would require us to commit ourselves to one particular theoretical position or model of democracy. We will not take this approach for a number of reasons. First, it would limit the range of institutions that could reasonably be discussed. No practical design can realistically hope to meet all the rigorous demands of any particular theoretical model. Only a few innovations come close to passing the strict theoretical tests of any one model and typically only squeeze through by overlooking certain aspects of their design. Such a deductive approach is likely to do disservice to the range of actually existing democratic institutions. It means that there is little comparison of the strengths and weaknesses of different types of innovation and how they might be combined to complement and overcome the deficiencies of particular designs. As Fung argues, whilst 'deductive approaches have produced compelling views of democracy', they have been less successful 'at producing policy or institutional reforms that might realize those views' (Fung 2005: 2).

Second, democratic theories or models tend to be incomplete, and, by their nature, their principles and rules drastically oversimplify the complexity of democratic practice (Jonsen and Toulmin 1998: 6). While theoretical work often proceeds as if it were an exhaustive account of democratic politics, theories offer only a partial analysis of our democratic condition. Democratic theory tends to develop in response to perceived problems in either democratic practice or weaknesses in current theories. Without wishing to offer a complete genealogy of democratic theory, we can understand the emergence of participatory democracy in the late 1960s and 1970s (Bachrach 1967; MacPherson 1977; Pateman 1970) against the backdrop and dominance of theories of elitist democracy that had developed post-war (Schumpeter 1976). More recently, deliberative democracy emerged as a corrective to the perceived focus on aggregative forms of democracy (Bohman 1998). This dialectical or reactive development of theory means that we tend not to develop fully-fledged theories of democracy (whatever they would look like), rather we theorise about particular elements of democratic practice that – for good reason – hold our attention at that particular moment in time.

Let us take deliberative democracy, which is arguably the most influential development within contemporary democratic theory. Deliberative democracy has provided a powerful theoretical critique of the tendency within democratic theory and practice to focus on the aggregation of preferences as the fundamental mechanism of legitimation. For deliberative democrats the process of formation of preferences is crucial. As James Bohman states, 'Deliberative democracy, broadly defined, is ... any one of a family of views according to which the public deliberation of free and equal citizens is the core of legitimate political decision making and self-government' (Bohman 1998: 401). Not surprisingly, when it comes to questions of institutional design, deliberative democrats are interested in the extent to which deliberation can be further embedded within the political process. But critics argue that there are many weaknesses in theories of deliberative democracy (Macedo 1999). For example, it is argued that as a theory it fails to provide a satisfactory account of how decisions should be made. If deliberation does not lead to consensus (a rare occurrence), how is conflict to be dealt with? Deliberative democrats are quick to point out how conflicting parties should engage with each other, but have less to say about how agreements short of consensus or a vague notion of workable agreement are to be reached. Under conditions of disagreement, where no workable agreement emerges, deliberative democracy offers little guidance on decision rules (Miller 1992). This is not to say that the insights from deliberative democracy are not significant – we will be drawing heavily on this literature throughout this book. Rather it is an argument for not imagining that one theory can offer us all the necessary resources to evaluate different democratic innovations. Deliberative democracy highlights the importance of considering how democratic innovations enable citizens to make considered judgements; other approaches to democratic theory may offer insights into other aspects of citizen participation. The danger of leaning too heavily on one theoretical position is that significant elements of democratic practice and institutional design can be overlooked.

Saward provides a useful corrective to the tendency to work from within a particular model of democracy. Using the example of direct and deliberative democracy, he argues that instead of viewing them as competing and often antagonistic models, we should recognise that their ideals and practices can be mutually supportive. In isolation, both theoretical models are (arguably) deficient; but mutual engagement indicates how their deficiencies might be overcome. For example, there is a tendency within deliberative democracy to criticise models of direct democracy for lacking an account of how citizens develop reflective preferences before decision-making. Equally, direct democrats are right to highlight the lack of any decision rule within deliberative democracy. But if they are not held as antagonistic positions, then we can see how mutual engagement may be productive: deliberation prior to direct decision-making creates a more legitimate democratic process where citizens are encouraged to reflect on their preferences before making political choices (Saward 2001).

Finally, our aim is to embrace a more ecumenical approach, rather than a single established theoretical perspective, that integrates the concerns of a number of different positions in democratic theory. This will allow for reflections on broad questions that cut across different streams of contemporary democratic theory.

Towards an analytical framework: goods of democratic institutions

If we are going to offer a comparative assessment and evaluation of different democratic innovations, the challenge is to sketch out the details of a more ecumenical analytical framework. Our approach in this book is to develop an analytical framework that allows for comparison of innovations based on the manner and extent to which they realise desirable qualities or *goods* that we expect of democratic institutions. This will enable us to compare qualitatively different types of democratic innovations. But it leaves open the question: which goods?

In assessing democratic innovations we will consider the extent to which they realise four explicitly democratic goods, namely *inclusiveness, popular control, considered judgement* and *transparency*. We will explore the nature of each of these goods in more detail later in the chapter. Briefly, inclusiveness turns our attention to the way in which political equality is realised in at least two aspects of participation: presence and voice. Popular control requires consideration of the degree to which participants are able to influence different aspects of the decision-making process. Considered judgement entails inquiry into citizens' understanding of both the technical details of the issue under consideration and the perspectives of other citizens. And finally, transparency centres reflection on the openness of proceedings to both participants and the wider public. These four goods are particularly apposite for evaluating the democratic qualities of innovations because, arguably, they are fundamental to *any* theoretical account of the democratic legitimacy of institutions. As we have already suggested, accounts of legitimacy in a particular democratic theory may well interpret and weight these goods in different ways. So, for example, theories of direct democracy tend to place particular significance on specific interpretations of inclusiveness and popular control, whereas theories of deliberative democracy privilege a different combination of inclusiveness, considered judgement and transparency. But however they are interpreted and weighted, it is difficult to conceive of a reasonable account of democratic institutions that did not consider these goods. In other words, a democratic theory that overlooked any one of these goods would likely be deemed severely deficient. We are not making any claims as to whether these goods are intrinsic or instrumental to democracy: different theories of democracy will offer different accounts of which of these goods (and others) are intrinsic and which are instrumental and their relative significance. Our approach avoids making any such claims beyond the perspective that the democratic status of institutions that fail to realise these goods in a compelling combination is likely to be challenged.[3]

But our evaluation of democratic innovations will not proceed purely on the basis of their democratic qualities. This book is interested in the potential for democratic participation to be institutionalised: we will be left in the abstract world of pure theory if we do not consider the practicality of innovations. We must therefore give consideration to the extent to which innovations are institutionally feasible. The four democratic goods in our analytical framework will be complemented by two additional institutional goods: *efficiency* and *transferability*. Efficiency demands that we attend to the costs that participation can place on both citizens and public authorities. Transferability provides an occasion to evaluate whether designs can operate in different political contexts, understood in relation to scale, political system or type of issue. Including these two institutional goods in our analysis means that we should avoid the unfortunate celebration of innovations that realise our four democratic goods in a compelling manner but which are entirely impractical: an unfortunately all-too-common occurrence in democratic theory.

A challenging way of confirming the significance of the goods that constitute our analytical framework is to consider the often uncomfortable arguments of sceptics and critics of citizen participation. While the dominant current within democratic theory is one that tends to valorise participation, there is a range of significant sceptical and critical voices that consistently argue that while enhancing citizen participation in political decision-making may (or may not) be a worthy theoretical ideal, there are good reasons why it is unrealistic and/or undesirable and may (perversely) have a damaging effect on the central institutions and practices of advanced industrial democracies. Many of these sceptical and critical contributions are from major democratic theorists who have strong democratic commitments. However, their reflections on our experience of existing institutionalised (and non-institutionalised) forms of citizen engagement – for example, participation in competitive elections and consultation exercises – lead them to contend that attempting to enhance citizen participation in political decision-making may actually

---

[3] Arguably these four democratic goods embody Robert Dahl's classic criteria of a democratic process, namely effective participation, voting equality, enlightened understanding, control of the agenda and inclusion of adults (Dahl 1998: 37–8).

undermine the democratic ideal. It is important that when applying our analytical framework, the challenges of sceptics and critics come to mind.

Considering the voices of sceptics and critics has advantages for our analysis. Primarily, it means that we do not side step significant challenges to increasing and deepening participation in the political decision-making process; instead difficult questions are confronted head-on. It is too easy to be swept along with the rhetoric of participation and not ask hard questions of institutional designs. By ensuring that our analytical framework requires engagement with the insights of sceptics and critics of citizen participation, we cannot be accused of wilfully avoiding controversies within democratic theory and practice. If it is a realistic proposition that democratic innovations should be more widely institutionalised, then it is essential that we are able to show, contra the sceptics and critics, that these designs actually promote rather than undermine the realisation of the goods we associate with democratic institutions.

The first challenge offered by critics and sceptics is that inclusiveness cannot be realised because of differential rates of participation across social groups. Studies of participation across a range of political activities provide evidence that very few citizens actually engage regularly in political action – whether conventional or unconventional – and that participation is strongly positively correlated to income, wealth and education (Pattie *et al.* 2005; Verba *et al.* 1978). These sections of the population have access to resources such as time, money and knowledge that enhance political efficacy. As such, Arend Lijphart argues that democracy's unresolved dilemma is unequal participation (Lijphart 1997). His particular concern is the differential rate of participation in elections across all advanced industrial democracies; a bias that is further exacerbated as the turnout rate falls (a trend that is occurring across almost all polities). If large swathes of the population do not vote on a systematic basis, their interests and opinions are less likely to be taken into account in the policy-making process (Lijphart 1997: 4). A similar concern emerges from studies of officially sponsored consultation exercises: typically it is the already politically interested and engaged who are motivated to respond to consultation documents and/or attend public meetings. Take, for example, the consultation exercise organised for the Oregon Health Plan in 1990 that is often held up as an exemplar of a thoughtful and well-structured process (Fung 2003b; Sirianni and Friedland 2001). As part of the exercise, forty-seven independently organised open community meetings were held across the state that aimed 'to build consensus on the values to be used to guide health resource allocation decisions' (Oregon Health Decisions 1990: 5). While these meetings attracted over a thousand citizens, even sympathetic commentators recognise the impact of uneven participation:

> The most obvious limitation of the community meetings process was that participation was less than hoped for and was skewed towards health professionals and those with above-average incomes and education ... Active outreach by the organisers and by those on the steering committee with strong links to medically underserved communities had not succeeded in getting a more representative group. Three of the community meetings were held in low-income housing projects, but only 14 percent of those who attended overall were either uninsured or Medicaid recipients, the initial target population of the reforms. (Sirianni and Friedland 2001: 158; see also Nagel 1992: 1976).

As Iris Marion Young argues, discussions of health care were 'dominated by white middle-class and college-educated perspectives' (Young 2000: 153).[4] The widely held concern amongst democratic theorists is that extending opportunities for citizen participation in the political process will simply reinforce and amplify the existing differentials of power and influence within society (Phillips 1991: 162; Sartori 1987: 114); in practice inclusiveness will not, or even cannot, be realised.

Second, sceptics and critics of extending participation argue that citizens tend to lack the skills and competence to make coherent political judgements: a direct challenge to the realisation of considered judgement. Without doubt this concern was most explicitly expressed by Joseph Schumpeter and was a crucial element of his defence of competitive elitism: 'the typical citizen drops down to a lower level of mental performance as soon as he enters the political field ... He becomes a primitive again' (Schumpeter 1976: 262). It is not clear from Schumpeter's writing whether he believes that citizens are inherently incapable of making good political judgements or whether they simply lack the motivation to make informed decisions (Beetham 1999: 8).[5]

There is plenty of evidence that most citizens are not that interested in politics and do not spend much time actively consuming political

---

[4] The organisers, Oregon Health Decision, note that although participants 'reflected a variety of backgrounds ... demographic sheets filled out by participants reflect an imbalance with fully 90 percent of participants being insured while only 4.4 percent were Medicaid recipients and 9.4 percent were uninsured'. Participants reflected the usual inequalities related to participation: 67% had college graduate education, 93% were white and 53% had an annual household income over $35,000, with 34% over $50,000 (Oregon Health Decisions 1990: 6 and 30). However, Lawrence Jacobs and his colleagues argue that to focus on the participants is to miss the political significance of the consultation exercise: 'reformers used the rhetoric of priorities to build a durable political coalition in favor of expanded access for the uninsured' (Jacobs et al. 1998: 178).

[5] For a recent re-elaboration and defence of the Schumpetarian position, see Posner (2003).

information. When they come to vote in elections they most certainly do
not interrogate party manifestos or records in any systematic or rational
manner. The majority of citizens have basic impressions about major political stories and the popularity of key politicians, and then use shortcuts
in making voting choices or what Samuel Popkin terms 'low information
rationality' (Popkin 1991). For example, voters may identify with a party
or party leader and/or look for guidance from particular organisations,
individuals or media outlets that they trust. There is ongoing debate about
whether such heuristics make up for a lack of political knowledge and
attention and whether similar choices would be made if individuals were
more fully informed (Bartels 1996; Lupia 1994; Popkin 1991). We can also
ask, following J.S. Mill, whether the private act of voting encourages citizens to make their decisions in the public interest, rather than for their
own private reasons (Reeve and Ware 1992: 97–8).

While citizens participating in elections are required to consider a range
of different issues, consultation has the virtue of generally focusing on
one area of policy, thus in principle reducing the complexity of decisions.
However, it is still pertinent to ask whether citizens are in a position to make
sound judgements. Public meetings typically attract politically interested,
strongly partisan citizens with well-established viewpoints. Participants
rarely hear the voices of those with different social perspectives, and even
on the occasions when a diversity of participants are involved, the length
of meetings – typically no longer than two hours – limits citizens' capacity
to absorb, understand and reflect on new information and perspectives.
These problems are even more acute with opinion polls, which are increasingly popular with public authorities: citizens are asked their immediate
response to questions on subjects on which they often have little or no
knowledge and with little or no opportunity to reflect on relevant information. Citizens are information-poor and have no opportunity to listen to
the perspectives of others. Opinion polls tell us what citizens think off the
top of their head – often a superficial understanding of the issues confront-
ing them. Whilst opinion polls may engage a statistically representative
cross-section of the public, what they provide is an insight into unreflective
public opinion. If such consultation has an effect, policy will be shaped in
response to fairly raw preferences. Mark Warren captures well the problem
faced by citizens in contemporary polities and the challenge that confronts
democratic innovations:

> democracy works poorly when individuals hold preferences and make
> judgements in isolation from one another, as they often do in today's liberal
> democracies. When individuals lack the opportunities, incentives, and neces-
> sities to test, articulate, defend, and ultimately act on their judgements, they
> will also be lacking in empathy for others, poor in information, and unlikely

to have the critical skills necessary to articulate, defend, and revise their views. (Warren 1996: 242)

A third issue commonly raised by sceptics and critics is not whether citizens are motivated and/or competent to participate effectively, but rather that participation will have little or no effect on political decisions – citizens' viewpoints will be ignored or the process and results of participation will be manipulated by political authorities to suit their own interests (Cooke and Kothari 2001). Critics contend that citizens are not given any meaningful popular control in the decision-making process and that transparency is not realised, because citizens are unaware of how (if at all) their contributions will be incorporated into decisions. Such concerns, implicit within Ricardo Blaug's distinction between 'incumbent' and 'critical' democracy (Blaug 2002), discussed in the Introduction, are explicit within the writing of theorists such as John Dryzek, who argues that extra-constitutional imperatives of the state (such as protection of capital accumulation) limit the potential for authentic citizen engagement and deliberation in political decision-making (Dryzek 2000).

For many theorists, the distance between the act of voting and the decisions made in their name helps explain the growing disconnection of citizens from their political representatives and institutions (Barber 1984; Offe and Preuss 1991; Phillips 1995). While periodic voting may entail 'a continuous discipline on the elected to take constant notice of public opinion' (Beetham 1992: 47), the extent to which this discipline leads to responsive rule is debatable – the wealth of evidence that citizens have little trust or confidence in their political representatives to take into account their interests and opinions suggests otherwise (see, for example, Dalton 2004 ; Pharr and Putnam 1999).

Evidence from consultation exercises suggests that the deep scepticism expressed by citizens about their capacity to affect the decision-making process is often justified. Reviewing a range of consultation strategies, Janet Newman and her colleagues argue that there is often an orientation towards 'enabling the public to operate within the norms set by the bureaucracy, rather than enabling bureaucrats to hear and respect the experience that participants bring to the process of participation. That is, it suggests a process of possible *incorporation* of the lay public into official institutions' (Newman *et al.* 2004: 211–12). The prevailing division of power between public authorities and citizens is far from challenged. In the UK, Vivien Lowndes and her colleagues found that 'only one-third of local authorities felt that public participation had a significant outcome on final decision making' (Lowndes *et al.* 2001: 452). Evidence from the Audit Commission comes to similar conclusions, finding that three-quarters of authorities surveyed had failed to effectively integrate the results of consultation with decision-making processes (Audit Commission 1999: 41). Investigating user involvement in health and local authorities in the UK, Mike Crawford and his colleagues could find very few examples of where citizen participation has actually led to improvements in services or changes in policy (Crawford et al. 2003). Daniel Fiorino, at one time the Director of the Performance Incentives Division at the US Environmental Protection Agency and a respected commentator on public participation, recognises the legitimacy of public scepticism, arguing that consultation exercises are often undertaken to 'give at least the appearance of individual and community involvement, legitimate decisions already made, warn the agency of potential political and legal obstacles, satisfy legal or procedural requirements, and defuse the opposition' (Fiorino 1990: 230–1).

While public policy may praise the virtues of participation (and may even make it a statutory requirement), evidence suggests that organisational and professional resistance to participation is often an obstacle for successful engagement (Crawford et al. 2003). It is not unusual to find the belief amongst agency officials that citizen involvement is not suitable for strategic level decisions – these require, for example, 'professional knowledge, managerial authority and political representation' rather than citizen participation. The public is too often viewed negatively as 'passive consumers; as a naïve, childlike and clamorous public; and/or as lacking skills, capacities or trust' (Newman et al. 2004: 210). Whilst there may be a belief among many public officials that participation will unrealistically raise expectations of citizens, it is just as likely that citizens' low expectations of participation and their scepticism towards the motivations and intentions of public authorities 'present a greater challenge for those pursuing democratic renewal' (Lowndes et al. 2001: 453). In institutional designs where power lies so heavily in the hands of public authorities, the potential for manipulation and co-option of citizens is high. Given the poor consultation records of many agencies, suspicion on the part of the public appears reasonable. To what extent can democratic innovations be designed to allay such suspicion and thus realise transparency and popular control?

A fourth challenge to embedding citizen participation is that it will place too many burdens on both citizens and institutions: in other words that enhancing participation cannot be considered an efficient mode of governance. Adapting Oscar Wilde, participation can take up too many evenings. For most citizens – in particular those from politically marginalised communities – the perceived costs of participation far outweigh any perceived benefits, and thus there is little or no motivation to engage. Warren rightly warns that 'radical democrats almost without exception hold that democratic participation is attractive activity, one that people would naturally choose if only they had the opportunity. They should dispense with this romantic dogma' (Warren 1996: 243). The demands of participation are just as likely to generate anxieties and fears and a reasonable preference to spend any spare time in other activities. Beetham has consistently argued that the 'economy of time' is a consideration for the design of all institutions and is particularly pertinent for innovations that aim to increase levels of citizen engagement.

> It takes time to grasp and discuss the complex issues involved in public decision-making, and there is only so much time that people will agree to devote to it. This is the only *democratic* argument for decision-making by proxy, by some smaller group which is in some sense representative of the whole, whose members can be released from other responsibilities to devote themselves more fully to deliberation of public issues. (Beetham 1999: 8–9)

Enhancing citizen participation can also place a significant burden on public authorities. Engaging citizens has resource implications, both in terms of organising engagement and the potential restructuring of administrative procedures and working practices to accommodate participation. Participation on the cheap is likely to be of a poor standard and will be detrimental to democratic practice. Poorly designed and implemented consultation is often down to lack of resources and tight time-tables. Effort and resources need to be expended if citizens, particularly those from politically marginalised social groups, are to be attracted to participate – capacity-building takes time and commitment on the part of public authorities. Often consultation is happening because it is what is expected – government guidance and legislation tends to place a high premium on consultation (Cabinet Office 2004), but without the support of adequate resources and professional experience. Although the climate of compulsion requiring participation in certain policy areas can lead to positive developments, it can have 'perverse consequences in terms of producing short-term and inappropriate strategies for engaging the public' (Newman *et al.* 2004: 208). 'If those responsible only carry out consultation because of the need to satisfy funding conditions, it will be poorly executed and half-hearted' (Commission on Poverty, Participation and Power 2000: 18).

Finally, there is a widespread assumption that the effectiveness of participation is constrained by scale, and thus the transferability of democratic engagement is limited. Warren contends that 'the transformative ideals of radical democracy … often seem beset by a fuzzy utopianism that fails to confront limitations of complexity, size, and scale of advanced industrial societies' (Warren 1996: 242). Robert Dahl sums up the challenge concisely:

> The smaller a democratic unit, the greater its potential for citizen participation and the less the need for citizens to delegate government decisions to representatives. The larger the unit, the greater its capacity for dealing with problems important to its citizens and the greater the need for citizens to delegate decisions to representatives. (Dahl 1998: 110)

Much of the focus in writing on citizen participation is on small-scale institutional structures: town meetings, workers' cooperatives, neighbourhood governance, etc. (Mansbridge 1980; Pateman 1970). Proponents of participation tend to take one of two approaches: either accepting that the size and complexity of contemporary polities means that opportunities for participation in political decision-making can be effective only at a local level, whilst 'politics-as-normal' occurs at higher levels of authority; or offering a radical prescription of decentralisation, where political control is exercised by smaller units. To what extent are democratic innovations able to buck these assumptions, embedding citizen participation in strategic policy, legislative or constitutional decision-making processes?

This brief survey of sceptical and critical voices offers considerable challenges to attempts to further institutionalise citizen participation in the political decision-making process and also indicates the relevance and compelling nature of the six goods of democratic institutions that make up our analytical framework. Calls for increased citizen participation are made against the backdrop of existing patterns of engagement that lead us to question whether democratic innovations can in practice fulfil our democratic hopes and expectations.

Three caveats need to be raised before moving on to a brief discussion of each of the six goods and their significance for the design of democratic innovations. First, in highlighting these six particular goods, we are not offering a definitive list of the goods associated with democratic institutions. Rather this particular selection of goods should be understood as significant 'ingredients' or 'components' (Saward 2003a: 88) of any reasonable understanding of what we expect from democratic institutions in general and democratic innovations in particular. Second, we should be aware that any particular institutional design is unlikely to fully realise all of these goods. And finally, we need to be attentive to the fact that institutions may realise these goods in different ways and in different combinations.

Inclusiveness

If uneven participation is a persistent concern across various modes of political participation, then inclusiveness is clearly a significant good of democratic institutions. Thus, a key question is: can democratic innovations buck the trend and institutionalise effective incentives for participation by citizens from across different social groups? In considering how inclusiveness can be realised we will need to attend to different institutional characteristics of democratic innovations. The most obvious is the fairness of selection rules and procedures. The first consideration is who has the right to participate: this takes us back to our earlier discussion in the Introduction of who counts as a 'citizen'. Robert Goodin terms this the problem of 'constituting the demos', a topic that has been much neglected in democratic theory (Goodin 2007). For Goodin, the democratic solution is enfranchising all affected interests rather than simply abiding by existing political boundaries. It is therefore pertinent to ask: how do democratic innovations constitute their demos? Second, once the demos has been established, institutions can operate a variety of selection mechanisms, from designs that are open to all, to those that restrict participation through mechanisms such as election, random selection and appointment. First impressions may suggest that inclusiveness would be best served through institutions that are open to all. Any restriction would undermine fairness – the equal right and opportunity to participate. But, as our brief discussion of the arguments of sceptics and critics indicated, when faced with opportunities to take part in political activities, we find differential rates of participation across social groups. Self-selection may well simply replicate existing inequalities. Difference theorists continually stress that presence can have a significant impact on the nature of decisions: if the politically excluded are not present, decisions are unlikely to fully respond to their concerns (Phillips 1995: 13). In judging the inclusiveness of democratic innovations, we will need to pay attention not only to the formal characteristics of the selection mechanism but also the extent to which in practice institutional inducements motivate the engagement of citizens from across social groups, ensuring that a particular social group is not marginalised or excluded from participation.

But consideration of selection mechanisms is not enough. We also need to be alive to the ways in which institutional design can affect fairness in making contributions: the presence of citizens from politically marginalised groups does not necessarily equate to equality of voice. To what extent does the design of an institution provide citizens with equal substantive opportunities to express their views and be heard on the issue under consideration *and* have equal chances to affect the output of the institution? Simply being present does not necessarily mean that citizens will be willing or able to make their views known. We know that citizens differ in their political skills, confidence and political efficacy: 'the feeling that one could have an impact on collective actions if one chose to do so' (Warren 2001: 71). We need to consider the ways that institutional rules, norms and expectations can exclude or undermine the contributions of certain citizens. According to Young, particular types of contribution, in particular dispassionate and disembodied reason-giving, are often privileged over other modes, such as narrative, thus perpetuating the dominance of citizens more skilled in these 'higher' forms of communication (Young 1990, 2000). Assessing the degree to which equality of voice is realised requires us to be attentive to the manner in which institutions encourage different types of contribution and offer support and resources to those citizens who have little experience and/or are intimidated by the thought of speaking in public. We can again distinguish between an institution where equality of voice is achieved in a formal sense in that all participating citizens have the equal right to contribute and one where that formal right is given substance by the provision of resources to support those with less experience and confidence.

We must also consider the extent to which equality of voice is realised through the rules and procedures that govern the generation of outputs from institutions. We use the term 'output' rather than decision, because institutions will vary in the extent to which they can affect the final political decision (see the discussion of popular control below). For some designs, their outputs are the final decision – they have direct policy, legislative or constitutional effect. But, more often than not, there is a distance between the output of institutions that engage citizens and the final decision of public authorities. In all cases, however, we need to consider the extent to which inclusiveness has been realised. How fair are the rules and procedures governing the output? Do citizens have an equal opportunity to affect the output? Overall then, the realisation of the good of inclusiveness is of crucial significance. Can democratic innovations be designed so that differentials that traditionally affect levels of engagement across social groups are reduced or even neutralised?

Popular control

Generally, definitions of democracy accentuate the equal right of citizens to take part in collective decisions. For example, Beetham's influential work on democratic audit is based on an understanding of popular control and political equality as the core principles of democracy (Beetham 1999). But much more attention is given to inclusiveness in both democratic theory and practice compared to realising popular control (direct democrats aside). What is often missing from the design of most democratic institutions is any sense that citizens have effective control over significant elements of decision-making. Given our earlier definition of democratic innovations and the concern that participation is often manipulated by political elites, one way in which their design should be judged is the extent to which citizens are afforded increased influence and control within the decision-making process.

In considering popular control we will draw on a highly stylised account of stages of the decision-making process, distinguishing between problem definition, option analysis, option selection and implementation. In reality the political decision-making process is far more complex and far from linear, but for our purposes this is a useful heuristic (John 1998; Parsons 1996). Democratic theorists are well versed in the ways in which powerful interests are capable of agenda-setting, defining problems in particular advantageous ways or avoiding or sidelining (whether overtly or covertly) contentious issues rather than subjecting them to public interrogation. Participation is often limited to 'safe' issues in order to suppress conflict. Additionally, agenda-setting can be constrained not by such a manifest exercise of power but by the division of labour across political institutions: the scope of participation will be limited by the powers of the relevant public authority. So, for example, the agenda-setting powers of a democratic innovation established by a local authority will be constrained in the extent to which it can have a direct effect on issues controlled by national government or other institutions. Given that most democratic innovations are established by public authorities, the process by which problems are defined and options analysed through forms of citizen engagement becomes crucial. An innovation may realise inclusiveness, for example, but citizens may be participating on an issue that has little political salience. Placing agenda-setting power in the hands of citizens requires mechanisms and procedures to be in place so that citizens are able to influence the selection of issues and the way in which they are to be considered, including for example the type of information they receive. To what extent can popular control be realised over the conditions under which citizens participate?

Even when participation occurs on significant issues, a common criticism that we will return to many times in this book is that it has little or no effect on decisions. Participation is either ignored by political authorities or is used to confirm decisions made elsewhere. This is where charges of co-option can have particular effect: citizens are drawn into a participation exercise as a mechanism of assimilation with little or no realistic opportunity to challenge established practices. In some designs, the outputs of innovations have direct policy or legislative impact, but this is rare. This leaves open the question of how the outputs of other designs affect final decisions. Are there procedures that can be put in place that ensure that outputs are given due consideration and weight in future political decisions? Finally, while most of the innovations in this book relate to the first three elements of our schematic decision-making process, a small number involve citizens in the implementation process and, as such, questions of the degree of influence remain apposite.

In considering all four stages of the decision-making process, we also need to be aware that the design of democratic innovations may involve citizens in 'sharing' power with other actors – for example, public authorities. Instances of co-governance – where decisions are taken and at times implemented through forums which include citizens and representatives from public authorities (and possibly other bodies) – raise important questions about the capacity of citizens to act in concert with actors that have more bureaucratic support and political experience. Given the increasing reliance on networks of governance in contemporary society (Stoker 1998), the ability of citizens to operate within these contexts is a significant consideration.

Considered judgement

While definitions of democracy tend to stress the goods of inclusiveness and popular control, the legitimacy of citizen participation in political decision-making arguably also rests on the capacity of citizens to make thoughtful and reflective judgements. Depending on the design of an innovation, these may be individual judgements that are collated in some way or collective judgements where citizens engage in problem-solving. If the role of citizens in the political decision-making process is to be enhanced, we will expect their judgements to be based not on raw preferences – on narrow private interests and pre-existing knowledge and prejudices – but rather on an informed and reflective assessment of the matter in hand. Arguably, this is an unfamiliar requirement in contemporary polities (Warren 1996: 242).

Considered judgement does not simply require citizens to learn more 'facts' about the issue under consideration, although such technical knowledge is crucial. It also requires them to appreciate the views of other citizens with quite different social perspectives and experiences. Hannah Arendt offers one of the most compelling accounts of considered judgement, which she terms 'enlarged mentality'. This requires a capacity to imaginatively place ourselves in the position of others, distancing ourselves from private circumstances that limit and inhibit the exercise of judgement (Arendt 1982: 42–3). For Arendt, then, considered judgement

> must liberate us from the 'subjective private conditions', that is, from the idiosyncrasies which determine the outlook of each individual in his privacy and are legitimate as long as they are only privately held opinions, but are not fit to enter the market place, and lack all validity in the public realm. And this enlarged way of thinking, which as judgement knows how to transcend its own

individual limitations ... cannot function in strict isolation or solitude; it needs the presence of others in whose place it must think, whose perspectives it must take into consideration, and without whom it never has the opportunity to operate at all. (Arendt 1968: 220–1)

Democratic institutions cannot be designed to *ensure* that citizens achieve such considered judgement, but there are different ways of providing information and exposing citizens to the views and perspectives of other citizens; to nurture and support the development of enlarged mentality. But, as Claus Offe and Ulrich Preuss suggest, within contemporary political thought: 'It appears to be a largely novel task to think about institutional arrangements and procedures which could generate a selective pressure in favour of this type of reflective and open preference-learning, as opposed to fixed preferences that are entirely derivative from situational determinants, rigid beliefs or self-deception' (Offe and Preuss 1991: 168). Analysing democratic innovations to discern the extent to which their structure enables participants to realise considered judgements can be seen as a contribution to this task.

Transparency

The ability of citizens to scrutinise the activities of institutions is crucial to any democratic system and is fundamental to building trust and confidence in the political process (Warren 1999). Increasing opportunities for participation will draw citizens into unfamiliar institutional settings where they are faced with unusual demands, in the sense that they are asked to make judgements that may have significant public impact. The transparency of proceedings becomes a crucial consideration in at least two senses. First, in relation to the citizens who participate in the process, transparency requires that participants have a clear understanding about the conditions under which they are participating – for example, how has the issue under consideration been selected, who is organising the process, how will the outputs of the process affect political decisions? In this sense the realisation of transparency may counter the fears of sceptics and critics who contend that engagement is little more than co-option of participants and is crucial if participants are to realise considered judgement.

If institutions that engage citizens are to have a significant effect on public decisions, then the process needs to be open to scrutiny not only to the participants, but also to the wider public (unless of course the innovation engages all citizens). Such external transparency is often referred to as 'publicity' – the transmission of information about the institution and its decisions to the wider public. The realisation of publicity is crucial if the public is to judge institutions and their outputs as legitimate and trustworthy. This is particularly the case when there is widespread suspicion about the motives of public authorities. Publicity can also act as a significant inducement for participants to come to public-spirited, rather than self-interested, judgements (Chambers 2004; Miller 1992). Organisers of democratic innovations can be more or less active in realising publicity: from a passive strategy of publishing documentation through official sources to a more energetic engagement with different forms of promotion and media.

Efficiency

Democratic innovations require citizens and officials to participate in new political practices and as such will involve civic costs as well as benefits. While theorists and practitioners are often quick to stress the virtues and benefits of participation for participants and sponsoring institutions, an assessment of innovations will also need to consider the demands they place on citizens and on other institutions and whether these are worth bearing individually and socially. Administrative costs and the burden placed on citizens can thus be a feasibility constraint on democratic innovations. For example, it is inconceivable that we would accept either the financial and bureaucratic costs or the levels of political activity expected from citizens associated with the participatory institutions of the ancient Athenian polis. It is, however, not possible to specify a general level of unacceptable burden. It is likely to be highly contextual and as such we will need to consider the perceived interests of participants and supporting institutions and the perceived effectiveness of particular institutional designs. Part of such a calculation will be a comparison with the perceived costs and benefits of *not* embedding participation within the decision-making process: the costs and benefits arising from alternative patterns of decision-making that do not offer structured opportunities for citizen engagement. The acceptable costs associated with particular innovations are likely to be different in different political circumstances.

Transferability

Given that we are interested in institutions that embed citizen participation in strategic level decision-making, designs will explicitly challenge the widespread assumption that citizen participation is limited by scale. Whilst it is accepted that some decisions can be made at a more local level, we take as given that significant political decisions will continue to be taken by public authorities at larger levels of organisation, such as city, national, transnational, global. We can learn lessons from smaller-scale designs, but our interest in this book is in whether democratic innovations can operate effectively at these larger scales.

Relatedly, we will need to discern whether certain designs will function effectively only within particular types of political system. Might differences in political, social, economic and cultural practices render problematic the import of particular institutions? Finally, we also need to consider whether particular designs are limited to dealing with certain types of issues. For example, particular institutions may be poor at dealing effectively with the complexity of particular scientific and technological issues.

In analysing these different aspects of transferability, the burgeoning literature on policy transfer offers helpful criteria (Dolowitz and Marsh 2000; Freeman 2006). For example, in cases where an innovation has been adopted elsewhere, it is well to consider, amongst other issues, the degree to which transfer has actually occurred (whether it is an example of copying, emulation, combination or inspiration), the type of actors involved in the process of learning (from elected officials and politicians through to policy entrepreneurs and supra-national organisations) and the degree of coercion involved. Studies on policy transfer provide insights into why the transfer of institutions can lead to failed implementation if the process is uninformed, incomplete or inappropriate (Dolowitz and Marsh 2000: 17).

Applying the analytical framework

The combination of the goods of inclusiveness, popular control, considered judgement, transparency, efficiency and transferability offers a powerful analytical framework for the evaluation of democratic innovations that aim to increase and deepen citizen participation in the political decision-making process. The democratic challenge is clear: innovations need to show how unequal participation can be overcome; how citizens can be empowered in the decision-making process; how the environment can be structured to enable informed judgements; and how proceedings can be open to participants and observers. Additionally innovations face the practical challenges of ensuring that costs placed on citizens and institutions are not too burdensome; and that the design can be used in a variety of political contexts. It is only if democratic innovations can realise an attractive combination of these goods that they will be deemed legitimate and worthy of institutionalising within our political systems.

In the chapters that follow we will use this analytical framework to offer a systematic evaluation and comparison of different types of innovation, before concluding with a discussion of the lessons that can be learnt for both democratic practice and theory. We are, however, faced with a plethora of designs that might be termed 'democratic innovations' (Smith 2005)

– arguably too many to analyse in detail. In an attempt to place some order on the diversity of practice, and to draw out meaningful insights into the implications of different design choices, we will focus our analysis around four categories of institutions. The innovations are gathered into categories on the basis of family resemblance: they have significant design features in common that mean that they realise reasonably common combinations of goods. The four categories are popular assemblies, mini-publics, direct legislation and e-democracy. A strategic decision has been taken to analyse a relatively small number of designs in some detail rather than simply provide a brief overview of a range of different designs.[6] This is for two reasons. First, it is only through a detailed explanation of design characteristics that we can understand the manner in which goods are realised. This will allow us to offer a more systematic comparison across innovations. And second, it is obvious from some discussions of innovations that political theorists and political scientists do not always understand the details and nuances of institutional design. Laying out the detail is essential in order to ensure that we are talking about the same thing. In each category, we will focus attention on innovations that realise a particularly compelling combination of goods: some of these innovations may be familiar to a few readers (the work is not intended to uncover completely new democratic experiments), but the value of our approach is that the variety of designs is evaluated using the same analytical framework. The analysis of innovations draws together material from a variety of sources rather than engaging directly in primary research. Most prominent are studies of particular innovations by democratic theorists and political scientists, independent (on some occasions more so than others) evaluation reports and materials produced by practitioners who organise or facilitate innovations. The aim is to interrogate the various materials in light of our analytical framework, a task that is not always straightforward given the different approaches and audiences of the sources.

The first category of innovation incorporates, as a central feature, popular assemblies: forums open to all citizens. The open assembly is arguably the most basic of democratic designs, taking us back to the central institutional body of classical Athenian democracy. In modern times, arguably the most long-standing example of assembly-based politics is New England town meetings; a more recent example, the neighbourhood meetings in Chicago Community Policing. Both of these designs operate at the relatively small scale. While there are significant lessons to learn from these institutions, our analysis will primarily focus on participatory budgeting (PB), in particular the design that emerged in the city of Porto Alegre, a much-lauded

---

[6] For those looking for such an overview, see Smith (2005).

example of engagement, where popular assemblies are a crucial element of an institution that operates on a much larger scale. What is especially attractive about this innovation is that it has influenced engagement strategies in other cities in Brazil and beyond (including advanced industrial democracies), and attempts have been made to transfer the basic design principles on to an even larger political scale in the Brazilian state of Rio Grande do Sul.

While open assemblies can be viewed as one element of ancient Athenian democratic practice, another significant aspect was the use of lot and rotation (or sortition) to allocate positions of political authority. The second category of innovation is those bodies that use forms of random sampling to bring together a diverse body of citizens to discuss matters of public concern, often termed 'mini-publics'. Over recent decades we have seen a growth in interest in and use of mini-publics such as citizens' juries, consensus conferences and deliberative polls. Arguably even more impressive, and the main subject of our analysis here, is the recent British Columbia Citizens' Assembly (BCCA) on Electoral Reform established in 2004. The randomly selected Assembly of 160 citizens spent eleven months investigating whether the province should introduce a new electoral system.

While the first two categories are different types of forums, the third has a completely different logic. This category is direct legislation, where citizens have equal decision-making powers through the ballot box. Propositions are either defeated by a popular vote or if passed have legislative or constitutional effect. Direct legislation – constitutional and popular referendums and initiative – is institutionalised in a small number of democracies, most notably Switzerland and California. Particular attention will be given to popular referendum and initiative because they also enable citizens to offer propositions. Successful initiatives introduce new laws; popular referendums repeal existing legislation.

The final category – e-democracy – differs from the other three in that family resemblance rests on the use of information and communication technology (ICT): other design features can and do vary quite dramatically. ICT-enabled or e-democracy innovations are thin on the ground, although their potential for enhancing citizen engagement in political decision-making would appear to be high. This category of innovation includes a quite diverse range of designs, from 21st Century Town Meetings where ICT is used to enable face-to-face engagement, to internet discussion forums, online deliberative polling and ICT-enabled direct legislation where engagement takes place online.

2

Popular assemblies: from New England town meetings to participatory budgeting

The classical Athenian assembly, where citizens (read Athenian males) gathered together to debate and decide law and policy, continues to transfix (Dunn 2005; Saxonhouse 1993). The idea of a popular assembly where citizens engage in face-to-face interactions and decision-making is arguably the touchstone for much writing on citizen participation: for example, the neighbourhood assembly open to all residents is a fundamental building block of Benjamin Barber's vision of strong democracy (Barber 1984: 267–73). For sceptics and critics, such participation is impossible and/or undesirable to institutionalise in large-scale, complex democracies. In most advanced industrial democracies, the nearest we come to such assemblies is the open public meeting that is often the central element of public authority consultation exercises. But, as we noted in the last chapter, such public meetings are a poor imitation of Athenian practice: self-selection leads to unequal participation; participants exercise minimal popular control; there is little time for citizens to develop considered judgements, and so on. Can innovations based on popular assemblies overcome these weaknesses and realise a compelling combination of goods of democratic institutions?

The New England town meeting, first established in the seventeenth century and arguably the nearest modern equivalent of the Greek assembly, receives surprisingly little systematic treatment within democratic theory.[1] This institution was much admired by Alexis de Tocqueville when

---

[1] There are, of course, exceptions that we will draw on in this chapter. See, for example, Bryan (1999, 2004); Zimmerman (1999); and Mansbridge (1980). Frank Bryan offers some pertinent reflections on why there has been so little interest within the US academy in one of the rare examples of open assembly-based democratic practice, given its presence on home soil (2004: 12–15).

he visited the United States in the mid-nineteenth century: 'Town meetings are to liberty what primary schools are to science; they bring it within the people's reach, they teach men [sic] how to use and enjoy it' (quoted in Bryan 1999: 195). Town meetings that are open to all residents, have legislative power over a range of local issues and allow citizens to elect town officials and hold them accountable for their actions still take place annually in a significant number of New England settlements (and in some Swiss communes). The governing autonomy of town meetings has been eroded somewhat by higher forms of political authority, and many towns have moved away from the traditional open meeting to the use of ballot referendum meetings, representative town meetings and town or city councils. However, a significant number, particularly in Vermont, continue with traditional practices of self-government.

While town meetings are primarily a rural phenomenon, it is possible to find open forums that take us beyond consultation in more populous urban settings. In sociological terms, inner-city Chicago is arguably as far removed from rural Vermont as one can imagine. Since 1995, the Chicago Police Department has been holding monthly community beat meetings in 285 neighbourhood beats across the city. In these beat meetings, police officers work with local residents to improve public safety in the neighbourhood. Community organisers are employed by the Police Department to mobilise local residents, and the open forums generate priorities and strategies for action and review progress. Given that decisions are made collaboratively, between citizens and the police, this mode of engagement is best understood as a form of co-governance. Evidence suggests that in comparison to traditional forms of consultation, Chicago Community Policing attracts a significant proportion of citizens from poor and less well-educated neighbourhoods (Fung 2003a, 2004).

There is one element of the design of both New England town meetings and Chicago Community Policing which limits the extent to which they can be classified as democratic innovations as defined in this book. In the Introduction, we placed an emphasis on democratic devices that offer citizens a formal role in policy, legislative or constitutional decision-making *beyond* the local: from the level of the city to the global. While radical programmes of decentralisation may be attractive in certain respects, it is the assumption of this book that power will continue to be exercised at these more strategic levels, and therefore the question of how citizen participation might be institutionalised to effect a change in the division of political labour at these levels remains highly pertinent. In these terms, the design of town meetings and neighbourhood policing is limited. That said, the apparent capacity of both designs to ameliorate to some degree the traditional differentials of participation and to empower citizens means that there may well be valuable lessons to learn from them.

Frank Bryan's impressive study of town meetings concludes: 'For real democracy small not only is beautiful, it is essential' (Bryan 2004: 136). If he is right, then our aim of embedding citizen participation across larger scales is futile. Is there any evidence that participation in open assemblies can be institutionalised in decision-making processes at more strategic levels? It is difficult to imagine effective assemblies that are open to citizens across large geographical areas, although, as we shall touch on in Chapter 5, advances in information and communication technology may make this more of a realistic proposal. Radical democrats (particularly those of an anarchist persuasion) often argue that the scale problem can be overcome through confederation. Harking back to the Paris Commune, proponents argue that local assemblies should associate through confederations, but with each assembly retaining its sovereignty (Bookchin 1992: 257–8). As Robyn Eckersley argues: 'a confederal body cannot proceed without the voluntary cooperation of its member units and cannot override the decisions of member units: the latter are determining, but not determined' (Eckersley 1992: 177). This option leaves power in the hands of citizens in their localities, but it is difficult to imagine how such an arrangement could effectively deal with strategic issues that require high levels of cooperation. Under current political, social and economic conditions it is no more than a utopian suggestion.

A set of practices that are often termed 'participatory appraisal' offer one potential approach to answering the question of how small-scale popular assemblies can be linked into larger-scale decision-making processes.[2] Participatory appraisal is most commonly practised in less economically developed nations, particularly because many international donor agencies such as the World Bank increasingly require such an appraisal within their loan and aid agreements (Norton *et al.* 2001; World Bank 1996).[3] Advocates argue that the nature of poverty is multi-dimensional and local people can be empowered and the legitimacy of poverty reduction strategies increased if there is community input through participatory appraisal. Advocates point to impressive examples of participatory appraisal in practice: one of the most celebrated was launched in Uganda in 1997 as part of the national Poverty Eradication Action Plan (PEAP).

---

[2] We are using the term 'participatory appraisal' to cover a range of designs that show a strong family resemblance, including participatory rural appraisal (PRA), participatory learning and action (PLA), participatory action research and beneficiary assessment.

[3] In recent years, there has been growing interest in how participatory appraisal could be applied in advanced industrial democracies. For examples in the UK, see Bennett (2004) and East End Health Action *et al.* (2003).

Participatory appraisal utilises a wide range of methods to engage traditionally marginalised communities and vulnerable social groups, including unstructured and semi-structured interviews, group discussions and exercises and biographies, alongside techniques such as preference ranking, mapping and drawing to make the process as accessible as possible to all participants, many of whom may be illiterate. While the commitment of many practitioners and development agencies should not be questioned, what is open to debate is the degree to which the rhetoric of empowerment is realised such that participatory appraisal can be classified as a democratic innovation as understood in this book. To what extent are citizens able to influence the political decision-making process? In practice, citizen participation remains localised, with professionals collating local appraisals into larger-scale plans. A growing number of critics suggest that the process fails to achieve its aims and that any empowerment is superficial, or even illusory. Critics question, for example, whether there is any real connection between participatory appraisal and decision-making: what evidence is there to suggest that local-level participation has any effect on broader macro-level policies that affect inequalities and injustices (Cooke and Kothari 2001)? In many ways, participatory appraisal is at best an impressive large-scale consultation exercise on the part of public authorities rather than a democratic innovation.

Are we left, then, with the option of radical decentralisation of power down to units such as New England town meetings and Chicago Community Policing or reliance on professionals to collate the views of open assemblies at higher levels of political authority? Neither of these is a satisfactory design option for democratic innovations as defined in this book. While we can draw some lessons from the experience of town meetings and Chicago Community Policing, this chapter will focus on a much-celebrated institutional design, participatory budgeting (PB). Typically we assume that the direction of learning about democratic practice will be one way – from the advanced industrial to more recently established democracies. We have nothing to learn; only to export. PB (in Brazilian, *orçamento participativo*: OP), initially established in Porto Alegre in Brazil in 1989, offers one celebrated example of where the direction of learning has reversed. Of all the participatory initiatives developed in less advanced industrial democracies, arguably it is PB that has caught the imagination of practitioners and researchers across the globe, including UN-HABITAT and the World Bank (Cabannes 2004; Wagle and Shah 2003). PB has spread to a growing number of Brazilian municipalities, one Brazilian state and beyond into Latin America and Europe: it is estimated that around 250 cities have embedded some form of PB (Cabannes 2004: 27). In this chapter, it is the original design as institutionalised in Porto Alegre that will be the main focus. This design offers an imaginative institutional arrangement where popular assemblies are combined with innovative representative forums that allow citizens to control and shape the distribution of a significant proportion of the city's budget. There is some criticism in the literature that Porto Alegre's PB process receives too much attention, to the detriment of other municipalities (Nylen 2003: 91–2). There are at least two responses to this criticism. First, almost all developments and analyses of PB make reference to Porto Alegre – it has become a mode of legitimisation for engagement strategies. Hence, it is important to have a clear understanding of how the often complex institutional design operates in this particular context. Second, having developed an understanding of the extent to which PB in Porto Alegre realises democratic goods, we will have the opportunity to draw lessons on the extent to which the design has been and could be effectively transferred and developed in other locations towards the end of the chapter. Not all designs that claim to be PB stand up to close scrutiny.

There are a number of features of this innovative participatory structure that make it particularly compelling. First, citizens are participating in an area of public policy that is rarely open to direct engagement, namely decisions about the distribution of significant portions of the city's budget: 'between 9 percent and 21 percent of a total budget that amounted to $160 million in 2000' (Baiocchi 2005: 14). Second, the design of PB combines very different forms of participation. Popular assemblies at the neighbourhood and regional (or district) level attract large numbers of citizens: over 16,600 citizens participated in the regional assemblies in 2001 (Harvard University Center for Urban Development Studies 2003: 40). From these assemblies citizens are elected to representative forums where decisions about resource allocation take place. Third, this democratic innovation has flourished in a city whose politics (like that of other cities in Brazil) was defined by corruption and clientelism. Traditional tutelage relations have been replaced by a more open and transparent form of governance. Fourth, the structure of incentives within PB has attracted significant numbers of poor citizens to directly engage in the governance of the city – a social group traditionally marginalised by the political system. Finally, the process has led to a redistribution of resources away from prestige projects towards investment in basic infrastructure and services that systematically favour poorer neighbourhoods that had often been neglected by previous administrations.

> The OP has approved hundreds of projects, including street paving, urban improvements in precarious areas, sewage, municipal public education, and health, with a completion rate of nearly 100 percent. These projects have contributed to an increase to almost full coverage in sewage and water, a threefold

increase in the number of children in municipal schools, and significant increases in the number of new housing units provided to needy families. Porto Alegre's expenditures in certain areas, such as health and housing, are much higher than the national average, and the municipality has tended over the years to spend less and less on administrative costs. From the perspectives of governance and quantitative indicators, the OP has succeeded in attracting broad-based participation from the poorer strata of Porto Alegre's citizenry and in effectively linking that participation to redistributive outcomes. (Baiocchi 2005: 14; see also Cabannes 2004: 40; Gret and Sintomer 2005: 64–5; Harvard University Center for Urban Development Studies 2003: 43–7; Santos 1998: 485)

PB was established by the Workers' Party (Partido dos Trabalhadores: PT) when its candidate won the mayoral elections in 1988. The PT came to power with an explicit pro-poor commitment, and PB emerged (falteringly at first) as a fundamental element of its governing strategy. The Brazilian system is notable in that there is significant municipal autonomy and fiscal decentralisation, with extensive executive powers in the hands of the mayor, particularly in relation to the city budget. The elected legislative assembly plays no formal role in the creation of the budget, but does have the power of veto.

The structure of PB has evolved over a number of years. The process takes place on an annual cycle, with citizen engagement occurring at three distinct levels: popular assemblies at neighbourhood and regional level (regional here referring to districts of the city which are made up of a number of neighbourhoods); regional budget forums; and the council of the participatory budget (COP), also known as the municipal budget council.[4]

It is the regional popular assemblies that attract the highest level of participation. These assemblies are open to all residents, whether or not they are members of officially recognised civic organisations. As Gianpaolo Baiocchi notes:

> Administrators rejected the proposal that participation be organised through existing neighbourhood associations in favour of an open system in which any citizen could participate. As explained by an activist, 'the participatory budget is for citizens, not for associations ... we work with direct citizenship and not associations'. (Baiocchi 2005: 37)

Until 2001, when the process was simplified, two rounds of popular assemblies were held in each of the city's sixteen regions, beginning in

---

[4] For detailed explanations of the workings of participatory budgeting in Porto Alegre, see in particular Abers (1998, 2000); Baiocchi (2003a, 2005); Harvard University Center for Urban Development Studies (2003); Santos (1998).

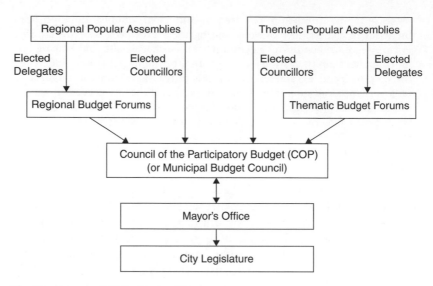

The Structure of PB in Porto Allegre

March or April. This has now been reduced to a single assembly in each region (Harvard University Center for Urban Development Studies 2003: 31). The popular assembly has three functions. The first is overview and scrutiny: holding the administration to account. Senior officials from the administration, including the mayor, review the implementation of projects within the region from the previous year's budget allocation and then are directly questioned by citizens about their record and policies (often beyond the realm of the budget). Second, participants vote on the priority issues for investment in the region as a whole, for example sanitation, paving, healthcare, etc. Third, the assemblies elect citizens to their respective regional budget forum and the COP. The method of selection for delegates to the sixteen regional budget forums provides a significant incentive for citizens to participate in the popular assemblies. Quite simply, the more votes, the more representation for a neighbourhood in the decisions about investment priorities. Selection of candidates for the COP follows a different logic – each region elects two councillors (with two alternates). There is equality of representation on the COP for each region, regardless of size, wealth or any other factor.

A parallel process of thematic city-wide popular assemblies was established in 1994, organised at the same time as their regional counterparts. The thematic strand was established to deal with issues that are not neighbourhood-specific, such as environment, education, health and social services and transportation: 'The emphasis of the thematic forums ... [is] on developing guidelines and long-term plans and policies for the whole city, rather than on short-term projects involving individual districts' (Goldfrank 2003: 44). Six thematic assemblies hold the administration to account, generate priorities and elect thematic budget delegates and two COP councillors (plus alternates). These thematic assemblies do not attract the same level of participation as the regional assemblies.

If popular assemblies were the only modes of participation, then the Porto Alegre process would likely have fallen foul of the same problem that appears to have ended PB in other locations, namely long lists of demands from citizens that the administration did not have the capacity to respond to, resulting in dramatic declines in participation and confidence in the process (Abers 2000: 56). After all, the limited resources available to the administration means that only about '30 percent of the demands originally formulated by the community can be taken care of' (Santos 1998: 493). In Porto Alegre, the structure of the budgeting process means that citizens do not simply make demands for investment, but are also involved in prioritising these demands and creating and applying the rules that guide distribution of resources across the city. These are the functions of the regional and thematic budget forums and the COP.

Each of the sixteen regions has a budget forum in which delegates review the investment priority lists presented by neighbourhoods and draw up an overall list of investment priorities for the region as a whole, in line with the broad priorities established by the regional popular assemblies. Although some regions use explicit needs-based criteria, most of the decisions are made through discussions and negotiations between delegates. This is why the mobilisation of citizens in each regional assembly is crucial – the larger the presence from a particular neighbourhood, the more delegates on the forum arguing the case for their preferred investments. Forum delegates are given training by the administration on issues of technical feasibility and make visits to neighbourhoods to inform their decision-making. Although the administration can question the technical feasibility of projects, the forums can overrule their advice. The forums are also responsible for ongoing negotiations and monitoring implementation of projects by the various city agencies. Forum meetings are open to all citizens to attend, but only the delegates have voting rights. Similar processes are established in the thematic budget forums.

The final element of PB is the COP (also known as the Municipal Budget Council) which consists of the two elected budget councillors from each region (regardless of its population size), two from each thematic area and one representative each from the union of neighbourhood associations (UAMPA) and the municipal employees' union (SIMPA). The COP has two main functions. The first is to produce the budget for investments prioritised by the budget forums. While the Council is charged with reviewing the whole of the city's budget, it has a specific duty to decide the relative distribution of resources among the various regions and between the various city agencies. Decisions are guided by a set of distributional rules: in the 2000/1 budget, for example, the three criteria guiding decision-making were 'the priorities established by the residents; shortcomings in services and basic facilities; and population base' (Gret and Sintomer 2005: 44).[5] Councillors are also responsible for making decisions on investment decisions proposed by the executive. Once the budget has been accepted by the mayor and presented to the city's legislative assembly, the COP attends to its second function: to reflect and decide on the rules that will guide the distribution of resources in the following year. In all of these tasks the Council works closely with officials from the administration. To defend against the abuse of power by particular citizens, councillors can be elected for only two consecutive terms of office and are subject to immediate recall. As with the budget forums, the meetings of the COP are open, although the public has only observer status.

The operation of the participatory budget has required significant administrative restructuring (Abers 2000: 77–8). The first element was the establishment of a centralised planning office, GAPLAN (Gabinete de Planejamento), to coordinate the technical aspects of the budget across the administration's different departments and to negotiate and support the work of the COP. As Rachel Abers argues, the existing planning office was 'too deeply entrenched in bureaucratic habits and technocratic ideology to carry out the innovative and politically charged projects that the government was hoping to implement' (Abers 2000: 77). The second important development was the creation of the Community Relations Department (CRC: Coordenação de Relações com a Comunidade), whose employees actively mobilise participants, supporting the development of associations and facilitating regional budget forums. Coordinators are assigned to each budget region. Finally, the administration invested in a computerised project management system that provides information on the status of projects and the budgets of city agencies. This allows citizens to keep abreast of developments and undertake research on the administration's activities.

The structure of PB is not what we would expect from standard forms of decentralisation. Decisions are being made by citizens in their neighbourhoods and regions, but also at the level of the city as a whole. As Abers

---

[5] For a detailed explanation of how the rules governing the allocation of resources is applied by the COP, see Harvard University Center for Urban Development Studies (2003) and Santos (1998).

notes: 'Ironically, the process of decentralizing decisions to the citizenry was compatible with the centralization of decisions within the bureaucratic structure' (Abers 2000: 88; see also Gret and Sintomer 2005: 28). To what extent then does this innovative participatory structure realise the various goods we associate with democratic institutions?

Inclusiveness

Most city officials promoting participatory policies are faced with half-empty meeting halls and a difficult struggle to engage politically alienated people in government decisionmaking. But in Porto Alegre, within a couple of years after the budget policy began, thousands of people were participating in the regional budget assemblies. In 1991, about 3,000 people participated in the big second-round regional assemblies. The following year this number doubled. By 1995, with the formalization of intermediary assemblies at the neighbourhood level, about 14,000 people signed their names on the rolls. Furthermore... this participation brought neighbourhoods and regions that historically had not been mobilized into the realm of collective action. The majority were poor rather than middle class. (Abers 2000: 135)

The number of citizens in the population of Athens during its democratic heyday has been estimated at around 30,000.[6] Quorum for certain types of decree stood at 6,000 – one-fifth of eligible citizens – and not many more than this number could have attended the Assembly given the size of the arena. As Mogens Hansen suggests, it is 'unique in history that the Athenians were able, forty times a year, to get a fifth of those with civic rights to participate in the Assembly' (Hansen 1991: 132; see also Saxonhouse 1993).

By chance, this is roughly the average percentage attendance in Vermont town meetings, although obviously the towns themselves are much smaller and civic rights more widely spread. Bryan estimates attendance at an average 20 per cent of all adult residents (Bryan 2004: 280); Joseph Zimmerman some 26 per cent (Zimmerman 1999: 196). Turnout in meetings in other New England states is lower.[7] Surveys of participation in Chicago Community Policing indicate that 14 per cent of citizens attended at least one beat meeting in 1997, with an average attendance of 17 residents per meeting, equating to a city-wide attendance of some 5,000

---

[6] This represents only around 10 per cent of the whole population and around one-fifth of the whole adult population (Hansen 1991).

[7] Attendance in Vermont is the highest across New England. In a 1996 study, Zimmerman estimates that attendance ranges from an average of 7 per cent of registered voters in Connecticut towns to 26 per cent in Vermont towns (Zimmerman 1999: 196).

residents (Fung 2003a: 139). In the late 1990s, as many as 8.4 per cent of the adult population in Porto Alegre (all residents over sixteen can participate in the process) stated that they had participated in budget assemblies at some point in the last five years (Abers 1998: 47–9). In 1999, the number of participants involved in the process reached over 20,000 (Silva 2003: 116), with a high degree of rotation amongst participants: one estimate puts the figure at 40 per cent rotation from one year to the next (Cabannes 2004: 36). In all cases (including the Athenian archetype), a minority of the enfranchised population participates. Is this a problem for the realisation of inclusiveness?

Archon Fung responds directly to this challenge in his discussion of local democracy in Chicago. He asks whether the participatory ideal of higher or even full participation is actually feasible or desirable for two reasons. First, can we realistically expect higher levels of participation given the demands of contemporary society? After all, such levels of engagement were never achieved in Athens, a polity that embraced the ideal of self-government. And as Bryan notes in relation to town meetings, attendance levels of 20 per cent compare favourably with turnout at local elections, where costs of participation are much lower (Bryan 2004: 286). Second, higher levels of participation may be unmanageable: when attendance increases dramatically (often in response to a perceived neighbourhood crisis), 'it becomes extremely difficult to conduct structured, much less sustained, inclusive, or effective, problem-solving deliberations' (Fung 2004: 105). What is crucial for the realisation of inclusiveness, according to proponents of assembly-based politics, is not sheer numbers, but rather who chooses to participate. Our attention should turn to questions of presence and voice across social groups. As Fung argues in relation to participation in Chicago:

> The democratic qualities of community-policing … depend not just upon the quantity and quality of participation inside the groups, but also upon connections between direct participants and other individuals. If direct participation roughly represents the interests and perspectives that exist outside of their groups, if groups are generally open to new participants who wish to join, and if participants are connected through networks of friendship or association to those who do not participate directly, then these bodies may generate fair decisions, despite the relatively small number of direct participants. If, on the other hand, community-policing … groups operate as exclusionary cliques in which one, or only a few, interests, dominate, then low participation rates may reinforce local oligarchic tendencies. (Fung 2004: 106)

As we discussed in Chapter 1, most citizens rarely engage in forms of political participation, but those who do tend to have higher than average income, wealth and education. Our knowledge of Athenian politics suggests that these were the characteristics of the few Athenian citizens who had the confidence to speak in the assembly. To what degree do New England town meetings, Chicago Community Policing and PB buck this trend?

Of those residents who attend town meetings, some 44 per cent speak during the proceedings (Bryan 2004: 280). Meetings tend to attract middle-aged and older citizens (Zimmerman 1999: 170), but apart from the very poor, who tend not to participate, evidence suggests that socio-economic status plays much less of a role in both attendance and voice than might be expected from our knowledge of other forms of partici-pation (Bryan 2004). Drawing on the experience of his own town meet-ing, Robert Dahl argues: 'Strong beliefs and a determination to have one's say are not by any means monopolised by a single socio-economic group' (Dahl 1998: 111). Bryan offers the explanation that the town meeting itself may well be crucial in developing relevant civic skills, in a way that 'neu-tralises the standard effect of social and economic status' (Bryan 2004: 120). He also provides evidence that the traditional gap between men's and women's attendance and contributions in town meetings is now almost closed, particularly for meetings that are held during the day and where childcare is available. The smaller the meeting, the more likely women are to contribute to proceedings (Bryan 2004: 189–231). On the basis of a quite staggering study of 1,435 meetings over three decades, Bryan tested a var-iety of variables, with size explaining much of the variance in town meet-ing attendance and distribution of contributions across participants:

> In general town meetings with the smallest number of people in attendance have the largest percentage of participators and the best distribution of par-ticipation among those present... Since the number of people who speak at town meetings does not keep up with the increase in the number of people who attend, the statistical relationship between the number of people at town meeting (its size) and the percentage participating is negative – strongly so. (Bryan 2004: 157–8)

While Bryan draws his conclusions from data collected from an impres-sively large number of meetings, Jane Mansbridge's famous study is based on a close analysis of a single town in Vermont. Her findings indicate that interesting dynamics are at play between 'old-timers' and 'newcomers'. For example, she notes how certain practices such as 'the friendly joking and informality, the attempts to cover up embarrassing incidents, and the unanimous votes' that have evolved over time to ease tensions, dissipate friction and enable the less confident, 'make participation easier for estab-lished members of the community', but in so doing 'make it harder for newcomers' to understand proceedings and participate fully (Mansbridge 1980: 68). In analysing who actually participates, she finds differential presence and voice within each of these two social groups: 'the very poorest old-timers and the lower-middle- or working-class newcomers ... are not even in the running' (Mansbridge 1980: 87). For these groups, participation is limited by a combination of the cost of attending (loss of a day's work, childcare costs, etc.) and the anxiety and fear of speaking in public, particularly the fear of criticism from fellow citizens (Mansbridge 1980: 60–71). These social differentials are also reflected in the selection of office holders (Mansbridge 1980: 78–9). Although there are not enough comparative data available, one factor that is likely to ameliorate to some degree the position faced by marginalised citizens is the capacity and, of course, willingness of the elected moderator to encourage contributions from those most reluctant to speak. As Zimmerman argues: 'The tone of the town meeting government is set, in part, by individual town officers, boards and committees' (Zimmerman 1999: 174). However, that assumes that the moderator recognises this problem and that marginalised citizens walk through the door of the meeting house in the first place.

Chicago Community Policing may be as far removed from rural self-government as is conceivable, but Fung's study suggests that the typical participation bias appears to have been reversed, with citizens from within poor and less well-educated neighbourhoods turning out at higher rates. The incentive structure is significant: like town meetings, Community Policing can exercise meaningful powers affecting the safety of neighbourhoods. Fung argues that contrary to expectations, 'disadvantaged citizens will overcome quite substantial barriers to participate in institutions that credibly promise to reward such activity with concrete improvements to the public goods upon which those citizens rely' (Fung 2004: 115). However, as with town meetings, there are different rates of participation *within* these poorer social groups, with relatively wealthier residents, homeowners and English speakers participating at higher rates (Fung 2003a: 129; 2003b: 359). Again, evidence suggests that the capabilities of the beat meeting facilitator are crucial in creating an environment in which citizens from more marginalised communities feel willing and able to contribute (Fung 2003a: 135–7).

To what extent does the more complex arrangement of PB ameliorate or reverse some of the worst differentials of participation across social groups? Are any gains lost with an increase in scale? The striking feature of PB is not simply that it engages large numbers of citizens, but that it mobilises significant numbers from amongst the poor of the city; citizens who are typically politically marginalised. It has successfully reversed the trends we associate with political participation, engaging a social group for whom the costs of participation (both direct expenses such as transport and opportunity costs) are high. Comparing her sample of participants in the popular regional assemblies in 1995 with the 1991 census on household incomes,

Abers provides strong evidence that 'socioeconomic inequalities did not reproduce themselves within the budget assemblies. Much to the contrary, the household incomes of budget participants are significantly lower than those of the population as a whole ... participants in the regional assemblies were poorer than the population as a whole' (Abers 2000: 122). A Harvard University study indicates that in 2002, the lowest twentieth percentile of the population accounted for 30 per cent of the participants in the popular regional assemblies (Harvard University Center for Urban Development Studies 2003: 10). Similarly, Marion Gret and Yves Sintomer argue that:

> working-class districts have mobilized more than the average in the participatory process. From as early as 1992, the zones with the highest per capita rate of participation have been the poorest and, to a lesser extent, those just below the municipal average in terms of median income. The poorest 40 per cent of the population account for 60 per cent of the participants in the plenary assemblies. (Gret and Sintomer 2005: 77)

How can we explain this engagement by the traditionally marginalised? After all, in our discussion of trends in participation in Chapter 1, we noted that open consultation forums tend not to be attractive to marginalised social groups? As Abers notes: 'Whereas often participatory policies are dominated by the wealthy, the well educated and representatives of business interests, the opposite is true in the case of the participatory budget' (Abers 1998: 54). The answer lies in the incentive structure implicit within the design of PB. There are at least four interrelated incentives in operation. First, there is a clear relationship between levels of neighbourhood mobilisation in regional popular assemblies and levels of representation on the budget forums in which delegates prioritise the demands of neighbourhoods into a regional list of investments. The more delegates from a neighbourhood, the more influence they can have on investment priorities. Second, the rules operated by the COP to guide the distribution of resources among the various regions of the city have always included at least one criterion related to relative poverty and infrastructure and service deficiencies of regions. There is a distributional bias that favours the poor. Third, the administration has been particularly active in promoting engagement and developing the civic infrastructure in poorer communities. Community organisers are employed to identify and support potential community leaders and to help establish and promote neighbourhood civic organisations. There is plenty of evidence that PB (including the activities of the community organisers) has been an enabling factor in a 'dramatic rise' in new associations across the city as citizens mobilise in response to the opportunities created by PB. This mobilisation often occurs in poorer areas with little tradition of civic organisation (Abers 2000: 166; Baiocchi 2003a: 59). And finally, participation has been enhanced by the 'demonstration effect' (Abers 1998: 138). Citizens in neighbourhoods that did not participate in the early years of the budgeting process witnessed the impact of investment in infrastructure and services in neighbouring communities that were mobilised. In the initial years of the budgeting process, much of the investment was focused in highly visible infrastructure projects, and, as Abers comments, the massive mobilisation of citizens often in areas with no tradition of community organising 'was related to the government's ability to respond to the participants' demands' (Abers 2000: 83).

As with New England town meetings and Chicago Community Policing, these figures mask stratification in participation *across* the poorest communities. One well-documented group who certainly do not participate to the same level is the 'very poorest' – those on the very lowest incomes.

> The very poorest inhabitants of Porto Alegre, who often live in the most unstable and dangerous conditions – such as newly occupied hillsides and flood lands – rarely participate. It is this group of people that probably have the least amount of time to do so – they are struggling hard just to scrape by... The populations of such communities are often transient: residents move out as soon as their financial conditions allow for it. For this reason too, they are unlikely to form neighbourhood associations and take part in processes that take several years to come to fruition. (Abers 1998: 54–5)

Even with dedicated community organisers, the administration has found it extremely difficult to reach and then mobilise this particular subsection of the population, for whom the costs of participation generally remain too high. This common finding across town meetings, Chicago Community Policing and PB indicates how difficult it is to fully realise inclusiveness understood as presence. And lack of presence amongst the very poorest citizens means that their needs and demands are unlikely to be given equal consideration, particularly in PB, where mobilisation can play a significant role in investment decisions. As we shall see later, there is some evidence to suggest that even without weight of numbers, the needs of some of the poorest neighbourhoods have been taken into account when they have been able to voice their perspectives in the regional popular assemblies, but in many cases they are not even present at these gatherings.

In terms of voice – making contributions within the popular assemblies – Gianpaolo Baiocchi provides apparently contradictory evidence on the extent to which different social distinctions have an effect on contributing to discussion and debates: 'Ethnographic evidence from district-level meetings did not show any pattern of women or the less educated speaking less often or conceding authority to educated men. Interviews among participants also revealed that they did not perceive such defects.'

However, his survey evidence found 'that women reported speaking less than men' (Baiocchi 2003a: 55–6). As with town meetings, experience of participation in the process appears to be 'a powerful predictor of whether persons will speak' and when this is taken into consideration, gender differences in voice are reduced. 'Once we consider only persons with a certain number of years of experience, we ... find that there is no significant difference between men and women reporting participation, or between persons with or without formal schooling' (Baiocchi 2003a: 56).

Distinctions between social groups become more obvious when we turn our attention to the selection of citizens for the regional budget forums and the COP: those citizens who have a direct effect on decisions. Here differences in income, gender, age and associational membership are more apparent. Baiocchi reports: 'Women are just over 50 percent of general participants, though they make up only 35 percent of councillors. Low-educated persons are just over 60 percent of the general participants, but constitute only 18 percent of councillors' (Baiocchi 2003a: 53). While the Harvard study reports that in 2002 the lowest twentieth percentile of the population accounted for 30 per cent of the participants in the popular regional assemblies, this drops to around 20 per cent for budget forum delegates and 15 per cent for councillors (Harvard University Center for Urban Development Studies 2003: 10). Baiocchi's analysis of these trends is interesting. He argues that 'neither gender nor education nor poverty significantly affected a person's chance of election'. Other variables have more effect, namely 'years of experience, number of ties in civil society, being on the board of directors of a neighbourhood association, and being retired or self-employed'. In Baiocchi's understanding of PB it is the 'availability of time and women's "second and third shifts" of household responsibilities [that] account for many, if not all, of these differences, particularly with respect to gender' (Baiocchi 2003a: 55). He quotes what he takes as a typical opinion:

> Men are always flying about. To be a councillor you have to be able to go to many meetings, in the evenings, and in many different places. So even if you don't have a job outside, you still have to take care of the house. So I'd say this is more difficult for women. (Baiocchi 2003a: 55)

This does not match the account provided by Abers from her earlier observations of PB in Porto Alegre. She agrees that time is certainly a factor in women's participation, but she argues that they also face two other barriers. The first is gender discrimination within the Brazilian culture. The second, related problem is one of self-confidence amongst women:

> All too often, at the regional forum meetings I observed, women bashfully declared that they were not *capable* of taking on roles, such as coordinator,

special representative to some assembly or municipal council member. Women elected to the executive committees of the Regional Budget Forums or other organisations more often acted as secretaries – taking notes during the assemblies, maintaining the files, and conducting much of the routine, administrative work or the organisations – and less often participating vocally in the discussions taking place. (Abers 2000: 128–9)

Whilst there is some disagreement about the extent and cause of differential participation rates across traditionally marginalised social groups, we should not lose sight of the fact that citizens from these social groups are present, contributing and participating in decision-making in higher numbers than most other institutions. For example, women representatives account for less than 10 per cent of the City Council in Porto Alegre and the number who are poor and without formal education is close to zero. Compared to the formal political institutions of the city (and elsewhere), PB has been effective in mobilising larger proportions of women, the poor, the less educated and minority ethnic groups (Baiocchi 2003a: 75). It is also significant that the level of women's participation in the budget forums and the COP has occurred without any positive discrimination. Although the city administration has expended a great deal of resources on mobilising poor communities, it is perhaps surprising that there have been no programmes specifically targeted at supporting and training women to engage in the process (Abers 2000: 128–9).

Associational membership is the most significant predictor of rates of participation for poor communities. Abers reports that 76 per cent of participants interviewed in the popular assemblies were 'members of some kind of association':

the vast majority of those who participated in the budget process were highly integrated into the civic life of their communities. Those who were more active in the budget process were also more active in civic associations. Of those who had been elected to the Regional Budget Forums, 94 percent were members of civic associations. Seventy-four percent of them attended meetings once a month, and 40 percent attended weekly meetings. (Abers 2000: 166)

At first glance this would seem to be a major limitation of PB. It would suggest that it is already mobilised neighbourhoods and their associations that dominate the process and monopolise the benefits of investment.

But again, the figures do not tell the whole story. First, many citizens have been drawn into civic activism and membership of associations *through* the PB process itself. Both Abers and Baiocchi provide evidence that significant numbers of these members of civic groups had not participated at all or had not been very active before their participation in the budgeting process (Abers 2000: 166; Baiocchi 2003a: 63).

PB has been a significant factor in the increasing associational density in Porto Alegre, particularly in those regions and neighbourhoods that had little tradition of civic organisation. And while many participants do have links to associations, Baiocchi reports that the opportunities to engage in PB generate new participants with no links to civic organisations: 'Each year, between 15 and 20 percent of participants had no previous OP experience and no ties to organised sectors like neighbourhood associations' (Baiocchi 2005: 43). His study of three districts of Porto Alegre shows how the budget process can be a powerful enabling factor, making it 'possible for new players to enter the civic arena. One of the greatest sources of dissatisfaction for many established neighbourhood association activists is, in fact, the appearance of so many new activists' (Baiocchi 2005: 67).

Most studies of PB tend to focus their attention on the popular regional assemblies and the activities of their delegates and councillors in the budget forums and COP respectively. This is not surprising given the degree to which this element of PB has not only ameliorated, but actually reversed established trends in citizen participation. Much less discussed and analysed is the thematic element of the budgetary process, where citizens engage with the administration in developing long-term, city-wide plans and policies in areas such as environment, education and transportation. The high level of participation by the poor is not replicated in the thematic element, and participation rates revert to more typical patterns: the majority of thematic participants have higher than average incomes and levels of education (Santos 1998: 486). The thematic element of the process was introduced in part to respond to the concerns of the middle classes, and it is citizens from this class, along with representatives from NGOs, unions and social movements, that tend to participate (Baiocchi 2005: 40). It appears that as we move to more strategic policy concerns and away from investment that responds directly to citizens' basic needs, the incentive for poor citizens to participate is much reduced and the resources necessary to participate effectively are unevenly distributed: for example, Abers suggests that the level of education and amount of time required for dealing with more general policy themes act as a barrier (Abers 2000: 122). This indicates an under-explored limit to the capacity of PB to realise political equality: once investments are no longer perceived to be of direct relevance to the lives of citizens or are more complex to understand, levels of engagement are likely to drop. The high level of participation from marginalised social groups does not transfer to the thematic stream of PB, nor is it evident in consultation exercises on broad policy themes in Porto Alegre – such as genetic modification and healthcare reform – which consistently fail to attract a broad cross-section of the population. As Abers

recognises: 'The irony here is that the same factor that initiated mobilisation in Porto Alegre – people's desire to address recognisable, immediate
needs – also put the brakes on organisation around less immediate, more
technically inaccessible issues' (Abers 1998: 213). Realising inclusiveness
is clearly tied to the incentive structure embedded within institutional
designs.

Popular control

New England town meetings can be viewed as the epitome of self-government. Members of a small community come together each year to debate
and decide on local decisions such as the level and distribution of local
taxation and to select and hold local officials (elected or appointed) to
account. Even though their governing autonomy has been much eroded
as powers over roads, schools, police, welfare and zoning have transferred
to state and federal level, town meetings still retain powers that can have a
significant impact on the lives of local citizens (Mansbridge 1980: 127–30).
However, Mansbridge's cautionary insights on inequality in Selby need to
be borne in mind in considering the extent to which popular control is
realised across the community: 'When machinists, carpenters, and factory
operatives decide not to exercise political power because they are not smart
enough or educated enough, they acquiesce in a pattern of domination
that undermines their self-esteem' (Mansbridge 1980: 95).

As a form of co-governance (rather than self-government), Chicago
Community Policing offers citizens 'a modicum of real decision making
power' (Fung 2003a: 132). Citizens are able to engage directly with local beat
officers in shaping priorities for action: the 'short feedback loop between
planning, implementation, and assessment increases both the practical capabilities and the problem-solving success of residents and police officers in
each beat' (Fung 2003a: 118). Residents and police officers work together in
an attempt to solve local problems. Fung's analysis strongly suggests that the
role of the beat facilitator is crucial in engendering a constructive and effective co-governance relationship, particularly in ensuring that all sections of
the community are involved in the process (Fung 2003a: 135–7). There are
limits to the governing autonomy of the beat meetings. While the central
Chicago Police Department provides training, resources and coordination
across the beat meetings, it also ensures the effectiveness of the process:

> central managers also monitor the deliberative process and performance
> outcomes of local groups. When they detect shortfalls in local process or per-
> formance, they can intervene and even apply sanctions. Thus neighbourhoods
> are subject to mechanisms of accountability that attempt both to check the

tendencies of autonomy to degenerate into license and to assure that limited devolution advances broader public ends. (Fung 2003a: 114–15)

Compared to New England town meetings, the governing autonomy of citizens in Chicago is limited in two aspects: first, they must negotiate and develop crime reduction strategies in collaboration with beat officers; and second, their activities are monitored by the central Police Department to ensure a satisfactory level of effectiveness.

Understanding the extent of governing autonomy or popular control of PB is more difficult given its relatively complex structure. Citizens are drawn directly into decision-making in a highly significant policy area: the city budget. But to what degree is popular control realised in the process? Against a backdrop of widespread public distrust in politicians and political institutions in Porto Alegre (and across the rest of Brazil), over 70 per cent of participants in the budget assemblies agreed that participants 'always' or 'almost always' 'decide about public works and services' (Abers 2000: 210–11). At the popular assemblies, citizens define the nature of local needs, select their priority areas for investment and elect delegates and councillors; at the regional budget forums, delegates prioritise investments across the region and oversee implementation; and at the COP, councillors decide on the distribution of resources across regions and the rules governing that distribution. What is particularly significant about the budgeting process then is not only that citizens make decisions about which investments occur on an annual basis, but also that they have agenda-setting power in deciding the rules under which that distribution takes place. Equally innovative is the way in which different types of decisions are made in different locations. The discussions and negotiations about regional priorities are kept separate from debates about the rules that should govern the allocation of resources across the city. The former take place in regional budget forums; the latter in the COP. This division of labour helps guard against the concentration of power and the re-emergence of clientalism and corruption.

To what extent is popular control actually realised in practice in the different bodies that make up PB? There are a number of issues to consider, including the official status of PB, the reliance on representatives in the budget forums and the COP, and the potential co-option of citizens who have been drawn into a bureaucratic process where they may be dominated by city officials. Let us take these issues in order.

PB does not have direct legislative power, neither is it codified into municipal law. Does this undermine claims of popular control? PB has only executive powers, delegated by the mayor, who retains the right to veto the budget on limited financial and technical grounds, although this right has never been exercised (Santos 1998: 491). Legislative power to veto and alter the budget rests with the City Council, which has never been under Workers' Party control since the budgeting process was established. Again though, the budget has never been vetoed: it is difficult for the legislature to apply its veto given the popular will that the budget represents. Second, the process is not codified into municipal law, which means that it could be abandoned or restructured by the administration if it so wished. As Baiocchi explains:

> Community activists and administration alike today resist making the OP an official municipal institution, regulated by municipal law, arguing that this would, for example, undermine the process that allows budget councillors to radically alter the rules from year to year. But this makes the OP vulnerable to ... electoral vagaries. (Baiocchi 2005: 154)

The desire of participants to keep the design flexible (it has changed in quite dramatic ways since its inception) must be weighed against the potential protection afforded by codification. Notably, when the Workers' Party lost the 2004 mayoral election, the opposition candidate stood on a platform of improving PB: participants and officials appear to recognise that it is a non-partisan process and one that is embedded (if not codified) in the governance structures of Porto Alegre (Baiocchi 2005: 157–61).

To make PB both a popular process – one that mobilises large numbers of citizens – and a process through which citizens have direct control over resource allocation and the rules governing that allocation at the strategic level (rather than simply devolving a portion of the available budget to each neighbourhood or region of the city), the design relies on the representative principle. It is the institutionalisation of representation that has allowed PB to extend over such a large scale compared to the town meetings of New England or Community Policing in Chicago. Whereas town meetings make final decisions, the popular assemblies of PB provide an occasion for citizens to make investment proposals, hold the administration to account and select representatives from amongst their number to make decisions throughout the coming year. While it is citizens who are making decisions in both the regional budget forums and the COP, they are elected by their peers in the popular assemblies. Does resorting to the representative principle undermine the realisation of popular control? After all, it is the limitations of representative political institutions of advanced industrial democracies that often lead theorists and activists to consider new forms of citizen engagement.

Iris Marion Young succinctly criticises the practice of principal–agent representation when she states: 'In most actually existing democracies, the moment of accountability is weaker than the moment of authorisation'

(Young 2000: 132). Citizens may exert power at the moment of election, but mechanisms of accountability between representatives and citizens are typically weak outside of these moments. While PB institutionalises a similar form of principal–agent representation that rests on the idea that budget delegates and councillors are able to deliberate and decide *for* others (Pitkin 1967: 42–3), has it institutionalised effective forms of accountability?

> Establishing and maintaining legitimate and inclusive processes of representation calls up responsibilities for both officials and citizens. Citizens must be willing and able to mobilise one another actively to participate in processes of both authorising and holding to account. Representatives should listen to these public discussions and diverse claims, stay connected to constituents, and be able to convey reasons for their actions and judgements in terms that recollect their discussions. Such mobilisation, listening, and connectedness can be either facilitated or impeded by the design of representative institutions. (Young 2000: 132)

There are important aspects of the way that representation is institutionalised in PB that point towards a more legitimate and inclusive process. Although in our analysis of inclusiveness we noted that elected delegates and councillors are more likely to be male and have a higher socio-economic status than other participants in the regional assemblies, they are 'still on average poorer than the population as whole' (Abers 2000: 127) and are drawn from the same neighbourhoods and associations as the citizens who have voted for them. Social proximity is a guard against the elitist tendencies of representative systems (Gret and Sintomer 2005: 94–5).

Second, the very rules of representation in PB undermine the ability of representatives to separate themselves from the broader population into a stable political class that concentrates power: a 'whole series of provisions curb the classic logic of representation' (Gret and Sintomer 2005: 121). Terms of office on both regional budget forums and the COP are limited to one year; and councillors are limited to two terms of office only. Both delegates and councillors are subject to recall at any time. Additionally, to reduce any suspicions of illicit influence on the part of the administration, it does not remunerate delegates or councillors (although this may have a negative effect on the capacity of poorer citizens to put themselves forward for election) and employees of the administration are not permitted to hold representative positions within the different bodies of PB.[8] Additionally,

---

[8] These are reminiscent of the type of institutional rules and principles implemented by Green Parties to defend against oligarchic tendencies. However, as parties such as Die Grünen in Germany have achieved electoral success, they have found that many of these

decision-making meetings are open: the decisions of delegates and councillors are made in public. The rules and practices of representation within PB reduce the possibility of corruption and clientalism, practices which have systematically undermined the democratic quality of Brazilian politics, although there are often complaints that budget councillors, in particular, fail to report back adequately to their communities (Santos 1998: 488). That said, the familiar patterns of clientalism are replaced by an institutional structure that facilitates something resembling the 'legitimate and inclusive processes of representation' advocated by democratic theorists such as Young (2000: 132). On the basis of his study of Porto Alegre, Boaventura de Sousa Santos argues:

> In my view, the way the different issues involving the quality of representation have been debated inside and outside the PB institutions bears witness to the engagement of the popular sectors of Porto Alegre in preventing the PB from falling into the trappings of the old clientalist, authoritarian system. (Santos 1998: 491)

Finally, given the way in which the whole process is facilitated by the administration, we need to consider carefully the extent to which citizens are actually able to exert control, or whether this is limited by the actions of officials. Again distinguishing between the different sites of citizen participation is crucial to understanding the degree to which popular control is realised. Citizens in the popular assemblies and their delegates in the regional budget forums have extensive autonomy over the prioritisation of investments in regions and neighbourhoods of the city. The main role that the administration plays is to facilitate meetings and to help mobilise citizens to participate. The one area where popular control is limited is in defining technical viability: city agencies are able to veto demands if they consider them to be technically inadvisable or economically inefficient. Even then, delegates have on occasion fought successfully to ensure progress for projects that officials originally considered unjustified (Abers 2000: 203–10).

The bodies where formal control may be compromised in practice are the COP and the thematic budget forums, where councillors and delegates are, by the nature of the decisions under consideration, more reliant on the technical knowledge of administration officials. In her detailed study of PB, Abers questions whether budget councillors have the capacity to effectively exercise their functions. Budget councillors have used their powers to change the rules governing the allocation of resources across the city. For example, they removed one of the criteria – the importance of

---

rules and principles militate against effective decision-making, understood as the capacity to respond quickly to changing political events (Rihoux and Rüdig 2006).

the district for the development of Porto Alegre – because it left too much discretion in the hands of the administration in defining relative importance. At times the COP has also effectively argued for an increase in the scope of the budget, often in the face of resistance from administration officials (Santos 1998: 497). Whilst recognising these occasional examples of resistance against the wishes of the administration, Abers argues that the Council is 'generally incapable of taking advantage' of its power (Abers 2000: 203). Budget councillors may have formal decision-making power, but they are almost exclusively reliant on information and technical advice from the administration: 'In such a system of co-government, the executive does have a very active role, if for nothing else because it controls technical knowledge and also because it either generates the relevant information or has privileged access to it' (Santos 1998: 492). The formal balance of power is different from the co-governance arrangements in Chicago Community Policing since citizens in Porto Alegre are the decision-makers. However, their reliance on officials can have a significant effect on the balance of power in practice. We will have more to say about the capacity of councillors to make considered judgements in the next section of this chapter. For now it is enough to recognise that the time constraints that councillors work under and their reliance on information from the administration make it difficult for them to fully scrutinise the administration's proposals, which include highly technical reports on the distribution of resources amongst agencies, agency investment plans, calculations based on the distributional criteria, and so forth. As Abers suggests, councillors' 'compliance suggests that GAPLAN's ability to convince the council members to favour its proposals was not just a matter of superior technical knowledge and explanatory capacities. The council members were simply overburdened with responsibilities' (Abers 1998: 202).

An important difference therefore emerges between different bodies within the budgetary process. As Abers notes:

> On balance, the regional forums were able to resist the positions of the government more effectively than was the Municipal Budget Council [or COP]. Whereas the council almost always passed government proposals, the forums often resisted government claims and fought for their priorities. The principal explanation for this difference lies in the organisational structures of the two forums. The council members were overburdened with responsibilities and were largely occupied with approving government proposals. The regional delegates, however, spent most of their time organising around the demands that they themselves brought to the table. (Abers 1998: 210)

Abers suggests that this difference may represent a dilemma for the design of participatory forms of governance. She draws an important distinction between participatory bodies that analyse 'top-down proposals' and those that involve a 'bottom-up priority formulation process', with the former (as represented by the COP) more likely to demobilise 'potentially powerful radical activists'. As she argues: 'In Porto Alegre, participants were much more likely to mobilise passionately against a government veto of their own proposals than to reject government-defined proposals' (Abers 2000: 211).

This concern with 'demobilisation' is shared by a number of activists in the city – particularly those with a long history of civic activity from before PB. For them, PB represents a process of bureaucratisation of once radical social movements. As one activist puts it, 'I am afraid we have become tools of the administration' (Baiocchi 2005: 121).

> Porto Alegre's citizens may have become overly involved in local questions at the expense of broader issues. Many older activists decry the 'excessive pragmatism' of a younger generation more concerned with urban services than ideological discussions … And many activists mentioned the decline in contention as a worrisome issue. The question that remains is whether civil society's focus almost exclusively on local issues, as a result of the success of the participatory process in delivering results, is to its detriment … While the municipal government has attempted to address these criticisms by expanding participatory processes to include broader areas of municipal governance, activists today express disappointment at the inability to mobilise around concerns aimed at the federal government. (Baiocchi 2005: 153)

This echoes concerns about the extent to which participation can be a form of co-option and reminds us of Ricardo Blaug's distinction between critical and incumbent democracy that we introduced at the beginning of the book, with PB enhancing incumbent activities to the detriment of acts of resistance (Blaug 2002: 107). The extent of protest activity has declined across the city as activists put much of their energies into the budget process and see returns for their communities. As such, Baiocchi questions whether 'the process has become *too* successful in attracting participants and channelling the energies of civil society' (Baiocchi 2005: 153). But whether this undermines empowerment as Blaug's distinction assumes is rather more difficult to assess. After all, ever-increasing numbers of citizens from politically marginalised groups – many of whom had never participated before – have been able to affect the distribution of resources across the city and in so doing improve their quality of life. Further, the uncodified nature of PB also means that citizens have the power to restructure elements of the institution. And, as we shall see later in the chapter, the budgetary process appears to have led to an increase in the numbers of civil society organisations, particularly in areas where activity was conspicuous by its absence. It is difficult to argue that this is not indicative of an increase in political efficacy and empowerment. It is also notable that much of the dissatisfaction with PB is amongst older activists who may have lost their former privileged status as new citizens have become active through the process (Baiocchi 2005: 67). It remains an open question then as to whether PB has been successful in providing an avenue for citizens to directly affect decisions about resource allocation, but in the process limiting their ambitions in broader political terms.

In summary then, the extent to which PB realises popular control can be contested. In formal terms, citizens – or at least their elected budget delegates and councillors – are given control over significant decisions about resource allocation. The popular assemblies play a significant role in legitimising the process, given the large number of citizens who attend on an annual basis. But to what extent is popular control actually realised in practice? Our brief discussion of the pressures that are on budget councillors certainly raises questions about their capacity to fully exercise the power that lies in their hands. Citizens are at a disadvantage when they are participants in bodies where they are required to directly engage and negotiate with officials, scrutinising their proposals and policies. The technical knowledge, experience and bureaucratic support available to officials places them in a powerful position vis-à-vis ordinary citizens. Finally, there is some disquiet amongst activists that the very effectiveness of PB may draw the energies of activists into the process and away from significant forms of injustice that operate through other channels.

Considered judgement

One of the virtues of localised self-governance (town meetings) and co-governance (Chicago Community Policing) is that citizens, at least in principle, have direct knowledge and understanding of the issues under consideration. According to Fung, the Chicago Police Department reforms 'presumed that problem-solving efforts would work best with deep citizen involvement. On this view, residents often possess superior knowledge of problems in their neighbourhood and might have different priorities' (Fung 2003a: 112). Additionally, the public nature of interactions means that open forums encourage participants away from making purely self-interested demands, particularly as the assembly is constituted by neighbours. As Zimmerman argues: 'The open town meeting is predicated on the theory that ordinary voters possess the native intelligence to weigh the pros and cons of an issue and the political acumen to make wise decisions' (Zimmerman 1999: 185).

Mansbridge's study indicates that in the town meeting of Selby, participants express a strong degree of empathy towards their fellow residents and a belief that their interests overlap: prime conditions for the realisation of considered judgement. However, she finds 'conflicting estimates of who can best pursue the common good' (Mansbridge 1980: 77), with old-timers appealing to their understanding of the town's traditions and newcomers arguing that their education and professional expertise give them more competence in making difficult judgements (Mansbridge 1980: 81–8). As we noted in our discussion of inclusiveness, more marginalised residents often choose to acquiesce rather than voice conflicting opinions. There is a danger within such a relatively small community that differences are not articulated, in order to avoid psychologically and socially damaging conflict amongst participants who must live with each other day-to-day. The perspectives of dominant actors in the community tend to define the judgements of the meeting. While there is an important role for the moderator in ensuring that conflicting voices are heard, the fact that the holder of this position is drawn from within the community means that latent conflicts may well remain hidden.

The important role that a moderator can play in constructing an environment in which considered judgement can be realised is highlighted in Fung's analysis of Chicago Community Policing. In his discussion of Traxton beat – a neighbourhood split in half between the west-side 'wealthy, mostly white, professionals' and the east-side 'lower middle class African-Americans' – he notes that in 1996 the elected beat facilitator 'conducted meetings in a laissez faire, first-come, first-served, style' such that residents from the west-side dominated discussions and consequently their interests were at the top of the local priorities, even though the east-side suffered the most serious crimes (Fung 2003a: 135–7; see also Fung 2004: 173–97). The election of a facilitator trained in problem-solving techniques in 1997 changed the dynamics of the beat meeting completely. She created space within which participants from either side of the neighbourhood learnt about the problems facing the other group and prioritised these problems together: 'Once charged with ranking and discursively justifying an agenda of public safety problems, the better-off residents quickly agreed that the east-side house, around which shootings occurred and drugs were trafficked, topped the list and therefore deserved the lion's share of their attention and that of the police' (Fung 2003a: 136).

The differing structures of sites of engagement within PB shape the types of judgements made by citizens. Crucial to any form of judgement is access to information. Given the complexity of the budgeting process and the need to guard against corruption, access to information is a guiding principle in the design of the process. This is realised through a variety of means: account-giving by officials at popular assemblies and at budget forum and COP meetings; the computerised project management system that ensures that information is available on the progress of investment projects and the funding of city agencies; and the activities of community organisers who provide participants with details of the workings of the budget process. Few participants complain about the quality of municipal information (Gret and Sintomer 2005: 85).

PB is, arguably, built on two logics that may at times be in tension: competition and solidarity. Neighbourhoods are enabled to bring forward their investment demands and priorities and the more participants they are able to mobilise, the more representation their neighbourhoods will have on their regional budget forum. Community organisers – employees of the administration – can play an important role in mobilising neighbourhoods with little history of civic activity, but it is the demands as defined by the citizens themselves that are presented to and considered at the popular assemblies and regional budget forums. This competitive logic within and between neighbourhoods is one of the main incentives to participate since there is a relationship between mobilisation and the ability of delegates to affect outcomes (Abers 1998: 223; 2003: 206). Elected delegates are expected to argue the case for their own neighbourhood's priorities – this pressure may impede more cooperative and deliberative interactions. Certainly the interactions in budget forums can be hostile and conflictual (Baiocchi 2005; Santos 1998). Such a competitive environment may appear inhospitable to the type of considered and reflective judgement that is perceived by many theorists as a good of democratic institutions. It leads to bargaining and negotiation between delegates as they manoeuvre to gain support for their priorities, often trading support for each others' projects. And under such circumstances, we would expect the less mobilised – typically the very poorest neighbourhoods – to be at a distinct disadvantage.

But there are aspects of the design and practice of budget forums that can temper this competitive logic, orientating delegates to the needs and interests of other neighbourhoods and common interests of the region of the city as a whole. First, the ongoing nature of the budgeting process means that delegates and neighbourhoods are able to build up trust across geographical areas. Given the size of regions, no one neighbourhood is generally able to dominate proceedings, so delegates often have to compromise, coming to agreements that different neighbourhoods will take it in turn to have their demands prioritised. The importance of these ongoing interactions should not be underestimated: 'through the budget process, neighbourhood groups learned to trust one another, engaging in long-term relations of reciprocity' (Abers 1998: 168). The building up of trust is also important in creating the conditions for support for collective projects across the region rather than in individual neighbourhoods. Baiocchi provides the example of the development of a new school in the Nordeste district. In 1998, activists in the district successfully persuaded delegates from different neighbourhoods to forgo their individual infrastructure demands to collectively prioritise education, receiving 'one of the single largest endowments for a project from the following year's budget, funds of over a million reais (roughly US$500,000) to build a new school' (Baiocchi 2005: 81).

Second, regional budget forums have been known to prioritise the needs of the poorest neighbourhoods even when they have low levels of representation. The presence of one or two delegates from the neighbourhoods can be enough to persuade the forum to prioritise their demands. As Abers notes:

> ethical questions about relative needs did have weight in the negotiating process. Although neighbourhood leaders often joined up to pursue their own neighbourhood's needs, awareness of bad conditions in other neighbourhoods made a difference when it came to ordering priorities. But arguments about the greater necessity of certain settlements could be ignored if no one was at the meeting to speak for them. When someone was present to remind people of a situation of great need, participants often found it very difficult to ignore. (Abers 1998: 183–4)

The needs of the very poor are often reinforced by forum visits to the different neighbourhoods so that delegates are able to witness at first hand the conditions people are living in. As Abers reports, this helped broaden perspectives. One delegate comments: 'These visits by the delegates changed things ... You think of yourself as needy, but then when you arrive in that other community and you see people even more miserable, you realise that your situation isn't that difficult. That you are even privileged' (Abers 1998: 183). Baiocchi recounts a similar view from a delegate from the Nordeste district, where they hired a bus to drive around the different settlements before deciding on priorities: 'it would be impossible to know what was going on in another settlement without seeing it' (Baiocchi 2005: 148).

Third, the community organisers play a significant didactic role in shaping discussions. Within PB, public education is not simply understood as the provision of information about budgetary rules and the condition of different neighbourhoods and development of political skills, but also the promotion of a particular orientation amongst participants towards cooperation and solidarity: 'Community organisers hired by the government worked closely with delegates all year-round, disseminating information about the workings of the budget and the kinds of investment possible, but also promoting ideas about distributional justice' (Abers 1998: 193). Baiocchi quotes a meeting facilitator:

> Another task ... is to preserve and help diffuse values. The participatory budget demands the construction of cooperation and solidarity, otherwise the logic of competition and 'taking advantage' becomes established, creating processes of

exclusion. Therefore, negotiations inspired by a solidaristic practice must be a constant in the pedagogical actions of facilitators. (Baiocchi 2003a: 56)

And it is not just community organisers who attempt to orientate participants towards common interests. Baiocchi quotes a pamphlet from the Partenon Popular Council, an independent civic organisation that has taken on the role of overseeing the activities of the region's budget forum:

> The resources destined for our district, as well as for the other fifteen districts, are not sufficient to attend to all our demands ... therefore, we need to define which of the demands will really attend to the principal needs of our residents, that is, works that have a social interest, such as: streets that lead to a school, hospitals ... We shall only reach agreement about the priorities of the Partenon district with broad and democratic discussions. Talk to your neighbours, find your neighbourhood association, participate in the meetings of the popular council, form a street committee, and let's clear up our doubts. (Baiocchi 2005: 87–8)

Against an apparently unpromising background of competition and negotiation, there is evidence that more reflective and considered forms of judgement are possible and do influence the decisions of regional budget forums. Whilst strategic forms of interaction often dominate, there is space for more deliberative interactions, where perspectives are broadened and justice is a prime consideration: 'many participants recognised that the participatory ideal would lose much of its legitimacy if it systematically ignored very needy neighbourhoods' (Abers 1998: 193). Whilst democratic theorists often wish to privilege the latter form of engagement, it is important to recognise that the celebrated levels of participation are achieved because neighbourhoods believe that mobilisation will have an effect on final decisions. If this competitive incentive were removed, active engagement and support for the process might dwindle.

Whilst it is apparent that regional budget forums exhibit 'mixed motives' (Abers 1998: 181), the COP is intentionally designed to reduce the impact of narrow self-interest and promote considered judgement. All regions have two councillors – levels of regional mobilisation do not affect representation in this body – who are elected for one-year terms, limited to two terms of office and subject to immediate recall. And the work undertaken by the COP is such that it orientates councillors towards questions of justice. Councillors are primarily concerned with establishing the rules of the game: what criteria should guide the distribution of resources across the city? What is particularly innovative about the design of PB is that councillors oversee the implementation of the budget using the criteria generated by the previous year's COP and then discuss the rules for the following year's budget. By separating the cycle of rule-making from distribution of resources, it is difficult for councillors to second-guess the priorities that will emerge from regions in the following year. Add to this the equal representation of regions, and it is clear that the context of engagement orientates councillors towards consideration of the fairness of rules and principles. It is notable that in the early years of the budget, councillors were quick to remove criteria that they believed were unfair: a criterion that distinguished between regions on the basis of levels of popular mobilisation which systematically gave preference to a minority of regions; and another that reflected the importance of the district for the development of Porto Alegre which left much discretion in the hands of the administration (Abers 1998: 80; Santos 1998: 478). As Abers notes: 'According to Luciano Fedozzi – the first strategic planning coordinator of GAPLAN – the main democratic accomplishment of the participatory budget was the proliferation of such "impersonal, objective and universal criteria in the allocation of resources"'(Abers 2000: 79).

In principle, the mode of selection and remit of the COP appear conducive to enlarged mentality. However, as we noted in the previous section on popular control, the actual operation of the Council may require us to temper such claims. Two aspects of the design of the council may limit the capacity of citizens to make considered judgements on certain issues. First, budget councillors are expected to consider complex technical proposals from the administration in the limited timeframe of an annual budget cycle. Abers questions whether citizens have the competence and/or the time to fully understand the implications of proposals.

> Most of the time, council members had neither the technical capacity nor the time to seriously evaluate them. Most members had little more than primary education and many had full-time jobs that severely limited the time they could devote to council activities. The result was that, with few exceptions, the council simply rubber-stamped government proposals. (Abers 1998: 201)

Apart from the burden of time, one of the problems facing councillors is effectively scrutinising administration proposals when their main source of information is the administration itself. Technical staff are paying more attention to making recommendations more accessible to lay citizens, and NGOs and the city's university provide intensive training to councillors (and delegates) in order to raise their level of budgetary knowledge and skills of engagement (Santos 1998). However, citizens still remain at a disadvantage in terms of access to information and technical knowledge and understanding. Whether they lack the intellectual skills to understand the administration's proposals, or whether it is simply the lack of available time and training is a moot point and one where there is little evidence from existing studies. What is clear is that councillors often find themselves in a position where they are forced to make judgements without fully comprehending the technical details of proposals. While the remit of the COP orientates participants to questions of justice and fairness, the sheer burden of information can overwhelm and as such impacts on their capacity to make informed and considered judgements.

Transparency

Arguably transparency – both internal and external – is most easily achieved in small-scale assemblies. After all, participants are neighbours. Residents of New England town meetings are generally well aware of when the annual town meeting takes place and the type of business that it deals with. However, as we discussed in relation to inclusiveness, Mansbridge's study of Selby indicates how informal practices of town meetings can be opaque to newcomers. The relatively small size of beat meetings in Chicago Community Policing improves the likelihood that internal transparency is high, and around 79 per cent of Chicago residents are aware of the programme, even if a much smaller number actually participate (Fung 2003a: 121).

Working on a larger scale, a much-lauded achievement of PB in Porto Alegre is the way in which it has replaced clientalist and corrupt relations with a much more transparent form of participatory governance. In a country where clientalism is rife, this is no mean feat. As a Harvard report notes: 'Even among those participants who do not get their project funded in a particular budget cycle, there is enthusiastic support for the opportunity to participate in decisions affecting the allocation of local resources. They are convinced that the OP reduces the potential for deal making, clientalism and corruption' (Harvard University Center for Urban Development Studies 2003: 63). Whilst few citizens can fully comprehend the complexity and technicalities of the calculations made in the COP, the broad criteria guiding allocation and the basic logic and structure of PB are well understood.

One of the main functions of the popular assemblies is account-giving on the part of administration officials. Once officials (including the mayor) have presented an overview of progress on investments from previous years, citizens are able to publicly question them about particular developments or broader policy issues.

> [T]his 'accounting' provides transparency and legitimacy, and participants repeatedly highlighted the importance of this part of the process. Owing to the fact that participants were vested with the power to demand accountability, it was impossible for the mayor's team to avoid having to answer for a range of governmental actions, much beyond the participatory budgeting. (Baiocchi 2005: 75)

Other features of PB are also designed to realise transparency and publicity. The regular meetings of budget forums and the COP are open to citizens, although they are limited to observer status in the COP meetings. The computerised project management system provides detailed information on the progress of projects and the way that money is spent across the city, offering further resources for popular oversight. Finally, community organisers actively promote the budget process, both in terms of educating participants and attempting to draw new citizens into the process.

Given the distribution of resources that has occurred, it is not surprising that there is fairly widespread popular support for the process from citizens in poorer neighbourhoods. Perhaps more surprising is the support from middle-class neighbourhoods that had traditionally enjoyed higher levels of investment and now tend to lose out under PB. Again, it is the transparency of the process and its impact on corruption that has been important in engendering broader support for the participatory experiment beyond those neighbourhoods that achieved direct investment: 'the policy acquired support of a middle class that wished for a government associated with social justice, transparency, and the battle against corruption' (Abers 2003: 202–3; see also Gret and Sintomer 2005: 91–2; Schneider and Goldfrank 2000: 15). Arguably, one indication of the impact of transparency and the support for PB is the decrease in tax evasion: 'in Porto Alegre, property tax delinquency dropped from 20 per cent to 15 per cent and, in less than ten years, property taxes grew from 6 per cent to almost 12 per cent of the municipality's revenues' (Cabannes 2004: 36).

Efficiency

Democratic innovations such as New England town meetings and Chicago Community Policing demand time and energy from citizens. To be an effective form of self-government, town meetings rely on a significant proportion of citizens being willing to give up a day's work (or other activities) to attend, and the willingness of a small group to stand for local office. Zimmerman argues that the fact that the annual assembly is no longer a holiday and pageant in most small towns, no longer plays its previous social function and must compete with other forms of entertainment and activity, explains why participation rates are not higher and why the number of citizens willing to put themselves forward for election to town offices is low (Zimmerman 1999: 166–8). Given the competing demands on time, levels of participation remain fairly impressive and compare well with turnout in local elections, which is much less demanding. The psychological barriers that often stop more politically marginalised citizens from attending and/or speaking often combine with fiscal limitations:

losing a day's labour or paying for childcare means that poorer residents and women can face increased burdens compared to other residents.

Community Policing places demands on both residents and the Police Department. More regular (but shorter) meetings must compete with other commitments and again place increased demands on poorer residents and parents (typically women) who require childcare. As a form of co-governance, it also places burdens on the Police Department. While there are gains to be had from developing neighbourhood strategies, the process requires police officers to engage in local meetings rather than in other activities. The Police Department has clearly decided that the gains in public safety and legitimacy outweigh the costs of the engagement strategy. This is also the calculation of a significant number of residents who have been willing to engage in the process.

Similarly, a process like PB places demands on both citizens and the administration. Since it has been operating successfully for over fifteen years, drawing in ever more numbers of citizens and extending its areas of competence, the costs involved are obviously not insurmountable. As Fung argues: 'The extravagant participation that Participatory Budgeting requires can be regarded as a cost, but one worth paying to reduce corruption' (Fung 2007: 455).

The design of PB explicitly creates a division of labour between tasks. While ensuring that there are meaningful opportunities and incentives for all citizens to participate in the large-scale popular assemblies, the more complex aspects of the budget process – e.g. prioritising of a region's investment demands, allocation of the budget across the city and reviewing the rules and procedures of allocation – take place in smaller representative bodies (the budget forums and COP). Elected delegates and councillors take on much of the day-to-day work in the budget process. The costs for these individuals are often high – in terms of expenses to attend meetings and opportunity costs – but it has important rewards in terms of community prestige and reputation as improvements occur in their often impoverished neighbourhoods (Baiocchi 2005: 110). But unlike the former clientalist relationships, the activities of delegates and councillors are far more transparent, and the opportunity to concentrate power in the hands of a select few is removed by the annual electoral process and the rotation of positions for councillors. Thus, potential community leaders are regularly held to account by residents. PB indicates that where the incentive structure is well conceived, forms of participatory governance can attract significant numbers of citizens and reverse the traditional socio-economic bias in political engagement.

The institutionalisation of PB also involves a significant cost to the administration, requiring considerable restructuring in its operations, in particular the creation of GAPLAN to ensure coordination across the administration and the CRC to promote community mobilisation in those areas with little civic activity. As a Harvard study on PB notes:

> As the scale of the operation expands with the size of the city, there is a significant but manageable cost to institute and implement the OP. Assessment of feasibility depends on the value placed on empowerment and participatory local governance. It is primarily a political decision because the constraint on successful implementation is institutional capacity rather than costs per se. (Harvard University Center for Urban Development Studies 2003: 63)

Internal administrative reform was necessary because the leaders of the Workers' Party recognised that there would likely be institutional resistance to changes in bureaucratic practice as citizens challenged the technical expertise of officials and agencies. GAPLAN's role was to ensure that the demands emerging from the budgetary process were met by the city's bureaucracy. The demonstration effect is crucial to the ongoing success of participatory governance in the city. Second, it was recognised that the administration would have to enable participation, particularly in those neighbourhoods where there was little tradition of civic organisation. An apparent civic benefit of the budgeting process has been the increase in associational activity, particularly in politically marginalised districts. In his study of the Nordeste district, Baiocchi notes that in 1989 there were only four active associations; in 2001, twenty-eight associations were electing delegates for the budget process (Baiocchi 2005: 148). 'Its residents, who were previously the most disenfranchised and without access to networks of power, have become the most enthusiastic participants' (Baiocchi 2005: 69). It is estimated that around half of the city's associations have been founded or restarted since the establishment of PB (Baiocchi 2005: 116). In calculating the efficiency of a mode of participatory governance, PB reminds us that we ought to consider its broad effects on civil society.

The benefits to the political life of the city are clear. Lines of accountability have been created where before corruption and clientalism were rife. No assessment has been attempted to compare the costs of PB to traditional budgeting processes. Once again, the Harvard evaluation notes:

> Such a study is technically feasible but its practical relevance should be questioned. In many ways, appraising the [PB] by the standard techniques of economic analysis would fail to capture the multifaceted impacts of a system that is primarily an instrument of empowerment. (Harvard University Center for Urban Development Studies 2003: 12)

The burdens of participation associated with active citizenship and institutional reorganisation appear to be worth bearing in Porto Alegre, where the effects on governance and civil society are so visible and beneficial.

Transferability

Most studies of PB point to a particular set of contextual factors that led to its establishment and success in Porto Alegre (see, for example, Baiocchi 2005: 137–55; Gret and Sintomer 2005: 69–70; Harvard University Center for Urban Development Studies 2003: 18). First, there was a favourable financial and legal situation. The financial autonomy afforded to Brazilian municipalities under the 1988 constitution meant that the mayor had discretion over a significant and guaranteed resource stream. Second, the 'spoils system' allowed the mayor to make strategic senior appointments: this was crucial in appointing officials within GAPLAN and CRC who were supportive of the goals of participatory governance and willing to initiate necessary administrative reforms. Third, the election of the Workers' Party candidate to the position of mayor came at a time when there was significant associational activity in the city in opposition to the culture of corruption and clientalism. And finally, the leadership of the Workers' Party in Porto Alegre was relatively pragmatic, eschewing a system of governance that privileged their own supporters and associations and instead developing a participatory process that aims to democratise access to power.[9] The question, then, is whether this specific set of circumstances means that PB is highly context-specific: can this form of governance be transferred, particularly to advanced industrial democracies?

The idea of PB has spread not only across Brazil, but also further afield in Latin America and into Europe (Allegretti and Herzberg 2004; Cabannes 2004; Talpin 2007). According to Baiocchi: 'The actual number of municipalities with such experiments, whether in name or spirit, is probably in the hundreds worldwide' (Baiocchi 2005: 154). Baiocchi is right to add the caveat 'in name or spirit' because it is clear from comparative studies that what is termed PB varies considerably. Given our definition of democratic innovation, we are interested in participatory budgets that have the following defining features. First, the process should engage citizens rather than the representatives of civil society organisations. A number of municipalities have established a budgeting process that is better understood as a form of community-based representative democracy rather than citizen engagement (Cabannes 2004: 28). PB in Belo Horizonte, for example, is based on engaging accredited community associations, rather than the 'citizen-focused' approach of Porto Alegre (Harvard University Center for Urban Development Studies 2003: 48). Second, citizens should have decision-making powers. A number of examples of PB are really nothing more

---

[9] It is undeniable that participatory budgeting was part of an electoral strategy to widen political support for the Workers' Party.

than an elaborate form of budget consultation where citizens only make demands. A defining feature of the Porto Alegre model is that citizens are drawn into the process of rule-making (through the COP), overseeing implementation and holding the administration to account. The third crucial feature is the capacity and willingness of the administration to respond to the participatory process. The administration needs to follow through in terms of implementation of projects. This is likely to require institutional reorganisation, both in terms of internal coordination and enabling participation through community organisers. These features of the budgetary process can be transferred, but it is unclear how many municipalities have fully embraced the political and bureaucratic implications of PB. As an assessment report produced at Harvard University argues: 'Political and managerial considerations rather than financial constraints are the determinant factors of success. Failures in the implementation process alienate citizens and carry a political risk' (Harvard University Center for Urban Development Studies 2003: 63).

PB has been established in a large number of Brazilian municipalities, particularly where the Workers' Party has or has had administrative control (Baiocchi 2003b). The idea has also spread into other Latin American cities, although they 'tend to favour participation through representatives of existing organisations' (Cabannes 2004: 36). There are some interesting examples where additional features have been incorporated into the original Porto Alegre design. In Belém (which has also received much attention from international agencies such as UN-HABITAT) citizens not only appoint budget delegates and councillors, but also overseers who are responsible for monitoring the implementation process (Guidry and Petit 2003: 62). Other cities have followed this lead and established specific commissions composed of elected citizens to inspect and oversee works (Cabannes 2004: 38). Developments indicate the extent to which the Porto Alegre design is being creatively extended, often in response to perceived limitations:

> Recife's PB has a committee dedicated to women, a singular experience at global level. Barra Mansa and Icapuí have been pioneers in introducing the perspective of children and youth, and this is now being experimented with in Recife, São Paolo, Goianna, Mundo Novo and Alvorada. Various cities are taking affirmative action to foster the participation of women and other excluded groups. Ilo (Peru) has established a system of quotas to ensure that 50 per cent of the delegates are women, and at least three of them are part of the directive committee of the participatory budget. In Rosario (Argentina), at least one-third of the councillors must be women. In Belém, delegates are elected for each specific committee: women, blacks, indigenous, homosexuals, elderly people, adolescents, children, disabled people and those who observe

Afro-Brazilian religions. It is an important contribution to the debate on participatory budgets and inclusion. Affirmative action has also been introduced into the participatory budget of São Paolo. (Cabannes 2004: 38)

Even where the context appears inhospitable to PB, there are examples of effective institutionalisation. Unlike Porto Alegre, where significant numbers of associations were supportive at the very inception of the process, in Alvorada PB was established in spite of associational opposition to a process that would lessen their political influence (Silva 2003: 117–23). There are, of course, examples where PB has been less successful: Cabannes reports a study by the Brazilian Forum of Popular Participation that 'indicates that, between 1997 and 2000, PB experiments were halted in 20 per cent of the 103 cases studied' (Cabannes 2004: 45). In some cases this appears to be when lessons from Porto Alegre and other locations are not fully understood or embedded. One of the main reasons why the budgetary process in both João Monlevade and Betim failed was because they were highly partisan, in that their design attracted only supporters of the Workers' Party. Not surprisingly, when the party lost control, PB was abandoned. Again though, there are examples of where PB has been continued when the Workers' Party is no longer in power. Porto Alegre is one such case, and Marchelo Kunrath Silva offers the example of Gravataí, where community organizations 'affiliated with opposition parties have pragmatically aligned themselves with the PB process; it has become difficult to defend a position that is against a process that introduces significant improvements to the population's quality of life' (Silva 2003: 126).

Significantly, Brazil has also witnessed the implementation of a participatory budgetary process at state-level in Rio Grande do Sul, offering some insight into whether it is possible to transfer the design to higher levels of political organisation. The majority of budgetary experiments have been in municipalities of less than 1 million people; in comparison, Rio Grande do Sul is 600 times the area of Porto Alegre, with a more ethnically diverse population of 10 million, around 20 per cent of whom live in rural areas. Policy transfer to state level was enabled by officials who had played similar roles in Porto Alegre: Governor Olivio Dutra, Budget Secretary Ubiratan de Souza and Community Relations Secretary Iria Charão. They were also building on the direct experience of over forty municipalities within the state (including Porto Alegre) that had already established PB (Goldfrank and Schneider 2003: 170).

The structure of PB at state level is broadly similar to Porto Alegre, although certain compromises have to be made, given the scale of activities, including an additional layer of representation (Harvard University Center for Urban Development Studies 2003: 35–9; Goldfrank and

Schneider 2003: 165). Given the distances involved, meetings are less frequent and quicker, making use of computerised voting and tabulation technology. According to officials in the state administration, this makes the process more 'efficient', although it is at the expense of the didactic and democratic quality of the process: there is less opportunity for face-to-face contact between citizens, which may have an effect on their ability to exchange information and become well informed before making decisions (Schneider and Goldfrank 2000: 4; Goldfrank and Schneider 2003: 167).

The process has engaged a significant number of the state's citizens, with the administration estimating that some '1.2 million people have been reached and participated in the OP over the four years, 1999–2002. This represents 16% of the electorate, and more importantly, includes 12% of the gaúcha population mostly in the rural areas and small towns' (Harvard University Center for Urban Development Studies 2003: 36).[10] There is evidence, however, that the larger scale has had an effect on women's participation across the state, 'which falls off rapidly the farther away from the community public meetings are held' (Harvard University Center for Urban Development Studies 2003: 38). State-level PB appears to have had progressive impacts on government expenditure, with positive social outcomes, including reduced infant mortality and increased numbers of gaúcha cities with a secure water supply (Goldfrank and Schneider 2003: 171).

Compared to Porto Alegre, the administration of Rio Grande do Sul has faced difficult political and administrative problems in institutionalising PB. First, compared to municipalities, the state is in a financially weak situation, with proportionally fewer resources available for distribution. Second, the process has been politically charged, with strong opposition from other political parties and within the administration itself. There have been difficulties in integrating planning and implementation, with less bureaucratic commitment to the process. In the face of such problems, Aaron Schneider and Ben Goldfrank still optimistically argue that:

> the experience of participatory budgeting in Rio Grande do Sul contradicts some accepted wisdom within theories of participation and theories of budgeting. First participatory democracy appears to be both possible and advantageous in large groups. Second, participation does not necessarily imply a loss of capacity to operate efficiently and plan effectively (Schneider and Goldfrank 2000: 20)

[10] These percentages are not completely accurate since the total quoted is a cumulative number over the four years and, therefore, includes people who attended in consecutive years.

And finally, what about transfer to advanced industrial democracies? To what extent has PB been effectively institutionalised within these polities? There is much interest in PB, particularly in Europe, although the majority of designs operating under the banner 'participatory budgeting' share little with Porto Alegre, except the name. Many of the European developments are little more than elaborate forms of consultation, with politicians and officials exercising a high degree of influence and control over the process and, as Yves Cabannes notes: 'Despite their much higher budgets per inhabitant, the European cities are not those that put more resources under discussion' (Cabannes 2004: 35). It is rare that citizens are afforded much political power beyond simply putting forward investment proposals (Allegretti and Herzberg 2004; Talpin 2007). There are a number of factors that may explain this situation.

First, the administrative structure of most European polities means that municipalities rarely have the political and fiscal freedom or the range of competences afforded their counterparts in Brazil. Two rare examples of participatory budgets that embrace many of the core aspects of the structure of Porto Alegre, in particular the COP, where elected budget councillors establish social justice criteria to guide the process, take place in Cordoba and Seville in Spain (Allegretti and Herzberg 2004; Talpin 2007). The federal system arguably provides for more political and fiscal independence for municipalities than most other European nations.

Second, the material conditions of advanced industrial democracies may require significant changes to the design of the process, changes that likely alter the important incentive structure embedded within the Porto Alegre model. The success of PB in Porto Alegre in attracting high levels of participation amongst lower socio-economic groups is tied to the capacity of the process to deliver investments in neighbourhoods. And the investments prioritised by citizens tend to be in areas such as sanitation, paving, basic healthcare and education, and so on. Projects are highly visible and respond to citizens' unmet basic needs. In advanced industrial democracies, the issues that mobilise such large numbers of citizens in Porto Alegre are not so relevant, because basic needs are generally already being met by public authorities. Is the answer then to organise PB around broader issues such as the form and management of health, education and social services, transportation, environmental protection, and other social goods? Evidence from Porto Alegre suggests that such a strategy may not mobilise citizens to the same degree. For example, participation in the thematic element of the process is much lower compared to territorially based mobilisation and it tends to be dominated by the more politically active citizens from the middle-class and from larger associations, unions and social movements. The traditional bias within participation is restored. The Harvard assessment report notes that 'Getting citizens to participate in discussions of development strategies is a major challenge. Benefits seem remote or unclear particularly to lower income populations for whom the cost and effort of participation are high' (Harvard University Center for Urban Development Studies 2003: 48). These issues are not as immediate as basic sanitation and paving and do not have the same demonstration effect as infrastructure projects. The lesson from PB as well as New England town meetings and Chicago Community Policing is that participation in popular assemblies is more likely to be higher and attract citizens from more politically marginalised social groups when the decisions of these bodies have obvious and direct effects on the lives of participants. This is a motivational challenge that institutional designers will have to face.

Third, most European political leaders lack the political will to enact PB in crucial policy areas where it might make a difference, for example in housing and social policy. Where PB has been established in advanced industrial democracies, it can best be described as cosmetic, with citizens having little material influence on significant areas of expenditure. While there is a general lack of political will to seriously empower citizens, there is a specific aspect of Brazilian practice that may cause concern: the competitive element within the logic of PB. Are public authorities willing to establish forms of governance that – at least in part – reward more mobilised neighbourhoods with resource allocation? Whilst needs-based criteria play an important role, decisions on prioritisation of resources are often affected by levels of participation. Policy-makers in advanced liberal democracies constantly proclaim the virtues of participation – whether they are willing to so explicitly link intensity of participation with investments is another matter.

Participatory budgeting – realising the goods of democratic institutions?

We began this chapter with a question about whether democratic innovations based on open assemblies could be effective beyond the local level. While designs such as New England town meetings and Chicago Community Policing offer impressive modes of engagement in self- and co-governance respectively, there are limits to the extent to which they can be used as a template for citizen engagement at higher levels of authority. What is particularly attractive about PB as established in Porto Alegre is the way in which engagement in an area of strategic policy is grounded in open popular assemblies and yet can realise a compelling combination of goods of democratic institutions. The institutionalisation of this form of participatory governance has mobilised citizens from social groups who are traditionally difficult to engage and drawn them into a transparent budgetary decision-making process. While the demands on delegates and councillors and the administration itself are high, they are costs that appear worth bearing, given the impact the process has on the living conditions of the city's poorest citizens, associational life and trust in political decision-making.

Fundamental to the design is an explicit recognition of the importance of incentives to motivate participation and to orientate citizens towards certain types of judgement. The self-selection of participants need not imply that traditional social distinctions will be replicated. The incentive structure of PB has successfully mobilised large numbers from poor social groups that have traditionally been resistant to political participation. This is because there is a visible return on participation – investments in neighbourhoods. While citizens are often motivated to participate on the basis of competitive self-interest, the design of budget forums and the COP orientates selected citizens towards judgements based on considerations of justice and fairness.

It is also important to recognise the commitment needed from public authorities to effectively embed this democratic innovation, both in terms of internal reorganisations to ensure coordination and delivery of investments and in promoting participation in the neighbourhoods and regions of the city. In Porto Alegre, the administration has ensured that the process is highly transparent and the public has good access to information. Even with a highly supportive administration, there remains the danger that the professional standing of officials (whether intentionally or not) unduly influences decisions of citizens, particularly in the complex decision-making of the COP. It is a conundrum that PB has not entirely resolved: how can we ensure that citizens have the capacity to make often complex and technical decisions without being unduly influenced by officials and other actors? Even though formal decision-making power rests with citizens, this does not always accurately reflect the balance of power in practice.

Our evaluation of PB indicates that with careful design, democratic innovations can be established that provide unambiguous incentives for citizens to participate effectively in political decision-making. It is an open question as to whether such incentives can be effectively institutionalised in the context of advanced liberal democracies and on larger scales of governance.

3

Mini-publics: assemblies by random selection

This chapter turns our attention to democratic innovations that are distinguished by their mode of selecting citizens, namely random selection. Random selection has a long democratic heritage: it was the preferred method for selecting positions of political authority in the Athenian polis and continued to play a part in republican thought and practice throughout the Middle Ages and the Renaissance and into the seventeenth and eighteenth centuries (Manin 1997). Given this democratic heritage it is perhaps surprising that it has played little or no role in contemporary political systems, where selection by competitive elections is generally perceived to be the democratic method of choice for positions of political authority. The most prominent exception to this rule is the randomly selected jury used in a number of legal systems in advanced industrial democracies: 'an obligation which may in principle fall upon any citizen, is almost the sole vestige of direct citizen participation in law-making and administration which survives in modern democracies' (Arblaster 1994: 18).[1]

Within the Athenian political system, lot and rotation governed the selection of magistrates, the council and the pool of volunteers for juries – all highly significant positions of political authority. As a selection mechanism, lot and rotation gave full expression to the principle of democratic citizenship by providing the occasion for citizens to rule and be ruled in turn: 'For Aristotle, this alternation between command and obedience even constituted the virtue or excellence of citizens' (Manin 1997: 28). By creating the conditions within which governors could understand the perspective of the governed (since they were one and the same), governors had

---

[1] On occasion, lots have been drawn to decide tied elections (Goodwin 2005: 55).

the 'means and motivation' to act in accordance with the ideals of justice (Manin 1997: 30).

A number of democratic theorists have argued the case for incorporating randomly selected bodies within contemporary political systems. For example, Robert Dahl has imagined the potential of a series of randomly selected advisory councils in both *After the Revolution?* (Dahl 1970: 149–53) and *Democracy and Its Critics* (1989):

> Suppose an advanced democratic country were to create a 'minipopulus' consisting of perhaps a thousand citizens randomly selected out of the entire demos. Its task would be to deliberate, for a year perhaps, on an issue and then to announce its choices... one minipopulus could exist for each major issue on the agenda. A minipopulus could exist at any level of government – national, state, or local. It could be attended... by an advisory committee of scholars and specialists and by an administrative staff. It could hold hearings, commission research, and engage in debate and discussion... In these ways... the democratic process could be adapted once again to a world that little resembles the world in which democratic ideas and practices first came to life. (Dahl 1989: 340)

More radically, a number of proposals have appeared that conceive of bodies based on random selection not as a complement to the institutions of advanced industrial democracies, but rather as a replacement or alternative. Selection for legislative assemblies would no longer be based on competitive elections, but rather on some form of random selection (Barnett and Carty 1998; Brighouse and Wright 2006; Burnheim 1985; Goodwin 2005: 181–6 and 244–6). We can even find proposals at the international level for the random selection of citizens from all nations to form a representative sample of trustees to oversee the constitution of international organisations such as the World Bank and International Monetary Fund. Such an arrangement, their proponents argue, would go some way to increasing the democratic legitimacy of these organisations (Frey and Stutzer 2006).

While these proposals remain just that – imaginative projections – we have recently witnessed a democratic experiment that has some similarities to Dahl's idea and in certain respects takes his proposal further. The innovation in question is the British Columbia Citizens' Assembly (BCCA). The BCCA was established by the government of British Columbia (with full support from the legislature) following a couple of perverse election results. The Assembly was charged with reviewing the province's simple plurality electoral system and if necessary recommending an alternative system. The Assembly involved 160 (near-) randomly selected citizens: a female and male from each electoral district, plus two citizens with Aboriginal backgrounds. For eleven months during 2004, citizens were engaged in learning and deliberating about electoral reform. Over a series of weekends for the first four months (January to April), members learnt about electoral systems. For the next two months, members were involved in fifty hearings across the province, taking evidence from fellow citizens and interest groups. The Assembly also took 1,603 written submissions. Finally, between September and November 2004, the 160 participants discussed and debated competing electoral systems, before coming to a decision. After eleven months of work the Assembly recommended that the current electoral system should be replaced by a version of single transferable vote (STV). In December 2004, the Assembly published its final report, *Making Every Vote Count*, explaining its activities and recommendation (Citizens' Assembly on Electoral Reform 2004).[2]

Where the Assembly can be seen as a more radical proposal than Dahl's suggested minipopulus is the fact that the legislature had committed itself to a province-wide referendum based on the Assembly's recommendation. This took place in May 2005 with the following question on the ballot: 'Should British Columbia change to the BC-STV electoral system as recommended by the Citizens' Assembly on Electoral Reform? Yes/No.' The government had placed two significant thresholds for the referendum to pass: at least 60% of votes across the province needed to be in favour; and at least forty-eight (60%) of the seventy-nine electoral districts needed to vote in favour. In the end, the referendum passed the second threshold, with seventy-seven districts in favour. However, the overall vote was 57.69%, missing the first threshold by only 2.31%.[3]

Reflecting on the work of the Assembly in the introduction to *Making Every Vote Count*, the chair, Jack Blaney, states:

> Never before in modern history has a democratic government given to une-lected, 'ordinary' citizens the power to review an important public policy, and then seek from all citizens approval of any proposed changes to that policy. The British Columbia Citizens' Assembly on Electoral Reform has had this power and responsibility and, throughout its life, complete independence from government...
>
> The members of the Citizens' Assembly – British Columbians who unstintingly gave their time and energy – demonstrated how extraordinary ordinary citizens are when given an important task, and the resources and independence to do it right. Over the eleven-month course of the Assembly, only one of 161 members withdrew and attendance was close to perfect. Their great and lasting achievement is the birth of a new tool for democratic governance.

---

[2] See the Citizens' Assembly's dedicated website for reports, videos and other information: www.citizensassembly.bc.ca/.

[3] See www.elections.bc.ca/elections/ge2005/finalrefresults.htm for details of the referendum results.

With an impressive commitment to learning so many new concepts and skills, and with a grace and respect for one another in their discussions that was truly remarkable, the Assembly members demonstrated a quality of citizenship that inspired us all. (Citizens' Assembly on Electoral Reform 2004: xiii)

Following in British Columbia's footsteps, two other Citizens' Assemblies have been organised, both on the question of electoral reform. Within Canada, the government of Ontario established a Citizens' Assembly on Electoral Reform which sat between September 2006 and April 2007. The Assembly had the same basic structure as the BCCA and engaged in similar activities. It was composed of 103 randomly selected members plus an independent Chair; participants were selected to ensure geographical, gender and age balance and the participation of at least one self-identified Aboriginal person. In its final report, *One Ballot, Two Votes*, the Assembly recommends a mixed-member proportional (MMP) system (Ontario Citizens' Assembly on Electoral Reform 2007).[4] Again, this recommendation was put to a binding referendum in October 2007, with 63 per cent of voters rejecting the recommendation.[5]

The third example is the Dutch Burgerforum Kiesstelsel – the Electoral System Civic Forum – which sat between March and November 2006, charged with reviewing and making recommendations on the electoral system of the Second Chamber (or Lower House). Again, participants were selected randomly using quotas based on gender, geographical distribution and age. The Civic Forum differs in two respects from the Canadian Assemblies. First, it operated at the national rather than sub-national level. Second, it was not linked to a referendum; rather it provided recommendations to politicians. In these recommendations the Civic Forum supported the continued use of proportional representation, but with a reform in the voting procedure (Electoral System Civic Forum 2006; Electoral System Civic Forum Secretariat 2007).

This chapter takes as its main focus the experience of these citizens' assemblies, but paying particular attention to the British Columbia experience, where academic commentary is beginning to emerge (Carty *et al.* 2008; Lang 2007; Warren and Pearse 2008a).[6] No other randomly selected body has been given the level of influence in the political process afforded

---

[4] See the Assembly's dedicated website for reports, videos and other information: www.citizensassembly.gov.on.ca/en/default.asp

[5] www3.elections.on.ca/internetapp/realtimereferendum.aspx?lang=en-ca&gf73=0&contestid=2&channel_id={923146e7-4d81-42a8-99f0-e61f5ab50387}&lang=en.

[6] I would like to thank Mark Warren and Hilary Pearse for giving me access to an early draft manuscript of their edited collection *Designing Deliberative Democracy*.

to these Assemblies, particularly the two Canadian examples that were tied to binding referendums. However, given the lack of informed evaluative material on the Assemblies, the chapter will also draw lessons and insights from a series of relatively more modest institutions that share similar design features, most prominently the use of forms of random selection. Over the past three decades, citizens' juries, planning cells, consensus conferences and deliberative polls have increasingly been used in advanced industrial democracies. Collectively, such designs (along with the Citizens' Assembly) have been termed 'mini-publics' (Goodin and Dryzek 2006).[7] Like the Citizens' Assembly, all four of these innovations use random sampling methods to bring together a cross-section of the population to discuss an issue of public concern and have been used at different levels of administration and in a variety of policy areas. Aside from the selection process, there are other common features: citizens are brought together for a period of between two to five days and are paid a stipend for their participation; independent facilitation aims to ensure fairness of proceedings; evidence is provided by expert witnesses who are then cross-examined by participants; citizens are given an opportunity to deliberate amongst themselves both in plenary and small-group sessions. While all four designs assume that ordinary citizens are both 'willing and able to take important decisions in the public interest' (Coote and Mattinson 1997: 4), there are some significant differences.

Citizens' juries have been run and promoted since the 1970s in the United States by the independent Jefferson Centre established by Ned Crosby (Crosby and Nethercut 2005; Stewart *et al.* 1994) and since the late 1990s have been popularised in other countries, particularly in the UK following a series of pilot projects run by the Institute for Public Policy Research (IPPR), the King's Fund and the Local Government Management Board (LGMB) (Coote and Lenaghan 1997; Davies *et al.* 1998; Hall and Stewart 1997; Kuper 1997; McIver 1997). Whilst Crosby has always found it difficult to attract government sponsors in the US, many of the juries in the UK have been sponsored by health authorities and local government; although other non-governmental organisations such as the Independent Television Commission and the Association of British Insurers have also sponsored juries (Smith and Wales 1999: 296–7). Citizens' juries tend to involve between twelve and twenty-four citizens who are required to develop a series of recommendations in response to a 'charge' (one or more

---

[7] A rare example of the use of random selection beyond mini-publics is the appointment process for Community Fund regional boards in England (Smith 2005: 61–2). The irony is that this public body uses a form of lottery to select citizens to sit on bodies that make decisions about the distribution of National Lottery funds!

questions). An interesting modification to jury practice is the Citizens' Council established by the UK's National Institute for Clinical Excellence (NICE) in 2003. The Council has a degree of permanence, meeting twice a year for a long weekend to deliberate and provide advice on ethical and moral questions related to resource use and allocation in health priority setting (Davies *et al.* 2006). At thirty members, the Council is slightly larger than the typical jury, and a portion of its membership stands down after a number of weekends to be replaced by new citizens – a rare example of the rotation principle.

Around the same time that Crosby was developing the citizens' jury model, Peter Dienel of the Research Institute for Citizens' Participation at the University of Wuppertal in Germany was independently establishing the planning cell. Unlike the US experience, the Research Institute has been commissioned on a number of occasions by German government bodies and agencies to organise planning cells on a range of issues such as town planning, local and national energy policy, highway developments and digital network and information technology. Further afield, planning cells have been used to help solve contentious planning problems in the Basque region of Spain and in Israel (Dienel 1996; Dienel and Renn 1995; Hendriks 2005; Smith and Wales 1999). Whilst often confused with citizens' juries, planning cells have some significant differences in design. First, although each planning cell typically includes twenty-five citizens, they are usually run concurrently or in series, thus involving larger numbers of citizens. To date, the largest planning cell project involved around 500 citizens from across Germany. Second, the educative aspect of planning cells is more formal – expert sessions are more akin to lectures. Third, Dienel is less concerned about the independence of facilitators, placing more emphasis on their ability to provide technical advice. Given the number of cells, Dienel believes that any influence on the part of particular facilitators will be marginal. Fourth, the larger number of cells and participants means that rather than citizens crafting collectively agreed recommendations, their views and perspectives are collated by facilitators who then draw them together into an overall report. Finally, Dienel requires commissioning organisations (typically public authorities) to enter into a contractual agreement to take into account the recommendations of the planning cell in future decisions, explaining publicly how and why recommendations were or were not followed. This practice has been adopted by many organisers of citizens' juries.

Consensus conferences have been run regularly since the 1980s by the Danish Board of Technology as a means of incorporating the perspectives of the lay public within the assessment of new scientific and technological developments which raise serious social and ethical concerns. Experiments with consensus conferences have also occurred in the Netherlands and the UK, although without the level of media and public interest or political impact observed in Denmark (Hendriks 2005; Joss 1998; Joss and Durant 1995). Consensus conferences differ from juries in two main respects. First, the organisers advertise for interested citizens, from whom the panel is selected. Second, the participants attend two preparatory weekends where they are involved in the process of selecting the questions to be answered by the conference and in selecting relevant witnesses that they would like to hear from and question. As with juries, consensus conferences produce a report of their recommendations – in Denmark these are sent to members of parliament, scientists, interest groups and members of the public.

Finally, the deliberative poll (sometimes termed deliberative opinion poll) is the creation of James Fishkin – a well-known democratic theorist (Fishkin 1997; Fishkin and Farrar 2005; Fishkin and Luskin 2000). Compared to other mini-publics, deliberative polling can involve large numbers of citizens – the largest to date being 459. More than fifty deliberative polls have been run at national, regional and local levels in the US, Europe, Australia and even China. Subjects have ranged from politically topical issues, including electoral choices, Britain's future in Europe, whether Australia should become a republic, through to regional planning for Texas electric utility companies (Fishkin and Farrar 2005: 75–6). In November 2007, arguably the most organisationally challenging Europe-wide deliberative poll was run involving citizens from all twenty-seven states of the European Union.[8] As with other mini-publics, participants hear evidence from witnesses whom they are able to question and have the opportunity to discuss issues amongst themselves in small groups. The distinctive feature of deliberative polls is that citizens are not asked to develop collective recommendations, but instead complete a questionnaire (with the same questions) before and after the event – hence organisers have a record of changes of opinion as citizens become more informed about issues. For this reason, Fishkin perceives the design to be a development of the traditional polling method. As he has continually argued:

> The deliberative poll is unlike any poll or survey ever conducted. Ordinary polls model what the public is thinking, even though the public may not be thinking very much or paying much attention. A deliberative poll attempts to model what the public *would* think, had it a better opportunity to consider the question at issue. (Fishkin 1997: 162)

Fishkin and his colleagues have begun to experiment with an online version of deliberative polling (Fishkin 2004) – a development that we will

[8] www.tomorrowseurope.eu/.

discuss in a later chapter on the impact of information and communication technology.[9]

There are then some potentially significant differences in the design of different mini-publics. For example, the BCCA differs from other mini-publics in at least three important respects. First, it sat over a period of months; second, it engaged in its own public consultation process though public hearings and submissions; third it was not simply an advisory body, but rather was authorised to set the political agenda, with its recommendations put direct to the population in a binding referendum. While the BCCA is the main focus of this chapter, there are enough similarities in the various designs discussed above to mean that insights from other mini-publics – in particular the way in which they recruit citizens and enable deliberation amongst participants – are also relevant to our analysis and evaluation.

Inclusiveness

Arguably the most striking aspect of mini-publics is the mode of selection. Although recruitment through random forms of selection has a long democratic heritage, its use in the political systems of advanced industrial democracies is negligible. Random selection, combined with regular rotation of positions of authority (lot and rotation), was the method of choice in Athenian democracy. As Barbara Goodwin notes, the 'choice of leaders by lot averted the danger that power would go to the rich or to those who desired it' (Goodwin 2005: 46). The use of lot and rotation acts as a defence against oligarchy and realises the principle that any citizen is capable of holding political office. As Benjamin Barber argues: 'Where every citizen is equally capable of political judgement and equally responsible for the public good, the rotation of responsibilities amongst citizens chosen by lot becomes a powerful symbol of genuine democracy' (Barber 1984: 293).

Whatever the size of the mini-public – from the 12 to 25 citizens in a citizens' jury through to the 160 citizens in the BCCA and the larger deliberative polls – participation in mini-publics is restricted. There is a division of political labour in the sense that a small group of citizens are recruited from the wider population. What is particular about mini-publics is the selection procedure. The equal opportunity to participate that is the hallmark of open or popular assemblies is replaced by an equal *probability* of being selected to participate (Brown 2006: 212–13; Saward 2000: 16). Is this a just and acceptable restriction? If the opportunity to participate is to

---

[9] For up-to-date information on deliberative polls, see Fishkin's Center for Deliberative Democracy, http://cdd.stanford.edu/.

be limited, then random selection appears to provide a fair mechanism to distribute this ineradicable inequality (Goodwin 2005: 45). It is a mechanism that ensures that no citizen or social group from the given population is *systematically* excluded from participation. As with popular assemblies, the relevant population from which citizens are drawn is typically related to the political boundary of the sponsoring public authority, which does not necessarily correspond to all affected interests (Goodin 2007).

In actual practice the Citizens' Assembly and other mini-publics rely on 'near-random selection' (Warren and Pearse 2008b: 6). There are three reasons why pure random selection is not achieved. The first two are well-known sampling problems that affect recruitment. The first relates to the incomplete nature of any database from which the sample of citizens is taken. For example, the initial sample for the BCCA was drawn from the province's voters' list. Not all residents of the province will be or can be registered. Similarly, deliberative polling tends to use random-digit dialling, but this tends to 'skew towards older populations, who have land lines and are more likely to be at home, and towards the better educated, who are more likely to be willing to talk with the pollster' (Fishkin and Farrar 2005: 74). The increasing use of mobile phones is exacerbating this problem. The new technology is predominantly used by younger generations, there is no general directory of mobile numbers and the numbers themselves tell recruiters nothing about the owner's place of residence (Traugott 2003).

A second sampling problem relates to the element of self-selection in the recruitment process. Citizens are under no obligation to participate. Since none of the innovations can *require* participation, those who are invited can choose not to participate. In the case of the BCCA, citizens from a large random sample drawn from the electoral register were asked twice whether they would be willing to participate:

> The initial letter, mailed to 23,034 randomly chosen citizens, invited the recipients to decide if they wanted to participate in the Assembly process. Those who responded positively and then attended a selection meeting were again asked to confirm their willingness to commit to the project and accept the responsibilities of membership. The Assembly members were then chosen by lot from this group of attendees. (Citizens' Assembly on Electoral Reform 2004: 39)

From the initial 23,034 invitations, 1,715 citizens responded positively; 964 attended selection meetings; and those who wished to participate were entered into a lottery. Even with this element of self-selection, organisers were confident that 'the final membership of the Assembly generally reflected the distribution of the provincial population' (Citizens' Assembly on Electoral Reform 2004: 40). The Ontario Assembly also reflected many of the socio-demographic variations across the province, including place of birth, languages and occupations (Ontario Citizens' Assembly Secretariat 2007: 47). The element of self-selection in mini-publics does appear to have some effect: in the BCCA, participants tended to be more politically knowledgeable and civically active than the general population; and tended to be more dissatisfied with British Columbia's political system (Carty *et al.* 2008: 149; Lang 2007: 41). Again, experience from deliberative polls suggests that '[t]hose who decide to attend are usually somewhat more politically active and better educated than the initial sample' (Fishkin and Farrar 2005: 74). However, the differences with the wider population appear fairly minimal and by no means reflect the wide differences in socio-economic characteristics between participants and non-participants in traditional political processes. Self-selection is perhaps more of a factor in consensus conferences, where volunteers are recruited through advertisements and make written applications. The panel is then selected from this pool of volunteers.

The third reason why pure random selection is not achieved in most of the mini-publics is actually by design. The Citizens' Assemblies, citizens' juries and consensus conferences all use a form of stratified sampling. This is to ensure that citizens from politically salient social groups are recruited. Pure random selection is likely to lead to citizens from numerically small social groups not being present. While no systematic bias would have been in operation, the lack of presence of certain groups may affect the perceived legitimacy of the body and, as we shall see when we discuss voice, mean that certain perspectives are not articulated. The BCCA used three criteria (where information on the population was readily available) – geographical district, gender and age – as the basis of quotas in its selection process. In comparison citizens' juries and consensus conferences often stratify the sample to include even more characteristics – for example ethnicity and on occasion political or social attitudes. Over-sampling of particular demographic characteristics ensures that the panel reflects politically salient characteristics from within the wider population. As John Parkinson recognises, the use of quotas ensures that 'small groups can be said to be statistically representative of a large population by the criteria chosen'. However, he warns that 'the downside is that such small groups are representative *only* on those criteria, leaving the risk of missing important differences which have not been selected for' (Parkinson 2006: 76). This may well have been the fate of the BCCA in its failure to select on the basis of ethnicity. There was a recognition that the selection process had failed to recruit citizens from Aboriginal communities – hence the Assembly chair requested that two additional members be included in the process, a request that was granted (Citizens' Assembly on Electoral Reform 2004: 39). But there were no criteria for other potentially salient minority ethnic groups, and, as we shall argue later, this may have had an effect on the proceedings (and hence the legitimacy of the process). Learning a lesson from British Columbia, the Ontario Assembly ensured that one self-defined Aboriginal citizen was selected, although again the presence of other minority ethnic groups was not ensured. Given their larger size, deliberative polls and planning cells tend not to use quotas, although deliberative polls have on occasion targeted particular populations 'to encourage participation by those who are less likely to attend (typically, this includes those with less formal education and those living in low-income or remote areas)' (Fishkin and Farrar 2005: 74).

Once citizens agree to participate in mini-publics, evidence suggests that they typically do attend. Even the BCCA – which ran for eleven months and was thus more demanding than other designs – suffered only one withdrawal. Commenting on the recruitment process, the Assembly's final report suggests:

> This process appeared to create a sense of 'buy-in' for the Assembly members that contributed significantly to their commitment to the process... the fact that only one member withdrew in the course of 11 intensive months, suggests that this process of recruitment deserves further examination. (Citizens' Assembly on Electoral Reform 2004: 39)

The formal invitation to participate, a modest honorarium and the sense that they are being asked to take part in a serious political endeavour appear to play a crucial role in motivating citizens' engagement in mini-publics and support for the process. Citizens who typically do not participate in open consultation processes and other forms of political activity are willing to participate in what are more intensive forms of political engagement. The fact that the invitation is limited to only a small number of (randomly selected) citizens appears to be an important motivating factor. Citizens perceive that they are being offered a rare opportunity to participate in a politically significant process. This was certainly the perception of participants in the NICE Citizens' Council, where citizens reported that their motivation to participate was based on a variety of factors: the belief that institutions should be more open to the public voice; that it is a public duty to make a contribution; and for reasons of personal growth and fulfilment. Citizens 'also frequently referred to a sense of being "privileged" to have been selected' (Davies et al. 2006: 80–1).

Given the well-known sampling problems involved in recruitment and the use of stratified sampling in many designs, it is necessary to temper any strong claims about statistical or descriptive representation on the part of mini-publics. Understanding representation in these terms can also be unhelpful if it assumes that participants are somehow representing 'people like them' in a strong sense (Smith 2003: 91). Jeffrey Abramson draws out this tension in relation to legal juries:

> We do not want to encourage jurors to see themselves as irreconcilably divided by race, selected only to fill a particular racial or gender slot on the jury. Yet we do want to encourage jurors to draw upon and combine their individual experiences and group backgrounds in the joint search for the most reliable and accurate verdict. The difference is subtle but real. (Abramson 1994: 11)

While there are different ways of conceiving the representativeness of mini-publics (Brown 2006; Warren 2008), some of which we will return to as our analysis progresses, random sampling techniques ensure that these innovations engage a broad cross-section of citizens with a diversity of social perspectives. The recruitment process generates a panel of citizens who differ markedly from the highly skewed characteristics of citizens who routinely engage in consultation processes. (Near-) random selection thus offers one mode of engagement that can overcome traditional differentials of presence in political participation and realise a particular understanding of inclusiveness.

Does presence translate into equality of voice? To what extent are mini-publics structured so that equality in contributions is realised, given the diversity of participants? Do more politically confident citizens with higher education and/or social status dominate proceedings?

The way in which the environment of mini-publics is structured to facilitate voice and interaction between citizens is one of the main reasons why mini-publics have proved particularly attractive to deliberative democrats (see for example Chambers 2004; Fishkin 1997; Fishkin and Luskin 2000; Smith and Wales 2000). A diverse body of citizens is brought together to discuss and debate issues of public concern. Diversity is crucial for ensuring that different perspectives are voiced – hence the importance of stratified sampling methods in certain designs. The BCCA gives us one example of where ensuring diversity was perceived to be crucial. For example, by ensuring geographical diversity, the needs of rural communities were consistently raised. However, by not ensuring that the Assembly was also stratified to include citizens from minority ethnic communities, such perspectives were not always voiced in the Assembly's discussions. The final decision to recommend STV rather than MMP (the former is arguably more sensitive to locality, the latter to ethnicity) may have been affected by the lack of minority ethnic voice (James 2008; Lang 2008). As Michael James argues: 'by stratifying for region and gender but not for race or ethnicity, citizen assemblies deliberating about electoral systems could potentially skew the agenda against the interests of racial or ethnic minorities and in favour of women and regional minorities' (James 2008: 120). That said, the Ontario Assembly also did not employ quotas to ensure racial or ethnic diversity, but did recommend MMP. While decisions about which criteria are salient may well have an effect on outcomes, the extent of the effect can be difficult to ascertain.

It may not be enough to simply have one or two participants from a particular social group, for example the two Aboriginal members who were recruited to the BCCA when it was realised that there was no Aboriginal representation in the original sample, or the single self-defined Aboriginal member required in the Ontario Assembly. James argues that a 'critical mass or threshold number' from minority social groups may be necessary for a number of reasons. First, to ensure that there are sufficient numbers to communicate – one voice can become isolated in a large assembly. Second, to provide support and bolster the confidence of speakers who may be offering a perspective that is uncomfortable for other participants. Third, to ensure that the perspective is heard in the different locations within the body – for example, the various break-out groups in the Assembly. Finally, in recognition of the fact that there is likely to be a plurality of perspectives from within social groups – they are not homogenous and closed communities (James 2008: 120–3). Achieving critical mass may require over-representation of small minority groups, something that could have been achieved given the size of the Citizens' Assembly. However, for whatever reason, it was not a consideration of the designers of the institution. In comparison, the small size of citizens' juries and consensus conferences means that although organisers can ensure the presence of different social groups, it is more difficult to recruit a critical mass. In a jury observed by my colleague Corinne Wales a lack of critical mass appears to have affected the ability of one juror to express her misgivings throughout the proceedings:

> I would have liked to hear other ethnic minorities' views in the Jury. As I am the only black female it was hard to get my views across … the minorities have no significant [voice] in the final decision. (Smith and Wales 1999: 307)

That said, even in the BCCA, where there was gender parity, some participants found it challenging to argue the case for women's representation and were not convinced that their arguments were given a fair hearing by fellow participants (Lang 2007: 55, 59).

Presence is obviously a precondition to being able to voice viewpoints. However, there are other aspects of the design of mini-publics that affect the fairness of proceedings and equality of voice, perhaps most significant being size and facilitation. Most citizens do not feel able or willing to speak in front of large groups where debates tend to be 'dominated by a small number of skilled and charismatic speakers … who count on rhetoric rather than argument' (Elster 1998: 107). Hence the larger mini-publics, for example Citizens' Assemblies and deliberative polls, have plenary sessions where witnesses make presentations and are questioned, and also break participants into smaller groups to enable discussions. In principle, working in smaller groups reduces the reluctance of citizens to contribute.

The 160-strong BCCA often broke up into 12 discussion groups of between 10 to 15 citizens. Citizens were assigned randomly to these groups and the membership changed each weekend, 'which helped members to get to know one another better while exposing them to a variety of perspectives' (Citizens' Assembly on Electoral Reform 2004: 66). As the report of the Assembly's deliberations and decisions suggests:

> members valued the groups. They provided many members with a less intimidating environment than the plenary in which to discuss issues and they provided all members with the opportunity to organize their thoughts before expressing their views in plenary sessions. (Citizens' Assembly on Electoral Reform 2004: 90)

In evaluating the work of the BCCA, participants noted that 'these small group discussions were crucial opportunities for learning, asking questions of clarification, sharing ideas, testing theories, building consensus, generating solutions, and so on' (Citizens' Assembly on Electoral Reform 2004: 240). The Assembly also established an online discussion forum to provide an alternative location for citizens to discuss their ongoing work. However, the 'digital divide' in both access (not all 141 members had internet access) and competence in the use of information and communication technology has some bearing on the extent to which this forum can be said to realise inclusiveness. This is a theme we shall pick up in a later chapter on e-democracy innovations.

Deliberative polls also use small discussion groups, but given that polls tend to last for only a couple of days, the time in groups is limited and membership is not rotated. Thus compared to Citizens' Assemblies, they suffer because citizens are unlikely to confront all the relevant differences in their group discussions and the limited time they spend together may not be enough 'to go through all the stages of breaking down barriers, expressing emotions freely, and searching for mutual understanding' (Parkinson 2006: 78). Here, the longer Citizens' Assembly and the smaller citizens' juries, consensus conferences and planning cells have a distinct advantage.

But even small groups can be dominated by 'the skilled and charismatic'. This is where the role of independent facilitation (sometimes referred to as moderation) is critical. In the BCCA, for example, discussions in both plenary and small-group sessions were not a 'free-for-all', but were instead facilitated. Facilitators in mini-publics use a range of techniques to ensure a degree of fairness in proceedings. Typically ground rules will be established which remind citizens of the need to respect the views of others and to encourage participation by all those present (Smith and Wales 1999: 303). The development of a 'statement outlining a set of shared values' was one of the first activities undertaken by participants in the BCCA. Assembly members committed themselves to:

- Respecting people and their opinions;
- Open-mindedness – challenging ideas not people;
- Listening to understand;
- Focus on the mandate – preparedness;
- Simple, clear, concise communication;
- Inclusivity – all members are equal;
- Positive attitude; and
- Integrity. (Citizens' Assembly on Electoral Reform 2004: 68)[10]

Such procedural values and rules set important parameters for acceptable behaviour and – where participants are involved in their drafting – help citizens to develop a sense of ownership and control over the process (Sang and Davies 1998: 48; Smith and Wales 1999: 303; Thompson and Hoggett 2001: 359).

Facilitators are generally alert to the way in which deliberations can be dominated by confident and outspoken individuals and to the fact that for some citizens, speaking in even a small group of their peers is still intimidating. In chairing the plenary sessions of the Citizens' Assembly, Jack Blaney was well aware of the difficult task of trying to create an environment where all citizens felt able to contribute. As Dennis Thompson observes:

> [E]qual respect does require that some positive steps be taken to ensure that the opportunities to speak are as equal as possible, and that the occasions for speech are as supportive as possible. The Chair of the Assembly made creditable efforts to create an environment that encouraged extensive participation. He informally solicited members' views and encouraged them to speak in the public forums. In most of the sessions, before recognizing the more active members, he made sure that first-time speakers had the chance to participate. (Thompson 2008: 45)

Some citizens' juries have experimented with two different facilitators – one whose role is to ensure the smooth running of deliberations (time keeping, ensuring the jury stays focused on the question, and so on); the other

[10] See also Smith and Wales (1999: 303) for an example of rules generated by participants in a citizens' jury.

acting as 'jurors' friend', encouraging particular individuals to contribute and ensuring that contrary voices are heard (Davies and Sang 1998). It is also common practice in citizens' juries and planning cells to break into even smaller groups (sometimes unfacilitated) to provide more opportunities for individuals to speak and to understand the views of others. Dienel rotates the composition of such groups to avoid systematic domination by particular individuals; Crosby often places the most vociferous citizens in a small group together, thus allowing others the opportunity to speak.

Establishing rules of conduct and other actions of the facilitator are fundamental to realising political equality in mini-public deliberations. Careful facilitation provides one way in which significant virtues, such as reciprocity, can be grounded and realised in practice (Thompson and Hoggett 2001: 359). Simon Thompson and Paul Hoggett are also particularly alert to the way in which different facilitation styles can affect the emotional dynamics of mini-publics: a non-interventionist 'hands-off' style can lead to domination by more vocal and confident citizens; a more interventionist, 'hands-on' approach that equalises opportunities for voice may be too domineering. Both extremes undermine deliberation: 'There is an inherent tension in the role of the moderator that cannot easily be resolved' (Thompson and Hoggett 2001: 361). In their careful study of the NICE Citizens' Council, Celia Davies and her colleagues provide a detailed account of how a desire to ensure fair proceedings can undermine interactions between citizens. 'In general, the facilitators of the Citizens' Council chose an inclusive style of facilitation, making sure that all who wanted to speak could speak, usually in order of request ... as a consequence there was little deliberation in the plenary sites' (Davies *et al.* 2006: 92). Their account of the plenary sessions suggests that the size of the Council – thirty citizens – made it difficult to chair a discussion and debate between citizens. As we will elaborate later, the situation in the Council was not helped by the fact that citizens were uncertain about the task they were being asked to undertake.

The operation of mini-publics suggests that the achievement of inclusiveness in the interactions between citizens requires a fairly structured environment, with clear rules and processes that orientate citizens towards mutual respect and reciprocity. Such virtues will not necessarily emerge naturally. The facilitator becomes a crucial figure in the promotion of free and fair exchanges between citizens, playing a central role in ensuring that citizens are able to contribute to the process. This is a difficult task, and judgements will be made about the extent to which different forms of discourse are valued – some facilitators may well value anecdotes and stories; others may promote more reasoned and principled forms of debate. As difference theorists have been quick to point out, emphasis on more dispassionate forms of reasoning can itself silence the already marginalised, reinforcing illegitimate relations of power (Sanders 1996; Young 1990). We need to be aware, therefore, that the extent to which political equality is realised in the exchanges between citizens can rest very much on the skills and styles of individual facilitators.

The final aspect of the design of mini-publics that can have an impact on inclusiveness is the form of decision-making. Whilst participants in the Assemblies in British Columbia and Ontario worked together in learning about and debating different electoral systems, in the end they made decisions using secret ballots. The results of deliberative polling are generated by individual participants completing a pre-prepared questionnaire. In comparison, in citizens' juries and consensus conferences, participants are required to craft a set of recommendations in response to a charge. This may involve voting, but unlike the other designs, typically not in secret. The difference in the way that citizens are asked to come to judgements (individually or collectively; in private or in public) may well affect the realisation of inclusiveness. Participants are more likely to face potential pressures to conform or agree in citizens' juries and consensus conferences, where decision-making is more collaborative. We shall have more to say about the effect of this difference between designs later in the chapter.

Popular control

Mini-publics are designed to empower citizens in at least two ways. First, they are given space to craft recommendations or reflect on their own individual judgements (depending on the design) free from the pressures that normally shape their opinions – the media, family, friends and colleagues – and carefully insulated from established political interests. Second, the design of mini-publics recasts the typical relations of power between citizens and experts. Selected experts (who are often representatives of interest groups) are given an opportunity to present evidence and to answer participants' questions, but this is the only impact they have on citizens' judgements and decisions. For some this might be a weakness of the design. However, if experts were given a more substantial role working alongside participants, their expertise would no doubt place pressures on citizens to defer to their authority. To a certain extent, then, we can understand mini-publics as a mode of 'democratising' expertise (Fischer 2000). Not in the sense that everyone becomes an expert, but rather that experts provide their evidence, answer citizens' questions and then stand aside to allow the citizens to weigh the different ideas they have been exposed to. Citizens are more in control of their relationships with experts.

There are, however, at least three elements in the design of mini-publics that potentially undermine the realisation of popular control: the selection of the charge and witnesses; the mode of facilitation; and the impact of the outputs of mini-publics on political decision-making. Selected citizens are brought together to work on a charge (or set of questions), listen to and cross-examine witnesses, discuss and debate with one another and come to judgements in a format that has been established without their involvement. As Amy Lang argues: 'The agenda problem is particularly relevant in large-scale processes like the BC Citizens' Assembly, where government defined the mandate of citizen discussions, experts were brought in to define the problem and the possible solutions, and organizing staff defined the roles and responsibilities of citizen participants' (Lang 2008: 86). Let us consider these different aspects of public control in turn.

There are understandable limitations on the extent to which citizens can be involved in process decisions, in particular setting the agenda. First, they are being asked to deal with a problem that has been defined as such by a particular public authority or other organisation that is commissioning the mini-public: if the charge is altered to something less relevant to the authority, it is difficult to see why it would finance and respond to the mini-public. Second, citizens often have little or no knowledge of the issue under consideration before they participate in the mini-public. It will be difficult for them to make reasoned judgements about which issues are most relevant for consideration. Crosby has experimented with total citizen control over the citizens' jury process, but – unsurprisingly – found that in the initial stages, citizens did not have enough of an overview of the subject to deal competently with setting the charge and witness selection (Crosby 1996: 18–19).

But how to ensure that the charge and selection of witnesses is not biased; that the mini-public has not been structured to deliver recommendations that are desirable to the sponsors? This was certainly the fear of the Association for Community Health Councils for England and Wales, which criticised the use of citizens' juries in health care on the grounds that the sponsoring body would be able to manipulate the process 'where questions are set and witnesses chosen ... in order to influence the jury's decision' (McIver 1997: 69).

We can see how the structure of a charge can affect deliberations and outcomes by looking at the BCCA. A seemingly simple charge of reviewing the current electoral system and (if necessary) recommending an alternative was affected by various limitations imposed within the mandate. For example, one non-negotiable aspect of the mandate was that the legislature should remain at seventy-nine seats. This apparently innocuous decision actually meant that one of the two options favoured by the Assembly – MMP – could not deliver the form of local representation based on small constituencies desired by most participants. It is arguable that this had an effect on the Assembly's decision to select STV (Lang 2007: 57–8; 2008: 92). Parkinson offers another example of agenda constraint: participants in two citizens' juries in Leicester and Belfast on aspects of health planning were frustrated because they were unable to challenge national policy frameworks that structured the local issues they were considering and therefore limited the remit of their deliberations (Parkinson 2006: 131). David Price, in his analysis of the use of citizens' juries in healthcare in the UK, has argued that the way that questions are framed not only influences the substantive area of discussion, but also the manner in which jurors discuss issues. He is particularly concerned that the form that charges take influences jurors to adopt 'the bureaucratic idiom of welfare maximisation', suppressing 'more commonplace' evaluative, non-welfare maximising language (Price 2000: 272). In a different context, an evaluation of the NICE Citizens' Council argues that the sponsoring body (NICE) was unsure of the role of the Council and was not willing for it to be involved in politically contentious decision-making (for example, decisions about the licensing of particular drugs). Instead the Council was asked to consider fairly vague 'value-based' questions about the general approach that NICE should take in its judgements on health priority-setting. The lack of direction and the confused nature of the charge played a significant part in the difficulties citizens faced in understanding their mandate and role (Davies *et al.* 2006; see also Parkinson 2006: 132–3).

Similar concerns can be raised in relation to the choice of witnesses: the balance of evidence can have a profound effect on the final outcome. In the BCCA, the research officers who put together the learning programme on electoral systems were independent and respected academics, seconded to the Assembly. Their programme was reviewed by an expert consultative committee. Unusually for a mini-public, the Assembly also engaged in a public consultation phase, taking evidence from interested parties from across British Columbia (a process that was repeated in Ontario). Having learnt about electoral reform, the design of the Assembly ensured that citizens were also aware of broader political debates within civil society. The design of the Assembly also clearly gave participants an advantage over their counterparts in other mini-publics. Having completed the learning and public hearing phases, citizens were able to work with the staff to plan the deliberation phase and to select additional witnesses (Citizens' Assembly on Electoral Reform 2004: 69). As their knowledge of the pertinent issues and the way that the Assembly operated grew, citizens were able to take a more active role in process decisions.

In other (shorter) mini-publics it is common to establish a stakeholder group that involves a range of interests with different perspectives on the issues under consideration who are then responsible for agreeing the charge and the range of witnesses. The consensus conference design is unusual in that it holds preparatory weekends before the conference, where citizens are not only given background information about the issue they will be considering but are also able to influence the shape of the charge and the selection of witnesses. A steering group makes its suggestions, but these are reviewed by the citizens before they undertake their more intensive deliberations – for example, citizens make the final choice of witnesses from a pre-prepared list.

A no doubt unintended way in which popular control can be diminished is the manner in which mini-publics are facilitated. We have already noted in the earlier discussion of inclusiveness the way in which different styles of facilitation can affect the types of contributions that are favoured and the form of deliberations. Facilitators are required to continually make decisions about when discussions should be terminated; who should speak, and so forth. Apparently small decisions can have potentially profound effects. In the BCCA, a decision was made to approach the evaluation of different electoral systems by first asking the citizens 'to debate the criteria that they might apply to assessing electoral systems'. These were then ranked and the first three values – effective local representation, proportionality of votes to seats and maximum voter choice – were used as the basis of 'the subsequent discussion of electoral systems' (Citizens' Assembly on Electoral Reform 2004: 90). This appears to be a sensible and logical way of evaluating electoral systems. However, the decision to limit the number of values to only the three ranked highest was arbitrary and meant that the fourth value, 'diversity', was not given much attention. Again, this apparently small decision may have had an effect on the final decision of the Assembly in that MMP is arguably more sensitive to certain forms of diversity. It also appears to have alienated women's groups, which then felt unable to support the Assembly's recommendation in the referendum process (Ratner 2008: 158).

R.S. Ratner's evaluation of the BCCA suggests that a few members of the Assembly 'objected to the unilateral power of the Chair to compose the speaker's list, cut off discussion, and interpret mandate restrictions. Some also saw the role played by facilitators as narrowing the parameters of debate in their manner of structuring the discussion sessions' (Ratner 2008: 158). However, overall, citizens' perceptions of the neutrality, professionalism and commitment of the staff was extremely positive (Citizens' Assembly on Electoral Reform 2004: 239); a perception that was reinforced by a reporter from the *Vancouver Sun* who stated that the presentations were 'an impressive demonstration of the professionalism and integrity of the Assembly staff' (Citizens' Assembly on Electoral Reform 2004: 96). An impression of independence is common amongst participants and observers of all the different forms of mini-publics.

The final aspect of the design of mini-publics that can materially affect the realisation of popular control is the way in which outputs from these events impact on the political process. The record of impact on political decision-making is patchy at best. Robert Goodin and John Dryzek are quick to admit that cases of mini-publics 'actually making policy... when a forum is formally empowered as part of a decision-making process' are rare (Goodin and Dryzek 2006: 7). Here, the two Canadian Citizens' Assemblies are the exception to the rule in that their recommendations on electoral reform formed the basis of province-wide referendums that the respective governments had committed themselves to implement if the propositions were accepted. In both cases the recommendations were rejected – a point we will return to in our discussion of publicity. However, this should not deflect from the fact that, unlike any previous mini-public, the Assemblies' deliberations and decision were clearly tied to a public ratification process.

This is a significant development in the practice of mini-publics, since many democratic theorists have been troubled by the way that such institutions challenge our traditional understanding of accountability. Whilst they have been explicitly authorised by a public authority to undertake their task and realise a high degree of inclusiveness, concerns are raised that the randomly selected citizens 'lack formal accountability mechanisms of re-election or removal from office' (Warren 2008: 59): they have 'no direct bonds of accountability to non-participants' (Parkinson 2006: 84). As we noted in the introduction to this chapter, there are some writers who argue that randomly selected bodies should be given the power of final decision-making, but these voices are rare. Even writers such as Fishkin – amongst the most vociferous of promoters of mini-publics – recognise that this would lead to a legitimacy problem and therefore argue that mini-publics (in his case deliberative polls) can at best have only recommendatory force.

> A deliberative poll is not meant to describe or predict public opinion. Rather it prescribes. It has recommendatory force: these are the conclusions people would come to, were they better informed on the issues and had the opportunity and motivation to examine those issues seriously. (Fishkin 1997: 162)

For Simone Chambers, Fishkin's assertion is troubling because it appears to 'bypass the general public altogether'. In comparison, 'the Citizens' Assembly model becomes completely dependent on the general public' (Chambers 2007: 6): both Assemblies 'gave account' in the sense of giving public reasons and justifications for their recommendations which were then subject to a public ratification process.

Aside from the Citizens' Assemblies, the relationship between the outputs of mini-publics and political decision-making is opaque. Even in Denmark, where consensus conferences are organised by the Board of

Technology, there is no guarantee of influence. Their recommendations tend to be taken seriously by politicians and at times influence public debates, and we can point to instances where citizens' judgements appear to have had an effect: for example, there is evidence that the recommendations of the consensus conference on genetic engineering in industry and agriculture led to the exclusion of transgenic animals from the first governmental biotechnology research and development programme (Klüver 1995: 44). But, this does not mean that all conferences have direct impact on policy decisions – the evidence is mixed (Joss 1998). Planning cells appear to have had fairly significant effects at the local and regional level in Germany, although 'independent evaluations are scarce' (Hendriks 2005: 92). Fishkin makes strong claims that the results of deliberative polls run for Texas utilities 'led to further investments in natural gas (which was regarded as relatively clean) and in renewable energy. In fact, the decisions resulting from the Deliberative Polls made Texas a national leader in renewable energy' (Ackerman and Fishkin 2004: 46). However, a more cautious assessment states that 'it would be disingenuous to suggest that the results of the deliberative polling process alone were responsible for the regulatory and legislative changes that followed' (Lehr et al. 2003, quoted in Goodin and Dryzek 2006: 9). We need to recognise that it is generally difficult to ascertain the impacts of mini-publics on substantive policy outcomes. As Carolyn Hendriks argues:

> Citizens' reports are conceived as advisory, and their recommendations invariably compete with other forms of advice from political parties, expert committees, and interest groups, for example. Moreover, when some of these other sources of policy advice happen to recommend the same policies and celebrate the same values articulated in the citizens' reports, it can be difficult to determine which recommendation held more sway. (Hendriks 2005: 91)

There is reasonable concern that commissioning bodies will simply 'cherry-pick' those recommendations or trends in opinions that support their perspective, while ignoring those that are uncomfortable. In recognition of this potential problem, Dienel developed the practice of drawing up a contract between the commissioning body, the organisers and the participants of planning cells, requiring the former to explain within a certain time-frame how it has responded to the recommendations of the citizens' report. This practice has been picked up by other mini-publics, in particular citizens' juries, although in reality it still leaves a great deal of room for manoeuvre on the part of sponsors. It is that room for manoeuvre that the innovative design of the Citizens' Assembly was able to overcome.

Considered judgement

Advocates of mini-publics place a high premium on their capacity to enable citizens to come to considered judgement. Reflecting on the experience of mini-publics, Chambers argues:

> In observing the quality of debate in many of these forums, one cannot help but have one's faith in the capacities of ordinary citizens renewed. These forums tend to bring out the best in people, showcasing such deliberative virtues as respect, toleration, common sense, fair mindedness, and most important, a willingness to be persuaded and change one's mind. The Citizens' Assembly was no exception. (Chambers 2007: 4)

Certainly the organisers and promoters of mini-publics are convinced by their capacity to create the conditions for sound judgements. As we have already noted, Fishkin often argues that deliberative polls provide an insight into 'what the public *would* think had it a better opportunity to consider the question at issue' (Fishkin 1997: 162). Similar sentiments are forthcoming from organisers of citizens' juries:

> If the jurors have enough information about the matter at hand, and if they have the opportunity to discuss the matter amongst themselves, they can be trusted to take decisions on behalf of the community, that others can safely regard as legitimate and fair. (Coote and Mattinson 1997: 4)

There are three specific features of mini-publics that motivate considered judgement. First, participants hear evidence from a range of witnesses who have been carefully selected to present an overview of the relevant issues. Citizens are given the opportunity to cross-examine these experts to not only clarify particular points, but also to raise issues that may not have been covered in presentations.

Second, participants have the opportunity to discuss the issue under consideration with other citizens with a diversity of social perspectives. They are not only able to consider the views of different experts, but also reflect on the way in which their fellow citizens understand and interpret this evidence in light of their own experiences. Diversity amongst participants has the potential to broaden the horizon of individual judgements.

Finally, the design of mini-publics can be said to orientate citizens towards considerations of the public interest, rather than their own self-interest. For example, citizens are not selected to represent particular social groups or interests in any strong sense (Abramson 1994: 11, 141; Smith and Wales 2000: 56–7). They are typically more open to changing their views as they hear new evidence and insights, since participation 'does not represent an opportunity for advancement, promotion or re-election'

(Dienel 1996: 114). Again, as we discussed earlier, the independent facilitation of mini-publics can help orientate citizens towards mutual respect and understanding and ensure that deliberations are free and fair. Mini-publics share these characteristics, because their designers believe that it is under conditions of inclusive and fair deliberation, free from external pressures, that citizens will be motivated to make 'public-spirited' judgements. And it is for this reason that deliberative democrats have shown an increasing interest in the experience and practice of these 'safe havens' (Chambers 2004).

What evidence is there that considered judgement is being realised in mini-publics? There is plenty of evidence of citizens changing their opinions as they hear evidence and deliberate with fellow citizens. So, for example, after the learning phase of the BCCA, MMP was the preferred option for a majority of participants, but by the end of the deliberation phase, STV was the overwhelming choice for a new electoral system. In citizens' juries in both the US and UK there is evidence that 'jurors almost always change their minds during the sessions, as they become more involved in the issues' (Coote and Lenaghan 1997; McIver 1997; Stewart et al. 1994: 25). But, without doubt, the most systematic evidence of opinion change comes from deliberative polling, since Fishkin and his colleagues apply both pre- and post-deliberation surveys (Fishkin 1997: 214–21; Luskin et al. 2002).

In itself, opinion change tells us nothing about whether judgements represent 'enlightened preferences'. Sceptics have raised questions as to whether (for example) the internal consistency of judgements has increased; whether irrational group dynamics have shaped judgements rather than reasoned argument; and whether results could be replicated with a different set of citizens (Merkle 1996; Price and Neijens 1998; Sturgis et al. 2005; Traugott 2003). Most sceptical commentary is targeted at deliberative polling – no doubt this is related to the extent to which Fishkin has promoted his design, not just as a democratic innovation, but also as a social scientific experiment that is an open challenge to traditional opinion-polling techniques. Whilst the evidence to fully refute these sceptics is not available, there is some evidence from the evaluation of mini-publics that considered judgement is being realised, often to a quite impressive extent.

The Citizens' Assembly, of which unfortunately we have only three examples to date, is where we would expect to find most evidence of considered judgement, since citizens have a relatively long period of time to reflect on relevant issues compared to other mini-public designs. This timeframe allowed researchers in British Columbia to observe deliberations and survey participants at different points during the Assembly's life. The citizens themselves believed that their capacity to make sound judgements had improved dramatically. In response to the question 'How informed about electoral systems do you feel?', the average response (on a 0–10 scale) jumped from 4.3 at the beginning of the process to 9.11 at the end of the learning phase (Citizens' Assembly on Electoral Reform 2004: 68). Observers of the BCCA attest that during the deliberation phase, citizens were involved in fairly sophisticated debates about the merits of different electoral systems. But it could be argued that the final decision was rather surprising, given that prior to the deliberation phase there was strong support for MMP. Evidence from André Blais and colleagues who undertook a series of surveys of participants' views during the life of the Assembly suggests that their decision was 'no mere random or unreasoned response' (Blais *et al.* 2008: 135). Throughout the year, the evaluative criteria that reflect citizens' 'basic predispositions to political values and institutional preferences' remained relatively stable over time (Blais *et al* 2008: 132). However, what does change during the learning and deliberation phases is the choice of electoral system – preferences shifted towards STV as citizens learnt about and discussed its potential impact on British Columbia. Blais and his colleagues argue that:

> Assembly members made choices that reflected a well defined set of criteria appropriate to the issue of how electoral systems are evaluated by experts. They rejected SMP because it is rightly understood to be an unfair – non-proportional – system. They chose STV over MMP because they believed that it would give them what they most preferred – greater individual voter choice at the ballot box – and they preferred the particular form of local representation it offered … Few electoral system experts would dispute the appropriateness of the full range of criteria they considered, few could dispute that their decision was appropriate given the priorities they assigned to the criteria they applied. (Blais *et al.* 2008: 138–9)

A significant factor in the Assembly's decision to recommend STV over MMP was the prioritisation of particular interpretations of voter choice and local representation as criteria of judgement; criteria that are not always prioritised by experts in electoral systems (Carty *et al.* 2008: 156). For Lang, the prioritisation of these criteria indicates that Assembly members experienced 'sufficient autonomy to decide what mattered to them'. She continues:

> It also answers another question often levied at citizen involvement efforts: what difference does it make to involve ordinary citizens in political decision making? The difference is that ordinary citizens thought differently about the issues at stake than experts or elected officials. (Lang 2007: 58)

Importantly, Blais and his colleagues are able to provide evidence that there was 'very little discrepancy in the evaluations of the more and less politically informed' members, or 'between those with more or less formal education' (Blais *et al.* 2008: 141). Their conclusion is that 'their collective choice made a lot of sense ... All in all, the rejection of SMP and the choice of STV appear reasonable, given the values of the Assembly members' (Blais *et al* 2008: 144).

Arguably, there are two particular features of the design of the Citizens' Assembly that aid participants in coming to considered judgements. The first is that the charge was clear: citizens were in no doubt as to the task they had been set. The experience in the Assembly could not be more diametrically opposed to the problems faced by participants in the NICE Citizens' Council. The first question tackled by citizens was 'What should NICE take into account when making decisions about clinical need?' Davies and her colleagues question whether "clinical need" set out in this way [gave] the Citizens' Council a viable task to do and one that would make sense to them?' (Davies *et al.* 2006: 77). Their study suggests not. Even though NICE recognised that future questions needed to be more carefully framed, they remained 'still too complex and abstract for participants and members of the Council continued to express a lot of confusion and dissatisfaction at those meetings' (Davies *et al* 2006: 112). In other words, the clarity of the charge can have a profound effect on the quality of judgements.

Second, participants in the BCCA had a distinct advantage in coming to considered judgements, since they had the luxury of almost a year to learn about and debate issues of electoral reform. Most other mini-publics take place over a few days. But even here, evidence of the capacity of citizens is promising. In their analysis of a series of citizens' juries in the UK, Jo Lenaghan and Anna Coote stress: 'right from the start ... we were deeply impressed – as were most other observers – with the level of competence with which jurors tackled their task' (Coote and Lenaghan 1997). A local councillor who observed another UK-based jury affirms this positive judgement: 'the jurors have spent more time considering this issue in an unbiased and deliberative way than most councillors have' (Hall and Stewart 1997: 14). Similarly, in a UK experiment with the consensus conference model on the politically controversial issue of radioactive waste management, representatives from government, the nuclear industry and environmental pressure groups were impressed with the panel's deliberations. For example, even though he did not agree with all their recommendations, Charles Secrett, Executive Director of Friends of the Earth, was generous in his praise of 'the common sense' of the lay panel's analysis and 'the process by which they arrived at these recommendations' (Palmer 1999: 100). Such impressions can only encourage confidence and trust in the decision-making capacities of ordinary citizens.

Fishkin is able to provide some evidence that participants in deliberative polls tend towards more 'public-spirited' judgements: 'They look beyond the most narrow and immediate constructions of their self-interest to support the provision of public goods' (Ackerman and Fishkin 2004: 55). Quoting John Stuart Mill, Ackerman and Fishkin argue that in institutions such as deliberative polls, the citizen 'is called upon, while so engaged, to weigh interests not his own; to be guided, in case of conflicting claims, by another rule than his private partialities' (Ackerman and Fishkin 2004: 57). As evidence of this transformation, they point to the results across the eight deliberative polls that have been held by Texas utilities, where 'the percentage of citizens who were willing to pay more each month for renewable energy rose from 52 to 84 percent at the end of the poll. Respondents were also willing to pay more to support conservation programs and subsidies for low-income customers' (Ackerman and Fishkin 2004: 55). They also highlight the evidence from a deliberative poll in New Haven, where residents were willing to engage in voluntary tax sharing, and a National Issues Convention where there was increased support for foreign aid and more stringent action on global environmental issues. Parkinson reports similar findings from citizens' juries: 'this is a common experience, that jurors generally do feel a sense of responsibility to the wider public interest, take their responsibility seriously, and so act *as if* they were being held to account' (Parkinson 2006: 80). The fear that citizens might 'make irresponsible recommendations... proved unfounded' (Parkinson 2006: 98) Arguably the findings from deliberative polls are most significant, given that in this design citizens record their individual views in private: they are not required to defend their final choices in front of their peers and are thus less susceptible to what David Miller terms the 'moralising effect of public discussion' (Miller 1992: 61). We will have more to say about this difference between the outputs of mini-publics below.

The evidence presented thus far suggests that the conditions for considered or reflective judgement appear to be in place. However, we need to remind ourselves of the earlier comments in our discussion of inclusiveness about the potential marginalisation of minority voices. Within the literature on deliberative democracy, we find a number of sceptical voices who believe there is a danger that deliberation can marginalise the already disadvantaged, with the perspectives of the already privileged dominating definitions of the common good (Phillips 1995; Sanders 1996; Young 1990). The design of mini-publics explicitly attempts to respond to such patterns of marginalisation by ensuring the presence of a diversity of participants, exposing participants to the views of experts, facilitating group discussions, rotating membership of small groups, and so on. However, especially in smaller mini-publics, there is unlikely to be the critical mass of citizens from minority social groups that may be necessary to effectively voice concerns and challenge dominant prejudices and perceptions. In the case of the Citizens' Assemblies, certain social groups – for example, minority ethnic communities – may not even be present since they were not subject to stratified sampling. But ensuring voice is not sufficient to ensure considered judgement on the part of participants. While facilitators are trained to be aware of marginal voices, we have already noted that their methods and techniques can themselves at times act as a barrier to voice. In the evaluation of the NICE Citizens' Council, for example, an episode is recounted where two participants – one a member with visual impairment, the other from a minority ethnic group – were left unable to challenge what they perceived as an inappropriate characterisation of minority groups, leaving 'the minority ethnic and disabled members of the Council at odds with the majority' (Davies *et al.* 2006: 139). In other words, even with explicit design principles that aim to overcome disadvantage, we cannot necessarily expect deep and long-lived prejudices to be recognised and/or challenged.

We also find concerns that the judgements of citizens in mini-publics may be shaped by irrational group dynamics rather than reasoned argument (Merkle 1996: 607). Cass Sunstein (2000) offers an overview of relevant social psychology literature, arguing that deliberation in small groups may lead to group polarisation – movement towards and adoption of more extreme positions. He argues that there are two broad mechanisms at work: a reputational effect where participants aim to maintain their self-conception in relation to the group; and the effect of limited argument pools, where participants tend to hear only arguments that reinforce their own point of view. However, his findings suggest that these tend to be properties of socially homogenous groups with a shared identity. He contrasts such groups with deliberative polls, recognising that the evidence of opinion change within the small discussion groups is not consistent with polarisation (Sunstein 2000: 116; see also Ackerman and Fishkin 2004: 61–5; Luskin *et al.* 2002: 477–8). The design of deliberative polls is a crucial factor in enabling *de*polarisation: participants are highly diverse in their social perspectives; the process is facilitated to ensure openness; balanced information is provided; and citizens are not required to make decisions as a group – their opinions are sought in private.

> Fishkin's experiments suggest that group polarization can be heightened, diminished, or possibly even eliminated by seemingly small alterations in institutional arrangements. To the extent that limited argument pools and social influences are likely to have unfortunate effects, correctives can be introduced, perhaps above all by exposing group members, at one point or another, to arguments to which they are not antecedently inclined. (Sunstein 2000: 117)

One of the characteristics of deliberative polls isolated by Sunstein – citizens are polled individually – is not common to all mini-publics. The design of the Citizens' Assembly shares this characteristic: while citizens worked together to evaluate different electoral systems, their final decisions were made through secret ballot. These designs differ then from citizens' juries and consensus conferences, where participants come to collective decisions after a period of deliberation, crafting a series of recommendations. This is a potentially significant difference that may have an effect on considered judgement. Citizens' juries and consensus conferences provide an opportunity for citizens to be creative in their decision-making, working together to develop novel solutions to policy problems. They also provide an opportunity for citizens to collectively justify their reasoning in the reports that are produced. In comparison, in deliberative polling, participants have little opportunity for creativity, since they are required to give their responses to pre-prepared questions. The preset nature of the survey instrument raises some questions about the extent to which it fully captures considered judgement: to what extent are organisers able to pre-judge the various directions that deliberations might take between participants and the different understandings of a policy issue that might emerge during the process? This is indicative of a significant difference in scope between deliberative polls and other designs: the function of the former is to provide a more informed sense of public opinion based on preordained questions; other mini-publics provide freedom for citizens to develop recommendations on how to respond to a current policy problem. But the freedom to craft recommendations may come at the cost of pressures to arrive at consensus and to avoid conflict, however much the facilitator attempts to create an environment within which all viewpoints are respected. On the other hand, it can be argued that if decisions are made in private – as in deliberative polling and the Citizens' Assembly – a degree of accountability is lost: accountability of citizens to their fellow participants. This recalls J.S. Mill's concern about the effect of the private act of voting. Whilst he recognised that privacy can defend citizens from illegitimate pressures, public decision-making requires participants to defend their judgements, arguably providing increased motivation to consider the public interest (Reeve and Ware 1992: 97–8).

Finally, concerns have been raised about whether the judgements of mini-publics can be replicated. Recall Fishkin's much-repeated contention: 'A deliberative poll attempts to model what the public *would* think, had it a better opportunity to consider the question at issue' (Fishkin 1997: 162). Patrick Sturgis and his colleagues ask: 'Would the same results have been obtained on a different sample? Or, perhaps more to the point, would the same sample have responded differently to a different set of speakers or a slightly modified set of briefing materials?' (Sturgis *et al.* 2005: 33). There are at least two ways of responding to this challenge. First, we can consider the evidence from mini-publics run on the same issue. This is a rare occurrence, but there are at least two examples we can draw on. In Texas, the deliberative polls run for utility companies shared many of the same questions. What is striking from the evidence presented by Fishkin is that the changes in opinion on a series of questions relating to the use of and willingness to pay for renewable energy and investment in conservation were similar and in the same direction across polls (Fishkin 1997: 220). However, the three Citizens' Assemblies offer a different story. All were established to review the relevant electoral system, but they came to different recommendations. The two Canadian Assemblies shared the view that their provinces' electoral systems should be replaced, but offered different recommendations: STV in British Columbia; MMP in Ontario. The Civic Forum in the Netherlands recommended a relatively small reform to the manner in which proportional representation is already practised. In all three cases the recommendations were well reasoned, but the Assemblies came to different decisions. But to expect the same result is to overlook the quite different political and social circumstances in which the three Assemblies operated. Why should we expect citizens in each polity, with its own political traditions and culture, to come to similar judgements? All we can reasonably hope is that they come to considered judgements that reflect the demands of their particular context.

The second response to Sturgis and his colleagues, then, takes a different tack and asks whether the conditions they lay down are reasonable and whether they hold for any other political institution, not just mini-publics. Would we be surprised that legislatures (for example) came to different political decisions if they had different legislators, if evidence was presented in different ways or if different legislators spoke? So why expect a higher degree of replication in mini-publics?

Transparency

One of the virtues of the BCCA is that, compared to other mini-publics, it realised transparency to a relatively high degree. Participants were clear about what was expected from them and efforts were made to publicise the workings and decision of the Assembly amongst the wider public of British Columbia. The same was true in Ontario.

Both Citizens' Assemblies had a clearly defined and easily understandable task: to review the electoral system. The reason why each Assembly was established, the expectations placed on participants and the role that the Assembly would play in the decision-making process (that any recommendation they made for reform of the system would be placed directly on to a referendum ballot) was made clear to citizens during the selection process. And as the work of the Assemblies progressed, staff made great efforts to ensure that citizens were aware of forthcoming topics and activities and had relevant information and papers in advance.

This level of internal transparency is not always achieved in other mini-publics. For example, the transparency of the NICE Citizens' Council suffered because the charge was generally vague and participants (and in fact NICE itself) were unclear about the role of their deliberations and recommendations in the decision-making process of the sponsoring body. As Davies and her colleagues bluntly state, for participants '[i]gnorance of their real position (they were not there as the recruitment advertisement had suggested to "have their say" about the NHS) had impeded their work' (Davies *et al.* 2006: 113). The NICE Council obviously provides an extreme example. However, as we have already noted in our discussion of popular control, for many mini-publics the relationship between their outputs and any future political decision by public authorities is often far from transparent. Dienel's use of a contract between the different parties involved in a planning cell is one way that promoters of mini-publics have attempted to make the relationship between output and political decisions more formal and transparent (Smith and Wales 1999: 305).

For mini-publics, publicity is crucial. Participants have gone through a process of mutual learning and deliberation, a process that distinguishes them from the general public. One way of beginning to overcome this gap is to publicise the workings and recommendations of the mini-public. Almost all mini-publics produce publicly accessible reports of their proceedings and recommendations, but rarely are these picked up by the mainstream media, hence public awareness is very low. The Citizens' Assemblies had a distinct advantage here given their significant funding: in both British Columbia and Ontario, a dedicated website provided background details and a running commentary on the Assemblies' work; and a summary of the final report was sent to every household. Unusually for a mini-public, both Assemblies engaged in their own public consultation exercise. In British Columbia this involved close to 3,000 people in 50 hearings, with over 350 citizens making presentations and generating 1,603 substantive written submissions (Citizens' Assembly on Electoral Reform 2004: 77). Many participants also acted as ambassadors for the Assembly during its lifetime, undertaking media interviews, giving talks, and so forth (Citizens' Assembly on Electoral Reform 2004: 100–1); many became active in the referendum debate that followed, promoting the recommendation of the Assembly (Cutler *et al.* 2008: 343).

To achieve significant levels of public recognition, mini-publics must rely on the media. Here, though, they face a range of problems. First, in most mini-publics, much deliberation takes place behind closed doors in small-group sessions: typically only the plenary sessions are open to the public and the media. Plenary sessions of the BCCA and a number of deliberative polls have been broadcast on television (typically on public broadcast channels) and on the internet. In contrast, small-group sessions, where much of the discussion between citizens takes place, are generally held in private, although they have been filmed in the coverage of deliberative polls. Removing the glare of publicity is seen as important for creating an environment free from the pressures that can undermine open deliberation between citizens (Chambers 2004; Elster 1998).

Second, media interest depends on the salience of the issue under consideration (Parkinson 2006). Again, the Assemblies had an advantage compared to many other mini-publics. They were high-profile institutions – the design had not been used before – and they were considering a politically charged issue, one which had caused public conflict and disagreement. There was a general recognition that the existing electoral system was unsatisfactory, but little agreement amongst political elites about the necessary shape of reforms. But even then, the proceedings of both Assemblies and their recommendations did not receive as much media attention as might be expected, particularly given that they framed province-wide referendums. One of the reasons in British Columbia is that prominent political actors, including the main political parties, did not engage with the referendum process (Carty *et al.* 2008: 158–9):

> [T]he dominant impression was of *silence*. No party took a position, nor did any currently prominent political figures. The usual non-party antagonists in BC's normally polarized political climate were also quiet. Official Yes and No committees did not exist, and the self-appointed unofficial ones had tiny budgets. (Cutler *et al.* 2008: 169)

A decision had been made to insulate the BCCA from partisan political activity, and this seemed to stretch into the referendum process: 'the BC debate was not dominated by party elites, the press and television did not play an overwhelming role, and there was very little partisan money spent to sway opinion' (Chambers 2007: 3). While around '100 Assembly members became active ambassadors of the Assembly and its recommendations and made presentations to interested groups in their respective ridings' (Ratner 2008: 146), very little government finance was made available to inform voters of the Assembly's recommendations and no official 'Yes' and 'No' campaigns were launched.

Evidence from British Columbia indicates the significant impact that a failure to realise publicity effectively can have. The analysis of post-referendum polling data by Fred Cutler and his colleagues suggests that knowledge of the BCCA had a significant impact on voters' support for its recommendation. Voters perceived the BCCA to be legitimate for one of two reasons: either because of its expertise or its inclusiveness and the fact that ordinary citizens had come to a near-consensus decision (Cutler *et al.* 2008: 176–82). However, the lacklustre and poorly funded referendum campaign meant that significant numbers of voters in British Columbia remained oblivious to the existence and recommendations of the BCCA until they read their ballot paper: 'With advance polls indicating that only one-third of the population had heard of the Citizens' Assembly or the referendum on electoral reform, one can imagine the surprise of many voters arriving at the ballot booth expecting to vote in a provincial election and being asked to approve or reject the voting system itself!' (Lang 2007: 36). As we shall discuss in more detail in the next chapter on referendums, it appears that many citizens take their political cues from elite actors and media discussions. Their lack of engagement in the post-Assembly referendum campaign meant that large sections of the public were unaware of the BCCA and its recommendations when deciding how to vote. The BCCA's name on the referendum proposition would have meant nothing. On this reading, the failure to fully realise publicity is the main reason why the proposition was rejected and in part explains the willingness of the BC executive to rerun the referendum.

In many ways, deliberative polling was designed with the media (in particular television) in mind (Fishkin 1997: 175), and it has been reasonably successful in achieving television coverage: two National Issues Conventions were broadcast by PBS in the US before elections in 1996 and 2003, and deliberative polls have been broadcast in the UK by Channel 4 on subjects including the future of the monarchy and the NHS and on ABC and Channel 9 in Australia as part of the run-up to the referendum on the republic. Parkinson's analysis of the NHS poll in the UK raises concerns about the way in which public deliberation is, or even can be, captured on television. He argues that the dramatic structure imposed on the three-part broadcast tended to highlight areas of conflict and polarisation – for example between the competing health spokespersons for the three main political parties – and the strong personality of the celebrity chair of the plenary sessions (Parkinson 2006: 108–13). What makes good television does not necessarily reflect the virtues of deliberation:

> The issue here is not that the television crew failed to capture the vast majority of the actual deliberating; it is that they *could not* do so using the medium of television in an environment where the needs of the audience are a significant factor…media dramatisation limits the access viewers have to any reason-giving that went on between participants over the three days, which gives

viewers little basis on which to judge the quality of conclusions to which the participants come. (Parkinson 2006: 112)

Rachel Gibson and Sarah Miskin offer a complementary analysis of the way that the Australian deliberative poll was televised, arguing that the crucial decisions about the structure and scheduling of the event 'were clearly made in deference to media concerns rather than for the optimal knowledge gathering and deliberation on the part of poll participants' (Gibson and Miskin 2002: 169). The current affairs programme *60 Minutes* was, like Channel 4 in the UK, highly selective in what it considered newsworthy (Gibson and Miskin 2002: 173). Gibson and Miskin highlight a paradox inherent in deliberative polling (and arguably in the practice of mini-publics more generally): Fishkin has long been a critic of the manner in which media coverage, in particular the focus on ever-shorter soundbites, undermines the possibility of democratic deliberation (Fishkin 1991: 62–3), and yet he must rely on the selfsame media to publicise the poll's existence and findings (Gibson and Miskin 2002: 172).

Efficiency

The main demand that mini-publics place on public authorities is financial. The actual organisation of a mini-public tends not to require any major administrative or bureaucratic restructuring – an independent facilitating body is typically commissioned to organise the event. But the financial costs can be significant. It is not surprising that the year-long BCCA is probably the most expensive mini-public to date, with a budget of $5.5 million (Canadian). It was a significant undertaking: the Assembly had a relatively extensive staff (compared to other mini-publics), financed a public consultation process, paid citizens' travel and accommodation costs, provided an honorarium of $150 per meeting day and published a report of its recommendations and proceedings that was then sent to every household in British Columbia. In comparison, citizens' juries tend to cost somewhere between £16,000 and £30,000; consensus conferences around £100,000; and deliberative polls in the region of £200,000. These costs may appear expensive until we consider the organisational effort and administrative support involved in terms of the selection process, engagement of witnesses, professional facilitation, transport and accommodation costs, and so forth. A number of mini-publics have been run on a much cheaper basis, but often by compromising the independence of the process (for example, staff from public authorities acting as facilitators and selecting witnesses) and thus a potentially significant aspect of their legitimacy. We have also witnessed such terms as 'citizens' juries' applied to simple consultation events, arguably in an attempt to improve public perception of the particular public authority.[11] Such misuse of the term can have a detrimental effect on public understanding of the specificity of mini-publics.

The attitude of governments towards mini-publics has been instructive. Clearly, the British Columbia and Ontario administrations viewed the Citizens' Assembly as a significant method for dealing with an intractable political issue, and the Danish administration recognises the importance of national consensus conferences on controversial scientific and technological issues. In comparison, the UK government has been less than enthusiastic. Although the New Labour government showed some initial enthusiasm for citizens' juries on coming to power in 1997, by 2001 its attitude had changed. In response to growing pressure to use mini-publics as a method for involving citizens in decision-making (see for example Parliamentary Office of Science and Technology 2001; Royal Commission on Environmental Pollution 1998), the Cabinet Office repeated the line that such approaches are generally too expensive (Cabinet Office 2001). However, in response, the House of Commons Select Committee on Public Administration reaffirmed its commitment to mini-publics, arguing that the government's attitude 'fails to take proper account of the cost – sometimes a very high cost – which can be attached to rushed government decisions based on contested scientific judgments' (House of Commons Select Committee on Public Administration 2001: para. 8). It is notable that the organisers of 'GM Nation?', the national consultation exercise on GM food that took place in the UK in the summer of 2003, had hoped to include one or more consensus conferences in the process (Agriculture and Environment Biotechnology Commission 2002: paras. 34–5). However, adequate funds were not made available by the relevant government department.

While there is some debate within official circles about the cost-effectiveness of mini-publics, the majority of citizens who are selected to take part are enthusiastic about the experience. For example, participants in the BCCA were strongly committed to the process: 97.4% of citizens felt that 'the work of the Citizens' Assembly is important' and 95% found the weekend sessions 'well worth my time' (Citizens' Assembly on Electoral Reform 2004: 240). As we have already seen, observers of the Assembly were highly impressed by the participants' commitment and willingness to fully engage with the process. Throughout the year, attendance was high, never dropping below 90%, with only one member withdrawing.

---

[11] On coming to power in 2007, the UK Prime Minister, Gordon Brown, used the term 'citizens' jury' to describe a set of consultation events that bear no resemblance to the structure of mini-publics (Revill 2007).

Similar findings emerge from other mini-publics (Ackerman and Fishkin 2004). Such commitment on the part of participants is interesting for two reasons. First, compared to most other forms of political engagement, mini-publics place a significant burden on citizens, both in terms of time and energy. The Citizens' Assembly is the most extreme, requiring commitment over a number of months. But the other designs still require intense engagement over a number of days. Second, mini-publics attract a cross-section of the population, many of whom do not choose to engage in other forms of political activity. As a sample, they may be slightly more politically active and interested than the general population, but it is only marginal – most do not have a history of political participation, but are willing to give up time and energy to participate in mini-publics. The main explanation for this is that citizens perceive participation in a mini-public as a serious undertaking. Earlier we referred to the evaluation of the NICE Citizens' Council, where participants justified their involvement in a variety of ways. Some citizens were motivated because they believed that institutions should be open to the public voice: 'people like me should be able to have a say'. Others stated that participation was a public duty and an expression of citizenship, that they wished to 'make a contribution', 'do something worthwhile', 'make a difference', 'benefit the future of our children' and 'put something back'. And other citizens perceived the Council as an opportunity for personal growth and fulfilment: being 'stretched', 'a knowledge adventure', and so on (Davies *et al.* 2006: 80–1). Participants in the higher-profile BCCA spoke not only of their interest in the issue, but also of the historic opportunity that the Assembly represented and the way that the Assembly made them feel important (Lang 2007: 41–2). That any recommendation would be placed before their peers in a binding referendum no doubt enhanced this motivation to participate. One crucial element of the motivational structure of mini-publics appears to be the invitation to participate: involvement is solicited. As we have already mentioned, the report of the Citizens' Assembly suggests that the selection process 'appeared to create a sense of "buy-in" for the Assembly members that contributed significantly to their commitment to the process' (Citizens' Assembly on Electoral Reform 2004: 40). This is confirmed by Davies and her colleagues, who find that the participants in the Citizens' Council 'also frequently referred to a sense of being "privileged" to have been selected' (Davies *et al.* 2006: 81). Participation in mini-publics is a rare opportunity – this makes it of additional value to citizens. While most governments and other public authorities remain to be convinced of the cost-effectiveness of mini-publics, the evidence from citizens is that they are more than willing to bear the apparently high personal costs involved in participating, since they perceive ample rewards.

Transferability

Mini-publics have been used at different levels of governance, by different types of public authority and across a range of different issues. There has been a tendency for a particular design to take precedence in particular polities. So, for example, consensus conferences were first established in Denmark, and although they have been used elsewhere, it is still the national Danish Board of Technology that commissions most conferences. In Germany, Dienel's planning cell design is the mini-public that is most often commissioned, usually by regional authorities. Citizens' juries have been commissioned in a number of countries, but their use is most frequent in the UK, where the think tanks, the IPPR, the Kings' Fund and the LGMB popularised the design in the 1990s, drawing inspiration particularly from the work of Ned Crosby in the United States. While early deliberative polls were run in the US in the run-up to national elections, Fishkin and his colleagues have been active in promoting the design in other countries. Finally, the Ontario Citizens' Assembly and the Dutch Civic Forum were heavily influenced by the experience in British Columbia, although it is an open question as to whether this design will be transferred further afield, given the referendum results that followed in both Canadian provinces.

There is widespread evidence that mini-publics can be run effectively at significant levels of governance: most are organised by local or regional authorities, but there are a number that have been run at national level. While we have not seen randomly selected bodies organised at the level of international organisations, as imagined by Bruno Frey and Alois Stutzer (2006), arguably the most impressive mini-public in terms of scale of governance is the recent Europe-wide deliberative poll 'Tomorrow's Europe' that took place in October 2007. The poll involved 362 randomly selected citizens from all 27 countries of the European Union and focused on social and foreign policy issues. What is particularly impressive about this event is that translation was provided in twenty-two languages to ensure that all participants were able to engage fully in the process (Tomorrow's Europe 2007).[12] The apparent success of this two-day mini-public indicates that a longer Citizens' Assembly could also be staged that crossed political and linguistic boundaries – the use of quota sampling means that it is possible to ensure the presence of citizens from different polities and also any politically salient social group, thus being sensitive to relevant differences and cleavages.[13] The limiting factor is obviously the logistical costs,

---

[12] For further information, including films and results, see www.tomorrowseurope.eu/ and http://cdd.stanford.edu/polls/eu/index.html#results.

[13] The Ontario Citizens' Assembly supported French speakers – at least one discussion group was always held in the French language.

in particular for translation, although they may be costs worth bearing, given the unusual democratic opportunities such a cross-national forum would bring.

Finally, the range of issues that have been tackled by mini-publics is impressive, including various forms of planning, controversial scientific and technological issues and, in the case of Citizens' Assemblies, electoral systems. There do not appear to be any obvious policy issues that mini-publics cannot deal with, although as we have already stated, the clarity of the charge is crucial. It is also important to remember the significant difference between deliberative polls and the other forms of mini-publics where citizens are able to engage in often complex and challenging problem solving. The reliance on opinion surveys in deliberative polls means that they can generate interesting data on informed preferences, but participants are not in a position to work on creative solutions to policy problems.

The development of the Citizens' Assembly design indicates one area where mini-publics may have a distinct democratic advantage over other forms of decision-making: on certain constitutional issues. Dennis Thompson argues: 'A prudent principle of constitutional design is that decisions about rules that affect who is elected should not be controlled by individuals who have a preponderant interest against (or for) change in the membership of the institution in question' (Thompson 2008: 24). For Thompson, this principle rules out institutions such as the legislature, courts and independent commission as 'unreliable to serve as final authority over the electoral system' (Thompson 2008: 23) and equally highlights the promise of mini-publics as a legitimate institution in aspects of constitutional decision-making.

Mini-publics – realising the goods of democratic institutions?

Mini-publics offer us something different in terms of institutional design. Their mode of selection and the form of interaction between citizens help realise the goods of inclusiveness and considered judgement to an impressive extent. Random selection has been generally overlooked within advanced industrial democracies – mini-publics can be seen as way of reinvigorating interest in the democratic credentials of this recruitment technique. Certainly it generates a diverse group of citizens, and the use of stratified sampling or quotas can ensure the inclusion of citizens from salient social groups. The ability to recruit a body of citizens with diverse social perspectives also proves crucial for the realisation of considered judgement. Deliberative democrats are quick to point out that the environment in which citizens interact in mini-publics can promote free and fair exchange between participants, providing them with an opportunity to learn about the issue at hand, understand the perspectives of others and come to judgements in the public interest. Whilst mini-publics cannot ensure that inclusiveness is always achieved in deliberations or that citizens have fully appreciated the views of others, they are structured to motivate citizens in these directions – and evidence certainly suggests that citizens take their task seriously.

Mini-publics have also been run on a wide variety of issues that are often ethically or politically sensitive. So, the three Citizens' Assemblies dealt with electoral systems, consensus conferences investigate controversial technological and scientific developments, planning cells – as the name suggests – tend to focus on planning issues and citizens' juries and deliberative polls have been employed across a range of policy areas. While the charge needs to be well defined, mini-publics do not appear to be limited to particular types of issues. Similarly, mini-publics have operated at a range of policy levels – from the local to the national – and the recent cross-Europe deliberative poll 'Tomorrow's Europe' indicates that mini-publics can be adapted to deal with transnational issues and constituencies.

Where mini-publics are arguably at their weakest is in realising popular control and publicity. Whilst the way in which they realise inclusiveness and considered judgement distinguishes mini-publics from traditional forms of consultation, they share the same problem: it is not always transparent how or even whether they have affected the broader political decision-making process; or that non-participants are aware of their deliberations and recommendations (or even existence). Here, the emergence of the Citizens' Assemblies in British Columbia and Ontario is a significant development and is indicative of increased ambition on the part of institutional designers. In this case, a mini-public was established that was asked to consider a highly politically charged issue with a guarantee that if it recommended reform its decision would go forward to a referendum. The virtues of mini-publics were – for the first time – complemented by a process of public ratification, thus increasing the extent to which popular control and publicity are realised in the design. The fact that the referendums were defeated should not detract from the significant development that the Assembly represents, although it should focus our attention on how to realise publicity effectively.

What our discussion indicates is that mini-publics offer a powerful way of motivating 'ordinary' citizens to participate in the political process. While their role has tended to be marginal, Citizens' Assemblies point to the possibility that mini-publics could play a more legitimate and formalised role in decision-making processes on controversial political and constitutional issues.

4

Direct legislation: direct democracy through the ballot box

Direct legislation is intuitively appealing for democrats, since citizens gain effective control over political decision-making, with each citizen having equal power to affect decisions through binding votes. Direct legislation has a long heritage: since 1848, Swiss citizens have had a binding vote on constitutional amendments proposed by their federal government; in 1874 they gained the right to challenge draft government legislation and force a popular vote; and since 1891 they have been able to offer their own propositions for constitutional change through the introduction of the constitutional initiative. And below the federal level, citizens are involved in a variety of different forms of referendum and initiative in their cantons and localities. Currently Swiss citizens vote on around ten propositions every year. Although there is no federal-level referendum process in the United States, a significant number of states and sub-state polities adopted some form of initiative or popular referendum in the first two decades of the twentieth century. Across the rest of the world, the use of referendum and initiative is generally more irregular.

Given this long heritage, does it make sense to consider direct legislation as a democratic *innovation*? In at least one sense it does. While the referendum is becoming a more commonplace element in the institutional architecture of advanced industrial democracies, it tends to be used sparingly; for the majority of polities it is not a significant democratic device. Most referendums are advisory and/or held at the behest of the government; in only a few polities do citizens have the right to launch their own propositions. For most, direct legislation is a relatively untried and untested form of governance. Additionally, referendum and initiative divide opinion. For some analysts, they represent the only feasible way of realising

111

political equality and responsive rule in large-scale, complex societies. For opponents, direct legislation weakens the institutions of representative democracy, handing decisions over to incompetent citizens whilst failing to protect the rights of vulnerable minorities. Recognising the divergence within academic and popular opinion, this chapter aims to evaluate the degree to which direct legislation can be viewed as an effective form of citizen engagement in political decision-making.

It is important to be careful about definitions, since there are different types of referendum and initiative and there is no consistent usage across different countries. In this chapter, we will use the term 'direct legislation' to indicate those forms of referendum and initiative where the vote is *binding*. Hence we will have little to say about advisory referendums where governments choose to put a proposition to the people but are under no compulsion to implement the decision.

We will primarily be interested in three forms of direct legislation, and much of our evidence will be drawn from experiences in Switzerland and the United States, in particular California. The first form is the constitutional or compulsory referendum where there is a requirement on the government to submit proposed constitutional amendments to a binding popular vote. This is the commonest form of direct legislation. Arguably of most interest are two forms of direct legislation that give citizens the power to enact a proposition. This can take two forms. The first is termed popular referendum in the United States (also known as the abrogative initiative or facultative referendum). The popular referendum allows citizens to challenge an existing law. If a petition is collected within a specified time period and with a specified number of signatures from citizens, a policy measure drafted or recently enacted by the legislature is tested by being put to a binding vote. If the vote is won, the policy is revoked. A small number of polities – Switzerland, several US states and cities and more recently Italy – have provisions for popular referendums.

The initiative shares some features with the popular referendum. In principle, however, it offers a mechanism for even more substantially altering the balance of power between political elites and citizens. While often confused with referendums, the initiative enables citizens to propose a legislative measure (statutory initiative) or a constitutional amendment (constitutional initiative) if they are able to submit a petition with the required number of signatures from fellow citizens. The initiative involves a binding vote by the citizenry on an issue generated from outside the legislature. The direct initiative, as used in California, bypasses the legislature, placing the proposition directly on to a ballot. In comparison, in the indirect initiative, the proposition is first considered by the legislature. If, after a period of time, there is no satisfactory action on their part, the proposition goes to a popular vote. This indirect version is used at the federal level in

Switzerland (only on constitutional amendments), where the government and both chambers of parliament have the right to consider the proposition and, if they do not accept the proposal, submit a counterproposal that also appears on the ballot.

There are significant differences in the institutional arrangements for direct legislation (Butler and Ranney 1994a). Qualification requirements – including the numbers of signatures required and the time allowed for collection of signatures for initiatives and popular referendums – and the type of majority required vary considerably between polities (including between US states). Within the same polity, the demands often differ between different types of direct legislation. For example, in Switzerland, a constitutional initiative requires signatures from 100,000 citizens (about 2 per cent of the population) collected within eighteen months, whereas a popular referendum requires only half the number of signatures, but collected within ninety days of a law's publication or an international treaty. Both initiative and popular referendum require a simple majority vote. Compare this to California, where an initiative requires higher number of signatures to be collected in only 150 days. Amendments to the constitution typically also involve a more demanding decision rule: in Switzerland, a constitutional referendum has a double majority provision where an amendment requires a majority of votes cast nationally and a majority of votes in over half of the twenty-three cantons. The formal role of political elites is also variable: our brief discussion of the difference between direct and indirect initiative indicates how the relationship between elites and citizens can differ depending on the institutional form of direct legislation and the wider institutional context in which it operates. Such differences in institutional arrangements can have a profound effect on the way that referendums and initiatives operate and the extent to which different goods of democratic institutions are realised.

Inclusiveness

Direct legislation is intuitively appealing in that, at the moment of decision, citizens 'enjoy precisely the same amount of political power' (Eisenberg 2001: 149). Political equality is, in principle, realised though a direct and binding popular vote on policy and constitutional measures. It is on these grounds that Michael Saward argues the case for increased use of referendum and initiative: 'equal effective inputs into the making of binding collective decisions in a given political community is the most defensible guiding principle in politics' (Saward 1998: 2). Direct legislation enables 'equal and regular opportunities for all adult citizens to set the public political agenda' (Saward 1998: 108).

When compared to other democratic innovations, referendum and initiative attract large numbers of citizens to make binding decisions for their political community, although a significant caveat is that the number who can actually participate is limited by the electoral rules and practices of specific polities: participation rights are rarely extended to the full resident population, and the boundaries of a polity do not always equate to the potentially affected population. For those with participation rights, the equal right and opportunity to participate does not always translate into high turnout or equal levels of engagement across social groups. As with elections, we typically find that a significant minority of eligible voters are not registered to participate. Additionally, turnout for referendums and initiatives is typically lower than in general elections. While there is normally a noticeable improvement in turnout on ballots that are run concurrently with elections rather than independently, there is usually a fall-off in terms of the numbers voting in the election and those that also complete the direct legislation ballot. What is particularly evident is that turnout is much lower in those polities where voting on direct legislation is common: the average turnout in Switzerland is just over 40 per cent; in California as low as 35 per cent. In comparison, the turnout figure is much higher in those countries that use direct legislation more sparingly. This is obviously a concern for those who support the further institutionalisation of direct legislation. As Matt Qvortrup argues:

> The conclusion that there is a negative correlation between turnout rates and the frequency of referendums leaves us with the apparently contradictory conclusion that referendums on the one hand increase responsiveness, as they potentially provide each citizen with opportunities for expressing his or her preferences as to the final outcome, but on the other hand decrease public responsiveness because the provisions for referendums apparently lead to lower turnouts. (Qvortrup 2005: 30)

But the picture is not so clear-cut: participation rates are higher for more controversial or emotive issues (Butler and Ranney 1994b: 16–17). Qvortrup contends that we may be witnessing 'selective participation': 'participation (the turnout) is a function of the perceived importance of the issue on the ballot. The ordinary voter sees no reason for wasting his or her energy on relatively uncontroversial issues' (Qvortrup 2005: 29). As evidence, he points to the 12% increase in participation in the Italian referendum on the abolition of PR for senate elections and state funding of parties; the infamous California Proposition 13 on property taxes in 1978 that increased turnout by 9%; and the Swiss referendum on membership of the European Economic Area which reached a high of 78.3% (Qvortrup 2005: 28). It appears that citizens have the potential to act when they deem such action necessary.

Arguably of more concern than sheer numbers is the differential rate of turnout across social groups – a similar problem that confronts elections across all advanced industrial democracies (see Chapter 1). The problem is particularly acute in polities such as California, where 'voter registration laws (and other aspects of American political culture) have substantially suppressed voter turnout amongst low-income voters' (Mendelsohn and Parkin 2001: 5). As Matthew Mendelsohn and Andrew Parkin argue: 'in situations of low voter turnout, such as in California, this means that the referendum may amplify the opinion of those most likely to actually vote: white, middle class, suburban voters' (Mendelsohn and Parkin 2001: 12). But even in Switzerland, where political authorities intervene to a greater extent to enable citizen participation, Wolf Linder argues:

> [D]irect democracy is demanding, and participation rates fluctuate fairly widely. So, especially when participation is low, the choir of Swiss direct democracy sings in upper and middle-class tones ... The most important restriction on the democratic norm of equal and general participation ... lies in the unequal representation of social classes. (Linder 1994: 95)

Qvortrup contends that this conclusion has been exaggerated, although his evidence still suggests an under-representation of citizens with low education and in unskilled manual occupations and an over-representation of graduates and senior managers in direct legislation across a number of polities (Qvortrup 2005: 31–5). Uneven participation across social groups can have a significant impact on the results of direct legislation, particularly when the outcome is close (Magleby 1984: 120). This is a widely-recognised problem, but one that has been inadequately addressed in most polities. Compulsory voting may be one answer to both low and uneven rates of turnout – a policy most prominently practised in Australia (Uhr 2002). For example, the 1999 republic referendum had a 95.1 per cent turnout.[1] While penalties tend to be low and enforcement lax, Arend Lijphart argues that 'the inducement of compulsory voting, small as it is, can still neutralize a large part of the cost of voting' (Lijphart 1997: 9).[2] For Lijphart, any costs of compulsion – for example, the violation of

---

[1] www.aec.gov.au/_content/when/referendums/1999_report/index.htm.

[2] In Australia citizens are required to attend a polling station and pick up their ballot for both general elections and direct legislation. There is no compulsion to complete the ballot. Hence, compulsory voting is actually compulsory attendance at a polling station. Although there may be a law mandating voting, the level of enforcement varies. In a number of countries, including Australia, if a citizen cannot provide a legitimate reason for abstention, then a fine is imposed. Compulsory voting for elections is practised at different levels of governance in at least thirty countries and the punishment varies: non-voters can be removed from the electoral register (Belgium, Singapore) and may be denied services and public-sector employment (Peru, Bolivia). Elsewhere, formal

individual freedom – are worth paying to reduce unequal participation (Lijphart 1997: 11; see also Watson and Tami 2001).

The initiative (and popular referendum) offers an additional, earlier opportunity for participation: the petition process in which all citizens have the right and opportunity to put issues on the ballot. Qualification requirements vary considerably. Even within the US we can find great variation:

> In the United States the requirement ranges from a low of 2% of registered voters in North Dakota to a high of 15% of votes cast in the previous general election in Wyoming. In addition to mandating numbers, some states require signatures to be collected from multiple regions of the state – to avoid sponsors soliciting signatures in only a handful of densely populated areas. Massachusetts, for example, allows no more than 25% of signatures to come from the Boston area. Another important variable is the time allowed for signature collection. In California, sponsors must collect all of their signatures within a 150-day window. In Florida, sponsors can take up to four years. (Lupia and Matsusaka 2004: 466)

It is understandable why such requirements are in place, otherwise citizens and political elites would be overwhelmed with proposals. It is also understandable that the qualification requirements for constitutional amendments are more demanding than other political changes, given their systemic impact (Frey 1994: 339). But, as Arthur Lupia and John G. Matsusaka note, these variations 'affect what kinds of policy proposals get on the ballot and the role of money in determining ballot access' (Lupia and Matsusaka 2004: 466). So, for example, in California a successful petition requires signatures that equate to 5 per cent of the turnout for the previous state election (around 400,000 signatures) to be collected within 150 days. This is a relatively high hurdle to overcome and it is almost impossible to achieve without paid petition circulators. But this is expensive: in excess of $1 million to qualify an initiative in California (Lupia and Matsusaka 2004: 471). As David Magleby argues, this limits who has the capacity to successfully qualify a petition:

> [I]t is clear that in order for initiatives and referendums to meet signature thresholds, legal challenges, and campaign costs, their sponsors must have

---

sanctions are much weaker or non-existent. In the two Austrian regions where voting is compulsory, turnout at elections remains higher than the national average even though enforcement is weak. See Institute of Democracy and Electoral Assistance (IDEA): www.idea.int/vt/compulsory_voting.cfm. In Greece turnout is around 75 per cent even though the imprisonment penalty is not generally enforced: 'Public awareness of the legal requirement appears to be sufficient in itself to secure general compliance' (Electoral Commission 2003: 2).

substantial political resources (money and manpower). Organised interests clearly have an advantage over most individuals in overcoming these hurdles. Thus, if a test for the popular sovereignty of initiatives and referendums is equal access in placing an issue on the ballot, the initiative and referendum fail. (Magleby 1984: 58)

There is no 'mythical citizen' who initiates petitions (Cronin 1999: 207), it is organised interests who are able to afford professional signature drives and/or call upon an army of committed volunteers. Most citizens cannot access such resources – particularly those from poorer and/or minority communities – and hence 'the issues placed before the voters reflect the interests of groups with money or highly motivated volunteers' (Magleby 1984: 76).

This is one obvious explanation as to why minority ethnic groups tend to participate in direct legislation at a rate lower than most other socio-economic groups. Evidence from Shaun Bowler and Todd Donovan (2002) indicates that minority ethnic groups feel disempowered in polities that have institutionalised direct legislation. There are additional reasons why minority ethnic groups may be alienated by direct legislation. First, direct legislation appears prone to repressive outcomes: 'One of the major concerns voiced repeatedly in discussions of direct democracy is that it raises the possibility of abusive majority rule' (Bowler and Donovan 2002: 125). While there have been a number of high-profile attempts to roll back minority rights, the actual impact has often been overstated: the number of anti-minority initiatives has been relatively low and they have rarely been approved (Butler and Ranney 1994b: 19–20). Bowler and Donovan suggest that in the US the success of repressive measures appears to be strongly correlated to factors such as community homogeneity, level of education and size of population: 'US anti-minority initiatives pass with relatively high frequency only at the local level, particularly in smaller places.' They go on to add that 'there is no evidence that the initiative results were different from those produced by municipal councils in similar places that have no provision for the use of the initiative' (Bowler and Donovan 2001: 133). Legislators can be equally as intolerant as citizens. And it is important to note that many of the more repressive initiatives have been sponsored (either directly or indirectly) by political elites:

> It is worth remembering that many dramatic recent examples such as California's Propositions 187 (immigration) and 209 (affirmative action) were embraced, backed, and in some instances largely authored by political elites. Insurgent outsiders and populist 'grassroots' activists – the ones we are supposed to suspect as agents of majority tyranny – have had less direct success with anti-minority initiatives than figures within the major parties. (Bowler and Donovan 2001: 135)

However, regardless of the frequency of success, it is clear that the initiative process can be used to challenge civil rights. As Magleby argues:

> Is direct legislation a danger to the rights of minorities? The answer seems to be yes, unless the courts are able and willing to protect these groups from attacks by direct legislation. In new democracies where traditions of antimajoritarian judicial protection of religious, ethnic, racial, and other groups may not exist, the potential for danger to minorities is greater. (Magleby 1994: 241)

Second, it is difficult for minority groups to use direct legislation to promote the types of special consideration that difference theorists frequently argue is due social groups that have suffered forms of systematic oppression (Young 1990). As an institutional mechanism, direct legislation tends to accentuate difference in a way that is often disadvantageous to minority social groups (Magleby 1984: 190). Avigail Eisenberg argues that direct legislation tends to reinforce an *undifferentiated*, rather than *differentiated*, understanding of political equality. In other words, where minorities are (or appear to be) appealing for distinct group rights or special status to protect against discrimination or rectify unjust disadvantages, then they 'are far more likely to find referendums an alienating event' (Eisenberg 2001: 158). In contrast, Eisenberg argues that direct legislation can be (and has often proved to be) an effective vehicle for minorities that are appealing to an undifferentiated conception of equality to ensure similar treatment to the majority community. Here, proponents of equal treatment are typically able to appeal to values that reinforce the self-perception of the broader political community. According to Eisenberg, 'one cannot justify the use of a referendum on the basis that referendums are a politically neutral means of resolving the issue ... the very use of referendums creates an atmosphere that biases the proceedings against claims for differentiated equality' (Eisenberg 2001: 164).

Are there ways that direct legislation can be designed to protect minority communities? One option is obviously to place constitutional limits on the range of issues that can be dealt with through this process. It would appear that the Italian practice of judicial review before a proposition is presented to the public is a better design than the practice in California, where court battles are common after the popular vote (Kobach 1993: 260–1). A second approach could be to ensure that qualification requirements force petitioners to collect signatures from diverse communities – earlier we gave the example of Massachusetts, where no more than 25 per cent of signatures can come from the densely populated and urban Boston area. And, in terms of the final vote, concurrent majorities can be required. For example, constitutional referendums and initiatives in Switzerland need a double majority to succeed – a majority of the overall vote and a majority in each canton. Whilst the qualification restrictions and concurrent majorities have tended to be geographic in nature, it is possible that they could be related to particular social groups (for example minority ethnic groups) in order to defend against repressive actions of the majority, although there is a danger that social divisions could become reified.[3]

Popular control

Compared to most other forms of citizen engagement, direct legislation offers a high degree of popular control. Citizens have the decisive voice in decision-making. According to Ian Budge and Saward, popular control, realised through referendum and initiative, delivers 'responsive rule', arguably the primary goal of democratic governance (Budge 1996; Saward 1998). Popular control is realised in different ways by different types of direct legislation. Popular referendum enables citizens to constrain the actions of political elites; the initiative places agenda-setting power in the hands of the electorate, providing an occasion for citizens to raise issues that elites may not wish (for whatever reason) to consider. According to Bruno Frey:

> Instances of voters breaking the politicians' cartel are no rarity: among the 250 referenda held in Switzerland between 1848 and 1990, the majority's will deviated from the stated will of the parliament in 39 percent of the cases. Important examples in which the classe politique was solidly in favor of a move but the electorate was strongly against are the decisions of whether to join the United Nations (1986) and the European Economic Area (1992). (Frey 1994: 341)

Analysis undertaken by Bowler and Donovan drawing on data from across the United States indicates that what they term 'internal efficacy' (individuals' perception that they have the resources and skills to influence government) and 'external efficacy' (their perception of the responsiveness of government) are higher in an institutional context within which direct legislation plays a role. They add that '[T]he substantive magnitude of the effect, moreover, rivals that of education, which has been demonstrated to be a consistent predictor of efficacy' (Bowler and Donovan 2002: 390). A significant caveat is that the results do not hold and are in fact reversed for citizens within minority ethnic groups – a finding that reinforces comments made in our earlier discussion of inclusiveness,

There is much evidence that responsive rule is better realised in polities with direct legislation *if* this is measured in relation to public opinion (a

---

[3] Where ethnic differences have been used in referendums, it has usually been to *deny* a particular social group access to the ballot (Qvortrup 2005: 173–4).

measure that we will critique later in the chapter). Analysts make much of the fact that policies in these political systems tend to reflect the median voter's preferences (Gerber and Hug 2001: 103–5). Direct legislation can be thought of 'as a "median-reverting" institution that pushes policy back toward the centre of public opinion when legislatures move too far to the right or left' (Lupia and Matsusaka 2004: 474). Again, Frey contends:

> Econometric analyses support the contention that direct democracies have the stated effect on policy outcomes. Based on data of Swiss communes it has been shown that the more developed the institutions of direct voter participation, the better the voters' preferences for publicly supplied goods are fulfilled and the more strongly public expenditure is determined by demand (i.e., by citizens' willingness to pay) rather than by supply factors, in particular by the politicians' and bureaucrats' own interests. (Frey 1994: 341)

Responsive rule is not only achieved through successful direct legislation – unsuccessful campaigns and the very threat of an initiative can affect the political landscape. For example, drawing on evidence from the Swiss experience of the initiative, Linder argues that even when initiatives are unsuccessful, they can have an effect on the political process by placing new issues on to the political agenda, accelerating the adoption of policies and expressing discontent with the political establishment (Linder 1994: 105; see also Parkinson 2001: 139). Most commentators on Swiss democracy argue that the *indirect* effect of direct legislation has been fundamental to the development of the country's 'consensus democracy'. Political elites have integrated different interests into the governing process as a way of anticipating challenges and overcoming the threat of initiatives and popular referendums. The process whereby the federal government and parliament are given time to consider initiative propositions and offer counterproposals means that there is a great deal of interaction between political elites and the authors of initiatives (Kobach 1993, 1994; Linder 1994). Simply counting the number of successful initiatives in particular policy areas does not give us a fair representation of the effect of direct legislation mechanisms: their indirect effect must not be discounted.

Summarising recent studies, Elisabeth Gerber and Simon Hug suggest that there is also evidence of the indirect effect of direct legislation in the US. Anticipating the potential for initiatives, public authorities tend towards policy that reflects the median voter's preference and hence majority opinion (Gerber and Hug 2001: 103–5). The potential indirect effect of initiatives is well understood by a range of actors. Gerber reports that 'economic groups, professional groups, and businesses ... attribute high levels of importance to signalling and pressuring the legislature and much lower levels of importance to passing new laws by initiative' (Gerber 1999: 83).

A number of caveats can be raised about how and the extent to which popular control is realised through direct legislation. First, we must remind ourselves of the earlier discussion of the potential for majoritarian tyranny. Whilst there may be relatively few examples of successful repressive campaigns, the indirect impact of direct legislation may be considerable. Where populations harbour anti-minority feelings, Gerber and Hug argue that there is a clear correlation between the policy preferences of citizens and the policy outcomes of states in the US with direct legislation, regardless of whether direct legislation has been used against these minorities (Gerber and Hug 2001: 105).

Second, there is a widespread fear that wealthy interests are able to 'buy' favourable outcomes through direct legislation – it has become an instrument of special interest groups. It is clear that organised groups, particularly in the US, are spending vast amounts on campaigns in an attempt to influence voters: at state level, over $129 million was spent on the campaigns for the twenty-nine propositions in California in 1988; $15 million on Washington's twelve initiatives between 1990 and 1994; and over $5 million on average for each initiative in Michigan in 1992 (Gerber 1999: 4–5). As Gerber notes: 'the *populist* paradox – the alleged transformation of direct legislation from a tool of regular citizens to a tool of special interests – undermines the promise of popular policy making at the ballot box' (Gerber 1999: 5). The phrase 'alleged transformation' is significant here. Gerber's detailed study of interest group influence on direct legislation in the US does not entirely support this rather simplistic account of wealthy interest groups manipulating citizens through high-spending advertising campaigns. Instead her work suggests that citizen interest groups are actually more successful at passing laws through the initiative process than wealthier economic interest groups. However, economic interest groups have a significant advantage when it comes to blocking initiatives that challenge their interests and using the process to exert indirect influence on political elites (Gerber 1999; Lupia and Matsusaka 2004: 470–2). As Gerber concludes:

> Certainly, the role and influence of economic interest groups is different from what modern critics charge. Economic groups are limited in their ability to achieve direct influence over policy, especially direct modifying influence. At the same time, however, direct legislation provides them with additional means for influencing policy in more subtle ways. In terms of ultimately influencing policy, these additional means may be every bit as important as passing new laws by initiative. To the extent that economic interests are able to influence policy through the legislative process, direct legislation provides them with an important mechanism for enhancing and protecting their legislative advances. (Gerber 1999: 146)

In their overview of recent scholarship on direct democracy, Lupia and Matsusaka argue that 'whatever the capacity of money to influence ballot proposition elections, it does not give narrow special interests any greater advantage than they already enjoy in the legislature, at least with regard to fiscal policy or the social policies that have been studied' (Lupia and Matsusaka 2004: 470). Given the ideal of direct legislation as a form of *citizen* empowerment, this appears to be a poor recommendation for institutionalization of this democratic device. It is for this reason that many observers of direct legislation, particularly as practised in the US, argue that we must begin to deal with the imbalances caused by differences in financial power through a firm regulatory framework that includes limits on campaign spending and declarations of the sources of funding (Budge 1996; Cronin 1999; Saward 1998). We will return to the question of the regulatory framework of direct legislation later in the chapter.

A third area of contention about the degree to which popular control is realised revolves around the role played by political elites. Formally, the level of elite control varies between the types of direct legislation – from government-sponsored referendums initiated by political elites through to direct initiative, where citizens control the agenda-setting process (Bowler and Donovan 2001: 128–9). We have already noted that in Switzerland, interaction between elites and the authors of proposals is built into the system. While the romantic image of referendum and initiative rests on the idea of citizen control of the legislative process, elites are far from passive bystanders. Unsurprisingly, government-sponsored referendums typically stem 'from a desire on the part of elites to achieve their preferred outcome, not from a normative commitment to greater public participation in decision making' (Mendelsohn and Parkin 2001: 3). Referendums can provide a strategic mechanism for governments to relieve tensions within their own parties when there are conflicts over policy direction, to further legislation that may be blocked by more traditional routes or to increase their public support. In comparison to initiatives, citizens have no say in the nature of the proposal. But even in initiatives we need to be aware that political elites play a significant role in the success or failure of proposals. First, as we have already noted, in many polities, a significant number of initiatives are launched by elite actors – rather than the 'ordinary citizen' – who believe that the initiative is the most profitable way of raising their profile and/or achieving policy change. Second, elites play a fundamental role in the success or failure of ballots. We will have more to say on this topic in the next section on considered judgement, but evidence suggests that elite actors play a significant role in shaping the decisions of citizens – many citizens rely on the signals from elites in making judgements about which way to vote. As Budge argues, 'Electors are clearly predisposed to follow party cues, as the strong discrepancies between the success rates of initiatives with and without government sponsorship show in both the US and Switzerland' (Budge 2001: 86). Further, in relation to anti-minority ballots, Bowler and Donovan note that the role of elites is not irrelevant: 'consensus among elected elites against anti-minority initiatives leads to the defeat of such measures, while tacit elite endorsement leads to greater popular support' (Bowler and Donovan 2001: 131).

The manner in which political parties (amongst other actors) play a crucial role in the outcomes of direct legislation makes a mockery of the common distinction drawn between direct democracy and representative democracy. There is a strong tendency in work on participatory democracy to privilege an unmediated form of democracy – a classical conception of direct democracy dominates, where citizens engage face-to-face and vote directly. Familiar mediating political institutions – in particular political parties – typically play no part in this model. But forms of direct democracy, in particular direct legislation, have long existed side-by-side with traditional institutions of representative government, such as political parties, in both Switzerland and US states. Direct democracy does not necessarily mean an end to the institutions of representative democracy. As Budge argues:

> [T]he essential feature of direct democracy – citizens taking the important decisions – is compatible with many types of institutional arrangements, including existing representational ones. The sole requirement by which we can judge whether direct democracy exists or not is the involvement of all adult citizens in directly debating and authoritatively deciding all the most important policy questions. (Budge 1996: 36)

Budge argues that we can take a more pragmatic approach to the idea of direct democracy; thus it is quite possible to imagine a system where all significant legislative matters are put to a popular vote and citizens are able to propose legislation through the initiative. The process would still be mediated by political parties, which would continue to play their policy-initiating and clarifying functions and guide and organise popular voting (Budge 1996: 40). According to Budge, recent advances in modern technology make regular popular votes and access to supporting information and discussion easier (Budge 1996: 24–8). Saward (1998) comes to similar conclusions in his study on democratic theory and practice.

A fourth concern is the tendency of direct legislation – in particular the initiative – to focus attention on single issues in isolation. Citizens are not required to have regard to the complexity of contemporary governance. As Magleby argues, 'the issue agendas created by groups that sponsor initiatives are narrower than the agendas of most state legislatures' (Magleby 1984: 197). Direct legislation may lead to myopic and irrational policies; for example, citizens 'will approve new spending programs while at the same time cutting their taxes' (Lupia and Matsusaka 2004: 474). This is a difficult criticism to evaluate, not least because government programmes are themselves often far from coherent. However, the direct initiative as practised in California does create the conditions under which a single proposition can radically impact on a range of public policies. So, for example, the (in)famous Proposition 13, carried in California in 1978, slashed property taxes and had a profound effect on the government's capacity to deliver other socially desirable and popular programmes (Smith 1998). Clearly the Swiss system of initiative has some advantages, in that there is an opportunity for political elites to negotiate and respond to the demands of petitioners, although this can often be used to cause delay. Summarising recent work on deficits in the US, Lupia and Matsusaka argue that 'neither initiatives nor referendums have a significant effect on the amount of debt issued. At least in this respect, the initiative process does not lead to prima facie irrational public policies – particularly when you compare such results to the deficit spending patterns of many professional legislatures' (Lupia and Matsusaka 2004: 474).

A fifth caveat relates to problems associated with implementation of successful citizen-initiated propositions. Direct legislation only cedes citizen control in the decision-making process: problems can arise when those decisions are implemented, since there is no oversight process built into the system. After a proposition has passed into law, popular control can be undermined by a reluctant or oppositional legislature or bureaucracy.

> [G]reat variation exists in how legislators, bureaucrats, and other government employees react to winning initiatives. Some measures, once passed, take full effect, whereas others are reinterpreted or ignored. These variations occur because the people who create and support winning initiatives are not authorized to implement and enforce them. Instead, they must delegate these tasks to legislatures and bureaucrats ... laws passed by voters against the wishes of legislative majorities or governors face powerful postpassage opposition that laws passed by these government entities do not. (Lupia and Matsusaka 2004: 475–6)

The capacity of citizens to use the court system or ombudsmen to challenge implementation deficit thus becomes a crucial aspect of the effectiveness of direct legislation.

Finally, we must question whether responsive rule should be evaluated in relation to public opinion as measured by the median voter's preferences. Public opinion tells us nothing about the extent to which citizens understand the issue (or issues) under consideration; it is likely to be at least partially constructed by raw, unreflective and ill-considered preferences. This brings us neatly to an examination of the extent to which direct legislation realises considered judgement.

Considered judgement

One of the consistent challenges to direct legislation is the charge that citizens lack the political knowledge and understanding to make sound judgements about the decisions put before them. As Giovanni Sartori bluntly argues: 'referendum democracy would quickly and disastrously founder on the reefs of *cognitive incompetence*' (Sartori 1987: 120). Summarising recent evidence on political interest and knowledge in the United States, Ilya Somin argues:

> Overall, close to a third of Americans can be categorised as 'know-nothings' who are almost completely ignorant of relevant political information – which is not, by any means, to suggest that the other two-thirds are well informed. Three aspects of voter ignorance deserve particular attention. First, voters are not just ignorant about specific policy issues, but about the basic structure of government and how it operates. Majorities are ignorant of such basic aspects of the US political system as who has power to declare war, the respective functions of the three branches of government, and who controls monetary policy. This suggests that voters not only cannot choose between specific competing policy programs, but also cannot actually assign credit and blame for visible policy outcomes to the right office-holders. (Somin 1999: 417, quoted in Lupia and Johnston 2001: 193–4)

This appears a far from conducive context for citizens to be making binding political decisions. However, while recognising these concerns, Thomas Cronin continues to defend direct democracy:

> The marvel is that all these devices of popular democracy, so vulnerable to apathy, ignorance, and prejudice, not only have worked but also have generally been used in a reasonable and constructive manner. Voters have been cautious and have almost always rejected extreme proposals. Most studies suggest that voters, despite the complexity of measures and the deceptions of some campaigns, exercise shrewd judgement, and most students of direct democracy believe most American voters take their responsibility seriously... In the absence of a convincing case that change is better, the electorate traditionally sticks with the status quo... Few radical measures pass. Few measures that are discriminatory or would have diminished the rights of minorities win voter approval, and most of the exceptions are ruled unconstitutional by the courts. On balance, the voters at large are no more prone to be small-minded, racist or sexist than are legislators or courts. (Cronin 1999: 197–8)

How can we have this wide divergence of opinion about the competence of citizens? One unsatisfactory response is that the less well-educated and informed tend to abstain from voting – their disenfranchisement therefore increases the reasonableness and rationality of decisions.

> [C]ompared with candidate election voters, referendum election voters are older, have more formal education, are of higher socioeconomic status and are

more involved and active in politics … Referendum voters, however, ignorant and unsophisticated they may seem when measured against the theorists' ideal citizen, seem nevertheless to be better informed and more sophisticated than voters in candidate elections. (Butler and Ranney 1994b: 18–19; see also Cronin 1999: 75–9)

This viewpoint is problematic on two counts. First – as we shall see below – even with low participation by more politically marginalised groups, there are still large swathes of citizens who vote with little or no substantive knowledge of the issue under consideration. And second, as we have already discussed in relation to inclusiveness, the democratic implications of such comments are deeply problematic. There is a failure to acknowledge that it is the voices of the more marginalised and oppressed groups in society that are more likely to be disenfranchised, and thus this position appears to be an apology for direct legislation being an instrument for the already politically privileged.

More recent analysis of the way in which citizens make decisions suggests that it is a mistake to focus attention on the poor results of 'political information' surveys. Drawing a direct causal link between such political information and the competence of citizens when faced with a ballot is to misunderstand how citizens make their judgements (Lupia and Matsusaka 2004). Here the work of Lupia (1994), following earlier studies on the use of heuristics or shortcuts in elections (e.g. Popkin 1991; Sniderman *et al.* 1991), has been particularly important in opening up the debate about voter competence. His analysis of an exit poll from a complicated insurance reform initiative held in California in 1998 isolated three categories of citizens. The first category was uninformed citizens who knew little about the issues and were unaware of the insurance industry's position on the five propositions. The second category could be classified as 'model citizens' – they were knowledgeable about the issues and were aware of the insurance industry's preferences. The third category was citizens who had little substantive knowledge about the issues, but were aware of the insurance industry's position. What is most interesting about Lupia's findings is that the voting patterns of the third category closely resemble the voting patterns of model citizens (Lupia 1994: 71; see also Lupia and Johnston 2001; Lupia and Matsusaka 2004). Lupia's conclusion is significant for debates about voter competence:

> [R]espondents who possessed relatively low levels of factual (or encyclopaedic) knowledge about the initiatives used their knowledge of insurance industry preferences to emulate the behavior of those respondents who had relatively high levels of factual knowledge. If we believe that well-informed voters make the best possible decisions, then the fact that relatively uninformed voters can emulate them suggests that the availability of certain types of information

cues allows voters to use their limited resources efficiently while influencing electoral outcomes in ways that they would have if they had taken the time and effort necessary to acquire encyclopaedic knowledge. (Lupia 1994: 72)

In a study that integrates a range of different ballot propositions, Bowler and Donovan offer corroborating evidence:

> While not being fully informed, voters nevertheless make successful attempts to reason by 'soft' criteria. In that they seek out available information and vote on the basis of ideology, party, cues, and instrumental concerns, we might say that they exercise their choices fairly competently over a very wide range of different ballot propositions ... Many of these voters thus appear able to figure out what they are for and against in ways that make sense in terms of their underlying values and interests. Failing that, others appear to use a strategy of voting *no* when information is lacking or when worries about general state conditions are greatest. Just as legislators do, these voters make choices purposefully, using available information. We might infer then, that outcomes in direct democracy – good or bad – represent the preferences of the voters. (Bowler and Donovan 1988: 168)

Such findings have focused analysts' attention on the way in which citizens use cues and shortcuts from credible information sources – sources that allow them to make judgements about the relationship between the ballot and their underlying values and interests. Again, this reinforces the significant role that political elites can play in the outcome of direct legislation (Budge 2001: 85; Gerber and Hug 2001: 131) and also the importance of the rules under which direct legislation takes place (Budge 2001: 74). If it is crucial that citizens are able to rely on credible shortcuts and cues, then a particular regulatory framework needs to be in place: 'truth-in-advertising laws, perjury penalties, or incentives to be known as trustworthy, each of which can minimize the range of false statements made about a particular initiative' (Lupia and Matsusaka 2004: 469). Summarising recent work on decision-making, Lupia and Johnston argue:

> [C]ommon stereotypes about voter competence rely on shaky foundations. If there are people who are willing to provide short cuts to voters and sufficient competition for voters to learn the motives or reliability of the short cuts they receive, then voters can approximate the decisions they would have made if better informed. (Lupia and Johnston 2001: 202)

This is clearly a much more nuanced account of how voters make their judgements in direct legislation. However, the conclusions need to be qualified. First, there remains a significant group of voters who lack or do not understand the available cues and heuristics (Kriesi 2002). Lupia and Johnston argue that in the case of the California ballots 'the outcome of the election was the same as it would have been had voting privileges been extended to only the more informed subset of respondents' (Lupia and Johnston 2001: 199). This may have been true in this particular case, but it cannot be a generalisable conclusion. Across the five ballots, the 'low information, no shortcut' group ranged from 10.9 to 20.9 per cent of the vote, and in close referendums this group of voters could well affect the result. Second, Lupia's findings may not hold for different types of direct legislation campaigns. The California insurance reform initiative involved 'narrow, well-financed groups taking on other narrow, well-financed groups'. Richard Jenkins and Matthew Mendelsohn question whether reliable information shortcuts and cues would be so easy to recognise on broader constitutional and economic issues where more diffuse constituencies battle each other and where we 'often find representatives of business, unions, and other prominent groups on both sides of the issue' (Jenkins and Mendelsohn 2001: 219). Bowler and Donovan's study appears to offer evidence that many citizens are able to access reliable heuristics across a range of different types of campaigns (Bowler and Donovan 1988).

Third, there is a problem with the way that Lupia and his colleagues conceive of competence:

> For the referendum context, we define the term as follows. A voter's choice is competent if it is the same choice that she would make given the most accurate available information about its consequence. Would she make the same decision if fully informed about the consequences of her actions? If yes, her choice is competent. (Lupia and Johnston 2001: 194)

As Mendelsohn and Parkin note: 'Those who believe that voters make reasonable decisions are interested in whether or not votes "make sense" based on the voters' interests and values' (Mendelsohn and Parkin 2001: 15). If recent work on heuristics is correct, then whether cues and shortcuts lead citizens to make decisions that are in a sense equivalent to considered judgements depends on whether the actors and organisations they are using as cues and shortcuts have themselves been through a reflective process, i.e. they are knowledgeable of the issue at hand and have an appreciation of the position of citizens with different social perspectives. Much then depends on the choice of heuristic. As we shall see below, critics of direct legislation often argue that political campaigns are rarely characterised by mutual understanding and sensitivity, and thus cues and shortcuts may end up reinforcing citizens' pre-existing prejudices, rather than reflecting a considered judgement. The use of heuristics need not undermine considered judgement, although the actual practice of direct legislation campaigns may have this undesirable effect.

Frey argues that the pre-vote public debate can generate important effects:

> Preferences are articulated, enabling mutually beneficial bargaining and exchange ... While referenda do not fully meet the criteria of unprejudiced talk and nonstrategic and nonpersuasive behavior among equals, every citizen who cares may participate (in this sense it is nonhierarchical). Unlike the rather academic and institutionally unbound notion of the ideal discourse ... the pre-referendum discussion is practically relevant, focused, and limited in time. (Frey 1994: 339)

While Frey is correct to stress the implausibility of any public debate achieving the demanding theoretical standards of communicative rationality, critics contend that the structure of direct legislation tends to generate a form of public debate that undermines reasonableness and empathy towards those with different viewpoints. The concern about repressive outcomes (discussed earlier in relation to inclusiveness) is indicative of an institution that fails to promote toleration and mutual understanding amongst citizens (Gerber and Hug 2001: 127). As such, deliberative democrats are typically the most vocal critics of direct legislation. This may be a surprise, given that a significant number of deliberative theorists focus particular attention on the associations of civil society – interest groups, political parties and social movements – as institutions that promote democratic deliberation (see for example Benhabib 1996; Cohen 1989, 1996; Dryzek 2000; Mansbridge 1996).[4] If this is the case, then we might expect that the public debates around direct legislation – in particular initiatives that can be launched by such associations – would be celebrated by deliberative democrats. But Simone Chambers is not alone in believing that the incentives embedded in direct legislation tend to undermine mutual respect and understanding and thus it is a poor mode of ratification.[5] She argues that direct legislation

---

[4] For a careful analysis of the various democratic functions of different types of associations, see Warren (2001).

[5] Chambers's concern here mirrors a more general uneasiness that the private act of voting *per se* may not be conducive to making judgements about the public good: citizens make judgements in isolation and are not required to articulate and defend their decisions in public. The secret ballot is so commonly practised in advanced industrial democracies that it is hardly ever commented on – it was introduced in Britain in 1872 as a mechanism to avoid the intimidation and manipulation of the electorate as suffrage was extended. Secrecy offers protection of political equality by reducing the impact of threats or offers. However, as J.S. Mill argued, citizens are more likely to consider their own private interests when voting in secret, compared to a public vote, where they may be required to defend their decision. For Mill, the potential costs of public voting are outweighed by the motivation it would generate to encourage citizens to make their decision in the public interest (Reeve and Ware 1992: 97–8).

has characteristics that act as a disincentive to considered judgement: first, it introduces 'an extreme form of majoritarianism'; and second, it embeds 'inflexibility and irreversibility' (Chambers 2001: 232). The need to reduce all decisions to a simple 'yes' or 'no' alternative embeds a majoritarian decision rule that hinders the cultivation of mutuality and reciprocity. It invites 'participants to approach debate strategically rather than discursively, that is it creates the incentive to find arguments that will sway only the needed number of voters ... as a decision rule it does not give citizens strong reasons to engage in mutual accountability' (Chambers 2001: 241–2; see also Dalton *et al.* 2001: 150). This is reinforced by the inflexibility and irreversibility of direct legislation – there is little or no room for negotiation, compromise and accommodation (the Swiss form of initiative being an exception to the rule in some respects), and its binding nature creates a fear of losing which will 'overwhelm any principled desire to reach cooperative agreement' (Chambers 2001: 246; see also Budge 2001: 69; Cronin 1999: 248; Uhr 2002: 82). Typically, there are 'few options for amendment and revision once the public has spoken' (Dalton *et al.* 2001: 150). The failure to institutionalise democratic deliberation means that direct legislation invests 'so much in numbers rather than arguments that it is hard for the losers not to read the outcome as "might makes right"' (Chambers 2001: 243).

Various institutional remedies have been suggested that aim to reduce (if not remove) such disincentives. For example, Benjamin Barber offers the multi-choice ballot as an alternative to the simple yes/no decision rule. This would be more sensitive to the complexity of many policy issues and the variation in citizens' preferences:

> The range of options would include: yes in principle – strongly for the proposal; yes in principle – but not a first priority; no in principle – strongly against the proposal; no with respect to this formulation – but not against the proposal in principle, suggest reformulation and resubmission; no for the time being – although not necessarily opposed in principle, suggest postponement. (Barber 1984: 286)

Barber argues that a more varied set of choices would elicit 'more nuanced and thoughtful responses', yielding vital political information. The preferendum shares similar characteristics: citizens are faced with a range of options rather than a binary choice. The approach taken by the de Borda Institute in Northern Ireland uses a points system of voting:

> If, say, there are five options on the ballot paper, voters would be asked to give 5 pts to their most preferred option, 4 pts to their second favourite, 3 pts to their next choice, 2 pts to their penultimate option and 1 pt to their least favoured option. In the count, we add up all the points cast by all voters, to see which option gets the highest. (de Borda Institute 2006)

This form of preferendum means that the most divisive option, which has a significant number of fives and ones, could have an average score of three and be beaten by a compromise option that attracted very few fives, but a significant number of fours. Advocates of the preferendum argue that it is particularly effective in situations of contentious social change – hence the interest in this proposal from organisations in Northern Ireland. While multi-choice ballots and preferendums may lead to more nuanced and sensitive decisions, the potential for confusion on the part of citizens is increased (an issue that we shall return to below).

Barber has also suggested the use of two-stage referendums: if a proposition achieves a majority in the first vote, a second ratification ballot is required after a specified period of time. This 'second reading' would provide an opportunity for citizens to reflect further on the implications of their decisions (Barber 1984: 288–9).[6] Chambers also argues that direct legislation should become more of an iterative process, where referendums, particularly at the constitutional level, 'should be treated as rolling drafts rather than final accords, so that amendments could be accommodated and suggestions solicited. Such an iterative model would focus on an ongoing process of consultation rather than a once-and-for-all ratification' (Chambers 2001: 250). Whilst this suggestion may reflect elements of the practice in Switzerland, Chambers appears to be arguing for the watering down of popular control: rather than effecting direct *legislation*, these institutions become no more than advisory, with power reverting to the legislature.

Finally, both Barber and Chambers argue that direct legislation should be accompanied by structured opportunities for deliberation between citizens. In Barber's vision of strong democracy, direct legislation would be strongly regulated (for example, limits on campaign financing; provision of fair information, and so on), a multi-choice format introduced and mandatory neighbourhood assemblies and interactive debates enabled by information and communication technology would help raise civic education amongst citizens:[7]

> The general aim of these regulations would be to maximise public debate and to guarantee open and fair discussion. With them, the dangers of plebiscitary

[6] The governments of New Zealand and the Australian Capital Territory (ACT) both experimented with multi-choice, two-stage referendums on electoral reform in the early 1990s (Hughes 1994: 170–1). While these were government-initiated referendums, so do not classify as 'direct legislation' as defined in this book, they indicate the potential of combining innovations – a topic we will return to in Chapter 6.

[7] Barber's institutional programme for strong democracy was developed before the emergence of the internet, hence his promotion of televised town meetings (Barber 1984: 273–8).

abuse of the referendum would be diminished and the utility of the multichoice format ... would be enhanced. (Barber 1984: 286)

Along similar lines, Chambers suggests that political authorities should be required to promote and enable unofficial and informal consultation involving civil society organisations to 'promote deliberation' and 'serve as a healthy counterbalance to the referendum dynamic', although it is unclear how these deliberations will be protected from what are often highly divisive campaigns and how far they will reach most citizens. It is noteworthy that she also suggests public authorities should be 'obligated to develop deliberative forums and opportunities to participate' that are 'properly insulated from majoritarian voting' (Chambers 2001: 250; see also Saward 1998: 118). Arguably this is what the governments of British Columbia and Ontario enacted in establishing their Citizens' Assemblies on Electoral Reform which we discussed in some detail in the previous chapter. In British Columbia, a near-randomly selected group of 160 citizens was charged with reviewing the province's electoral system and, if it deemed it necessary, proposing an alternative system. In 2005, the BCCA proposal for a form of STV was put to the electorate in a binding referendum. Although the referendum passed in all seventy-nine electoral districts, it did not pass the second threshold established by the government – the overall vote of 57.69 per cent in favour of the proposition was just short of the required 60 per cent. The Assembly in Ontario proposed a version of MMP, and in this case the vote was lost much more decisively.

Regardless of the referendum outcome, evidence from the BCCA indicates a particularly interesting effect that the Assembly had on the vote. The BCCA appears to have offered a trustworthy decision-making heuristic for those citizens who were aware of its existence. As Rafe Mair, one of British Columbia's best-known political voices, stated: 'we should start with the thought that 160 of our fellow citizens, in an overwhelming favourable vote, and after the most careful of examination of plenty of evidence, have made a recommendation. While that doesn't mean we must agree with them – it does tell us that since none of us have gone through that exercise, we should give considerable weight to the recommendation made' (quoted in Cutler *et al.* 2008: 174). However, as we mentioned in the previous chapter, the referendum campaign was poorly resourced, with minimal elite engagement: as a result, only a minority of the population knew of the BCCA's existence and thus could use it as a shortcut or cue.

Fred Cutler and his colleagues suggest that the perceived democratic legitimacy of the Citizens' Assembly was crucial to its impact on voters' judgements. For those citizens for whom the BCCA was available as a heuristic, it had one of two effects: for some, the Assembly's expertise was significant in their support for its recommendations; for others it was its representative quality and the fact that ordinary citizens had come to a near-consensus decision. Where voters were aware of the Assembly's existence and its role and structure, they were more likely to vote in favour of the proposition: 'Focussing on the CA [Citizens' Assembly] really was a heuristic, a fall-back strategy in the absence of information on substance. Voters who are sceptical of elite manoeuvres and who do not gather enough information on substance were able to learn enough about the CA to be brought on side with its recommendation' (Cutler *et al.* 2008: 186). Arguably, if political elites had been more active in the referendum campaigns this would have raised the profile of the Assembly within the media, and it is likely that the proposition would have comfortably passed. The British Columbia experience offers an interesting example of how deliberation amongst citizens might be embedded within the direct legislation process, such that a group of (near-) randomly selected citizens have a distinct role in framing the proposition and their considered judgements have a meaningful effect on the decisions of their fellow citizens. The potential of combining different democratic innovations – in this case, mini-publics and direct legislation – will be considered further in a later chapter.

Transparency

In principle, direct legislation should be highly transparent to participants. Propositions are put forward for public consideration, either from fellow citizens or the government. The wording of the proposition, background information from official sources and a public debate between the main protagonists inform citizens of the pertinent issues and allow them to make an informed judgement – whether this is based on their own direct weighing of the evidence or through the use of reliable heuristics. However, if we break direct legislation down into three aspects – petitioning, campaigning and the ballot itself – we find that in the actual practice of direct legislation, transparency is often undermined and perverted.

Collecting signatures for an initiative or popular referendum petition is a time-consuming and costly process. The romantic image of hundreds of volunteers pounding the streets engaging their fellow citizens in debate over the merits of a particular proposition has in most cases been replaced by professional petition circulators who are increasingly using direct mail techniques to gain signatures. This should not be surprising, particularly in polities such as California, where the qualification requirements are particularly demanding – hundreds of thousands of signatures in 150 days. Given the costs involved in signature collection, there is little or no incentive for petition circulators to ensure that citizens fully understand the proposition that they are supporting. As Cronin argues:

> By using slogans such as 'Do you want to make politicians honest?' 'Let's get tough on muggers,' 'Don't let the government push you around,' and 'Sign here to stop big business pollution', signature collectors often talk citizens into signing something they do not understand. (Cronin 1999: 208)

Too often literature can be deceptive and citizens are not given information about which groups are supporting the proposition. The assumption that any proposition that qualifies for a popular vote already has significant support cannot hold. While some reformers have gone so far as to argue that paid petition circulators should be prohibited, Colorado's attempt in 1984 to do just that was overruled by the US Supreme Court (Cronin 1999: 125–6). Cronin, amongst others, has argued that there need to be stiffer penalties for deceptive petitioning, and balanced and accessible information must be provided from independent sources, not only explaining the nature of the proposition, but also indicating which organisations are circulating the measure (Cronin 1999: 217 and 236–7).

The campaign that precedes the ballot can also affect the extent to which transparency is realised: this good is often subverted through deceptive and fraudulent claims and advertising and the withholding of information about financial support. Reliable information is key. If citizens are to come to sound judgements, they not only need information about the consequences of the proposed measure, but also details of who is supporting and opposing the proposition. Most news coverage tends to focus on and be structured by the activities of political elites, and attention tends to dwell on strategy and events rather than an analysis of substantive issues (Jenkins and Mendelsohn 2001). This may be enough to provide citizens with necessary cues, although the effect of misinformation can be particularly pertinent where the debate is dominated by one side that has access to significantly larger financial resources. This can occur particularly when political elites line up together on one side of the argument. In some countries, such as the UK, parts of the news media aim for fairness in their coverage of the competing sides, although this is not universal practice across polities.

In an attempt to ensure the provision of 'balanced' information, a number of polities – for example Massachusetts, Oregon and Washington – circulate voter information pamphlets that provide an explanation of the proposition and its consequences, and some Californian cities make simplified hundred-word 'ballot digests' available (Cronin 1999: 238).

Saward forcefully argues that if direct legislation is to be effectively and fairly institutionalised, then there is a strong case for an independent notification and information agency: 'The role of this agency would be to foster the preparation and dissemination of unbiased information in a variety of forms and outlets, and to oversee the realization of the ideal of openness in processes of governance' (Saward 1998: 105). John Uhr offers similar arguments, suggesting that political claims could be subjected 'to independent review by a non-partisan public authority or specialist referendum commission' which might arrange for 'a public retraction by offending parties' or 'rights of reply or rebuttal from those misrepresented' (Uhr 2002: 193). Ensuring that advertisements from partisan actors are not the only source of information is crucial, and most commentators on direct legislation argue that the rules that structure campaigns need to be tighter. Thus we find a series of recommended safeguards including mandatory disclosure of campaign contributions to ensure that citizens are aware of who is promoting and opposing propositions and to guard against the excessive influence of money; public financing and/or expenditure ceilings to ensure that campaigns are not dominated by one well-financed side; fair access to the media; and stiff penalties for false advertising (Cronin 1999: 232–40; Kobach 1993: 248–9).

A final aspect of direct legislation that can undermine transparency is the make-up of the ballot itself. Magleby cites a series of studies that conclude that on average around '10 percent or more of the voters cast incorrect or confused ballots' (Magleby 1984: 144) – they fail to vote in the way that they had intended. There are a number of related explanations of mistaken votes. The first is connected to misleading campaigns: partisan actors use deceptive advertising explicitly to confuse citizens. Second, individual propositions can be highly complicated and difficult to understand: the technical and legal language of many ballots is impenetrable for a significant number of citizens. Magleby contends that the level of education needed to understand propositions is often too high. On the basis of a survey of ballots over a decade between 1970 and 1979, he argues: 'In terms of formal schooling, less than one-fifth of the adults in California, Massachusetts, Oregon, and Rhode Island would have the capacity to read and understand the actual ballot question and description printed on the ballot' (Magleby 1984: 119). For Magleby, the frustration caused by their inability to understand the details of propositions may help explain the relatively low turnout by citizens with low levels of education and the apparent mistakes they make when they do cast votes: 'while direct legislation may lessen the alienation of some, it may serve to heighten the sense of alienation and frustration of others' (Magleby 1984: 142). Relatedly, the counterintuitive nature of some propositions can affect transparency. Again, Magleby cites a number of cases where propositions are worded so that a Yes vote is actually a vote against the particular policy (Magleby 1984: 141–4). Finally, there are a number of examples where opponents of a particular measure have qualified counter-initiatives in a blatant attempt to confuse voters – as we have already noted, where citizens are uncertain about particular propositions, their tendency is to vote against measures (Mendelsohn and Parkin 2001: 19). Such experiences may warn against proposals to use the multi-choice ballots or preferendums that we discussed earlier, since the potential for confusion may be even higher. The idea of an iterative process, which involves more than one ballot before ratification, may offer more scope for dealing with such confusions in that citizens are given time between votes to consider the implications of their decisions.

Efficiency

Compared to those democratic innovations based on participation in assemblies (whether open or selective), it can be argued that the demands placed on most citizens by direct legislation are relatively modest. Citizens are not expected to give up large swathes of time in specialised forums and are required only to attend a polling station on a particular day. The costs associated with voting on direct legislation are often reduced by holding ballots at the same time as major national or other elections. This neglects the costs associated with accessing and assimilating reliable information and coming to informed judgements, although as we have seen, many citizens take shortcuts to reduce this burden. Developments in information and communication technology (ICT) offer a way in which voting – and the provision of information – can be made easier. For Budge, such technological advances are one of the reasons why his model of party-based direct democracy is a realistic possibility (Budge 1996). Citizens with relevant computer or TV equipment need not be required to visit voting booths and can easily access official and partisan information. The first binding referendum that made use of the potential of ICT appears to have taken place in the small commune of Anières in Switzerland in January 2003, with almost half of the votes cast via the internet (Kersting and Baldersheim 2004: 293; Trechsel et al. 2003: 50). We will have more to say about the possibilities opened up by ICT in the next chapter, but it does raise questions about the impact of the 'digital divide' – differences in ICT ownership and proficiency that tend to reinforce existing participation differentials (Norris 2001) – and potential security risks.

The costs associated with successfully placing a proposition on a ballot through the initiative or popular referendum are obviously much higher, and we have noted that the qualification requirements can place an unacceptable burden on ordinary citizens. Qualification requirements need to be reasonably high otherwise there would be an endless stream of propositions that would overwhelm both government and the people. However, too high a hurdle and the initiative and popular referendum is accessible only to organised and well-financed special interests groups who are able to facilitate effective signature drives.

While there are concerns that the opportunity for citizens to make binding legislative and constitutional decisions does not seem to motivate higher turnouts, especially in those polities where direct legislation has long been established, public support for direct legislation is impressive. As Linder notes: 'The popularity in Switzerland of direct democracy is enormous. In a 1991 survey for instance, just 14 per cent of interviewees agreed with the idea of restricting the referendum in favour of more parliamentary power' (Linder 1994: 134). Similarly, Cronin reports on various surveys from across the US during the 1970s and 80s where, consistently, two-thirds or more of respondents signalled their support for direct legislation and were critical of the idea that powers should rest with the legislature instead of allowing initiatives (Cronin 1999: 78–80). Russell J. Dalton and his colleagues provide similar evidence from across Europe. Reporting on the 1997 Eurobarometer survey, they note: 'Among those Europeans who express an opinion, 70 percent are positive about the direct democracy of the Swiss system' (Dalton *et al.* 2001: 145). What is clear from this European analysis is that there is a strong link between support for direct democracy and political dissatisfaction with existing political institutions and incumbents.

There appears to be a paradox here: large swathes of citizens (often from particular social groups) choose not to participate in direct legislation, yet they strongly support the idea that decisions should be made directly by the people rather than by a distrusted political elite. It is important to recognise that even the 35 and 40 per cent of the population regularly participating in Californian and Swiss ballots respectively represent significant numbers, although legitimate concerns remain about uneven participation across social groups. Whilst the popular vote is binding, individual citizens may well calculate that their own contribution will make minimal difference to the outcome. It is pertinent to recall Qvortrup's observation that many citizens may engage in selective participation. Given their general lack of interest in politics, it is only when they perceive that their interests and values are at stake that large numbers of citizens participate (Qvortrup 2005: 28–31). This can be seen as a rational response to the opportunities offered by direct legislation. As Albert Hirschman argues: 'the ordinary failure, on the part of most citizens, to use their potential political resources to the full makes it possible for them to react with unexpected vigor – by using normally unused reserves of political power and influence – whenever their vital interests are directly threatened' (Hirschman 1970: 32). If this analysis is correct, the efficiency of direct legislation lies in the fact that it is a relatively simple device through which these 'unused reserves of political power and influence' can be directed when citizens perceive the time to be right.

For public authorities, the institutionalisation of direct legislation is demanding, requiring significant institutional commitments. For direct legislation to be most effective from a democratic perspective, specialist agencies are needed to facilitate and regulate the process – for example, providing guidance for potential petitioners, overseeing the collection of signatures and ensuring fairness in campaigns – and to provide balanced information to citizens about the nature and consequences of propositions. These functions all have resource implications.

And the results of direct legislation also have implications for public authorities. The initiative and the popular referendum can generate pressures on the government, legislature and bureaucracy that they were not necessarily expecting and may well not support. The nature of direct legislation means that citizens can dramatically alter the course of policy – in fact reverse it on occasions – and it is often the very politicians and bureaucrats whose ideas and work has been challenged and rejected who are then required to change their practices. As we have already noted, public authorities can play an obstructive role in the implementation of propositions. Direct legislation requires a certain type of enabling authority, where politicians and bureaucrats appreciate the value of direct decision-making, otherwise the system will be placed under stress. It is noteworthy that the Swiss approach, where the federal government and legislature are given time to respond to a successful proposition, provides an opportunity for officials and proponents to come to a mutually satisfactory outcome. However, there are concerns that this delay simply allows the government to obstruct the passage of propositions it finds unfavourable.

Transferability

In terms of scope and scale, referendums and initiatives in principle know no boundaries: '[they] can be used regardless of the size of the political unit, in terms of either geographical extension or population size' (Saward 1998: 83). We already find examples of direct legislation being used at the local through to federal or national level. In Switzerland, for example, different forms of direct legislation are in operation at all levels of governance. Beyond the nation state, transnational direct legislation is certainly conceivable, although practical questions of isolating the affected population and establishing requisite qualification and majority requirements would need attention (Budge 1996: 168–71; Held, 1995: 273; Saward 1998: 135–8). It does not take much imagination to see how the use of concurrent majority rules, for example, can be extended from the federal/national level to the transnational context to ensure that propositions achieve widespread support from across different nations. The finding that it is direct legislation at the local level that is often the most repressive suggests that in terms of protection of minorities, direct legislation may be most appropriate at larger scales. Here we typically find more heterogeneous populations that express a number of cross-cutting cleavages. Empirical evidence suggests that in such diverse communities, minorities are less likely to face a consistent threat from majoritarianism (Bowler and Donovan 2001: 144). However, the existence of structural minorities and highly divided communities may affect the desirability of direct legislation, or at minimum require careful consideration of suitable constitutional constraints on its practice.

There is no single approach to institutionalising direct legislation – there is actually a range of devices (referendums and initiatives) that can be institutionalised at different levels and with different forms of regulation. The form of regulation (whether access to media, funding limits, and so forth) will affect practice as will the manner in which direct legislation is integrated with existing institutions. The comparison between the direct initiative in California and its indirect cousin in Switzerland is instructive: the former institutional setting tends towards a divisive politics; the latter, a more consensual approach. Whatever the form, however, direct legislation tends to affect all aspects of the political system:

> As the referendum becomes a more regular component of decision making, it leaves few if any of the institutions, processes, and values of liberal, representative democracy untouched. Legislatures, courts, political parties, interest groups, and citizens each respond in different ways to the opportunities and challenges offered by the use or potential use of the referendum. The end result is a different kind of representative democracy than existed before. (Mendelsohn and Parkin 2001: 2)

The variety of forms of direct legislation also indicates the extent to which it can be used across a variety of issues – from policy-making to constitutional change – although the simple yes/no format means that it is not appropriate to use for complex political issues (unless the multi-choice ballot or preferendum is being considered).

Direct legislation – realising the goods of democratic institutions?

The promise of direct legislation is that, at least in principle, it can real-ise both inclusiveness and popular control within and across large-scale polities: the vote of each citizen has equal worth, and their collective deci-sions are binding across a significant range of constitutional and legislative issues. As Saward argues, 'direct democracy need not ... be face-to-face democracy; it does not depend upon the capacity of the members of the political unit to gather together in one place to make decisions' (Saward 1998: 83). Polities such as Switzerland provide examples of how direct legislation can be institutionalised as a central democratic device within representative systems:

> The Swiss system is at odds with much political theory and with the mainstream of political thought. It provides evidence that intensive political participation beyond the occasional election of a political elite is possible and can play an important role. It shows that a substantial proportion of the population are willing to discuss and express their preferences, even regarding the most complex political issues. And if there are shortcomings in direct democracy, Switzerland has neither suffered anarchy as some feared in the nineteenth cen-tury, nor has it experienced the political revolutions others dreamed of. Direct democracy and the complexity of modern society are not mutually exclusive. (Linder 1994: 130)

This is an important reminder that the rather tortuous debate that casts direct democracy against representative democracy is highly misleading. In many ways the institutionalisation of direct legislation makes sense only *within* a system of representative democracy. Parties and other mediating political institutions do not simply disappear – they play a critical role in the effectiveness of direct legislation.

But our discussion has indicated that in practice direct legislation does not fully realise the goods we associate with democratic institu-tions. Whereas the promise of direct legislation rests on the binding col-lective decision of free and equal citizens, the realisation of the different democratic goods that we are interested in – inclusiveness, popular con-trol, considered judgement and transparency – is often subverted by the manoeuvrings of powerful special interests and political elites. Does the existing practice of direct legislation show that its promise cannot be fulfilled? Certainly we need to recognise that there are problems that are unlikely to be overcome – for example, we cannot seriously expect every citizen to come to a fully considered judgement on each proposi-tion, and achieving higher and more socially representative turnouts is certainly challenging. However, the degree to which democratic goods are realised and problems at least ameliorated in large part is related to the strength of the regulatory framework that establishes the rules and practices of direct legislation. If direct legislation is to be institutional- ised to a greater degree across advanced industrial democracies, it is the establishment of an effective regulatory framework that most needs our attention.

5

E-democracy: the promise of information and communication technology

We are witnessing a quite extraordinary pace of change in information and communication technology (ICT), which is enabling ever more inventive forms of interconnection and communication between citizens across global space: with the 'ubiquity of computer networks, new spaces for public discussion and exchange are invented, introduced, and updated on an almost continual basis' (Sack 2005: 242). But given the pace of change, the political, social, economic and environmental impact of new technology is not easy to discern. Visions and scenarios of the impact of ICT on democratic governance differ widely. At one extreme, ICT represents the dawning of a new age for democracy, offering new opportunities for citizens to participate in local through to global public spheres and grassroots movements to challenge corporate dominance; at the other extreme, ICT leads to increased surveillance by the state and commercial actors and the further marginalization and fragmentation of politics in favour of highly personalised forms of entertainment (Barber 1998; Gibson *et al.* 2004; Kamarck and Nye Jr. 2002; Latham and Sassen 2005b; Sunstein 2001; Tsagarousianou *et al.* 1998). Arguably, however, the distance between rhetoric and reality is vast: 'little empirical research has been done on the claims of either supporters or critics of e-democracy, or the specific practices with which democracy is being brought into the public sphere' (Schlosberg *et al.* 2006: 211). The jury remains out on the impact of ICT on democratic theory and practice.

Whilst there have been staggering developments in the commercial world, the potential for using ICT to increase and deepen citizen participation in political decision-making has lagged somewhat behind. Public authorities and agencies have tended to prioritise two areas. The first is service delivery: authorities are particularly interested in potential efficiency savings and also the possibility of using ICT to tailor services to individual citizens' needs. Although highly significant, this development does not have a direct impact on the area of political activity that we are examining in this book: it is more accurate to consider these new modes of service delivery as a form of e-government rather than e-democracy. The second related area where public authorities have been active is in the provision and dissemination of information: most public authorities have websites that provide access to reams of official documentation. While such information is a necessary resource for informed political participation and can increase transparency, public authorities have tended to view the internet as a 'one way publishing and distribution network rather than as a many-to-many medium' (Sack 2005: 266). As David Schlosberg and his colleagues note: 'The majority of government uses of the Internet provide information to citizens without offering the opportunity for interaction and the accountability that follows from such interaction' (Schlosberg *et al.* 2006: 210). Great claims have been made for the potential impact of ICT on citizen participation in decision-making, but most of the attention has focused elsewhere.

> It is striking that, although the initial promise of most electronic democracy projects was to develop and implement active local democracy which would enable citizens to express their views, opinions and preferences in binding or consultative polls, this promise has not been fulfilled – at least not to the extent initially anticipated by advocates of electronic democracy. (Tsagarousianou 1998: 170)

This leaves us in a slight quandary. Unlike the devices under examination in other chapters, it is difficult to identify an outstanding ICT-enabled democratic innovation that is representative of the field. Instead, we will discuss a range of promising designs from which we can develop a sense of the potential impact of ICT on citizen participation in political decision-making. Our focus will predominantly be on computer-mediated communication, although, as we shall argue, ICT-enabled participation does not necessarily have to take place entirely in virtual space. The analysis in this chapter will be arranged around a briefer evaluation of five quite different e-democracy designs: 21st Century Town Meetings; open discussion forums; Womenspeak; online deliberative polling; and ICT-enabled direct legislation. Many of these designs can be understood as building on the developments in face-to-face innovations that we have already discussed in this book, although the creation of new forms of virtual interaction means that we are witnessing both continuity and change in modes of engagement. Given the diversity of technological possibilities, it is not surprising that we find a diverse range of democratic experiments that enable quite different patterns of interaction (Latham and Sassen 2005a: 5). We should also remember that the rapidly changing characteristics of ICT mean that many of the designs discussed in this chapter are relatively recent developments, and we can expect new, more imaginative experiments to emerge in the coming years. With this proviso in mind, it is still pertinent to ask: to what degree do emerging e-democracy designs realise the goods we associate with democratic institutions?

21st Century Town Meetings

In previous chapters we have noted how judicious use of ICT can increase the effectiveness and efficiency of democratic innovations. The computerised management system employed in Porto Alegre ensures that participants in participatory budgeting (PB) have access to information on the status of projects and the budgets of city agencies. The transparency of information allows citizens involved in different elements of the budgetary process to keep track of investments, undertake research on the administration and its agencies' activities and hold the administration and budget delegates and councillors to account. Beyond Porto Alegre, the European Union-funded project 'e-Agora' is experimenting in PBs in Brazil and Chile with the use of SMS text messaging and email as a method of voting (Pratchett 2006: 12). The British Columbia Citizens' Assembly (BCCA) also made use of ICT. First, the Assembly was able to accept and organise the large number of public submissions in a relatively short space of time and in a way that was easily accessible to participants. Second, the public was able to access the Assembly's website and keep up-to-date with proceedings. Finally, Assembly members were able to access a members-only internet-based forum to discuss relevant issues between formal gatherings (although not all members signed up). In both PB and the BCCA, ICT arguably improves the effectiveness of the innovation, but is not essential to its basic operation. 21st Century Town Meeting differs in that ICT is fundamental to its design. But, unlike other e-democracy designs discussed in this chapter, ICT is used to enable engagement between large numbers of citizens in the same physical location.

The 21st Century Town Meeting developed by the organisation America Speaks evokes the traditional New England town meeting (discussed in Chapter 2), but, according to its organisers, updated 'to address the needs of today's citizens, decision makers and democracy'.[1] These impressive one-day events have engaged between 500 to 5,000 citizens on a range

---

[1] www.americaspeaks.org/.

of different issues, including planning, resource allocation and policy formulation: for example, the mayor of Washington, DC held a series of seven 21st Century Town Meetings on the city's spending priorities between 1999 and 2005 (Lukensmeyer and Brigham 2002; Lukensmeyer *et al.* 2005). The most widely discussed America Speaks event is 'Listening to the City: Rebuilding Lower Manhattan', which took place in the aftermath of September 11, attracting 5,000 citizens and (arguably) affecting decisions about the future of the World Trade Center site. 21st Century Town Meetings combine face-to-face deliberations in small groups with large-scale ICT-assisted interactions and collective decision-making. ICT is crucial to connect the small and large scale.

Organisers work hard to ensure as diverse a range of participants as possible, engaging in targeted outreach to attract traditionally hard-to-reach sectors of the population. On entering the venue, citizens are faced with a series of small tables, each with a networked computer, electronic keypads for all participants and large video screens. Typically, participants are broken into demographically diverse tables of ten to twelve citizens, each with an independent facilitator. Each table uses the networked computer to offer ideas and comments as their discussions progress. These are quickly collated and synthesised by a specialist team who distil comments from tables into themes that are presented back to the room via the large video screens, either for further comment or votes. The electronic keypads provide for instant voting. The large video screens present data, themes and information in real time for instant feedback. America Speaks runs these events only where there is commitment from decision-makers to attend and respond to the outcomes. The sheer scale of the meetings makes them difficult to ignore and means that they often generate substantial interest from the media and public authorities. The combination of small-group discussions and large-scale collective decision-making on a single day could not take place without the use of ICT.

In attempting to realise inclusiveness, organisers face familiar problems. Targeted outreach is considered essential to attract politically marginalised groups, although even then the events typically fail to attract young people and minority ethnic groups in proportion to their presence in wider society. In many ways, the design of 21st Century Town Meetings does encourage voice for those who participate: facilitated small-group discussions, the capacity to feed ideas and concerns from small groups to the whole hall and voting on priorities using touch pads.

Such intense engagement by large numbers of citizens within a short time-frame (one day) is enabled by information specialists who facilitate the process by making quick decisions about the relevance of the information being sent to them from each of the small groups. Their rapid selection

of emerging themes is the key to the effectiveness of 21st Century Town
Meetings, but arguably also its most controversial element from a democratic
perspective. The extent to which popular control is realised over the themes
that develop during the day rests on the capacities of these specialists to
make sound judgements under pressure. There is no opportunity for review
or oversight by participants. The pressure to make near-instantaneous decisions is the price that is paid to ensure that 21st Century Town Meetings
are exciting events that can integrate the contributions of large numbers
of participants into collective discussions and decisions. Rapid feedback is
essential. For organisers, it is sheer numbers that are critical to influencing
political elites and in making 21st Century Town Meetings media-friendly.
There certainly appears to be evidence that these events can influence political decisions. In the 'Listening to the City' event, for example, participants
rejected the six proposals put forward by the Port Authority and the Lower
Manhattan Development Corporation for the redevelopment of the World
Trade Center site following the September 11 attacks. As the official report
of the event states, it was difficult for decision-makers to ignore the views of
such a large body of citizens:

> The messages generated by this committed, energized assembly – one of the
> largest gatherings of its kind – reached decision-makers quickly and unmis-
> takably… 'Listening to the City' had a direct and swift impact on the fate of
> these concept plans. Just weeks after the six plans were introduced as a starting
> point for discussion, the program they were based upon was set aside, largely
> because of sharp criticism at 'Listening to the City' and other public feedback.
> (Civic Alliance to Rebuild Downtown New York 2002: 2, 11)

In summary, 21st Century Town Meetings indicate how ICT can be integrated into the design of democratic institutions in a way that increases
efficiency: it enables large numbers of citizens to be engaged in policy
discussions and collective decision-making over a relatively short time-
period. Certainly if events were longer than a single day, the drop-off in
attendance would be noticeable. And it is the involvement of large numbers, organisers argue, that leads to policy impact. But the capacity of these
events to engage large numbers can be achieved only by relying heavily on
information specialists: their central role in problem definition and agenda-setting arguably has a negative impact on the realisation of popular
control and transparency. Yet again the design of an innovation involves
compromises between different goods.

Finally, there are interesting ways in which the design of 21st Century
Town Meetings could be extended. First, because of the way that ICT
is incorporated, events do not necessarily have to take place at a single
venue. It is technically feasible that parallel Meetings could take place

in different geographical locations, and thus across political boundaries. Second, there may be lessons to be drawn for other innovations in the way that 21st Century Town Meetings utilise technology to increase the number of citizens who can be involved in relatively short timeframes. For example, with a different selection mechanism – random selection – the 21st Century Town Meeting could be converted into a different form of mini-public.

Open discussion forums

The emergence of the internet has led to a blossoming of virtual discussion forums that enable citizens to communicate across space and time to an extent that was previously inconceivable. Only a small number of these forums explicitly focus on political issues, although it is not uncommon for conversations between participants on social networking sites to raise political issues (as in normal face-to-face conversation). Rarely do these discussion forums exert any meaningful influence on the formal political process. A rare counterexample is the oft-discussed MN-POLITICS organised by the non-partisan organisation Minnesota E-Democracy in the US.[2] Its forums attract a significant proportion of users who might be classified as 'activists' and who have a high degree of interest in politics. A small, but significant, proportion work in the city's public administration or are journalists. The characteristics of the users help to explain why there is some evidence that Minnesota E-Democracy has, at times, played an agenda-setting role in the broader politics of the city – for example, the press has covered online debates. There is also anecdotal evidence that debates have had an effect on local political decisions (Jensen 2003).

Public authorities have begun, often tentatively, to integrate some of these new technologies into the political process as a way of engaging citizens in the political process.[3] Early developments tended to be one-way, in the sense that participants were able to post their contributions electronically, but were unable to view other contributions or engage directly with officials or politicians. In the UK, the independent, non-partisan Hansard Society has been particularly active in promoting and organising more innovative internet-based consultations between citizens and government departments, ministers, legislative committees and individual parliamentarians, making use of a variety of web-based technologies, including online surveys, blogs, webforums (all asynchronous)

---

[2] See www.e-democracy.org. MN-POLITICS was established by the e-democracy activist Steven Clift. See www.publicus.net/.
[3] See Pratchett (2006) for an overview of e-democracy developments across Europe.

and webchats (synchronous). It is becoming more commonplace for parliamentary committees to establish webforums as a mechanism for generating evidence in pre-legislative scrutiny and in the select committee process (Coleman 2004; 2005; Ferguson 2006a; Ferguson 2006b). In the US, Schlosberg and colleagues point to the development of 'open-docket' forms of participation for environmental rule making by federal agencies such as the Department of Agriculture (USDA), the Environmental Protection Agency (EPA) and the Department of Transportation. The open docket system allows participants to post comments online and to read and comment on the postings of others and therefore, at least in theory, to consider the perspectives of participants with whom one disagrees – a prerequisite for considered judgement (Schlosberg *et al.* 2006: 211–12). While most of these developments are little more than a new mode of consultation, it is worth considering some of the design characteristics of both independent and government-sponsored webforums, as their use as a mechanism of democratic engagement is likely only to increase.

One of the main challenges facing internet-based engagement is the well-documented 'digital divide' that exists in terms of access to and proficiency in ICT. A significant proportion of citizens in advanced industrial democracies, let alone less-industrialised nations, do not own the relevant equipment and/or have the knowledge and confidence to use electronic media such as the internet (Norris 2001). Whilst access to the internet may be on the rise, it is far from universal. Globally, according to 2007 figures, internet penetration stands at only 19%, with Northern America achieving access levels of 70% of the population compared to Africa's 5%.[4] Across Europe, while internet penetration is increasing, it still only stands at 42%.[5] This figure hides a high level of variation in access between nations, from a high of 86% in Iceland to a low of only 6% of the population in Albania. Differential access to ICT may lead to the emergence of new forms of inequality and social exclusion (Cederman and Kraus 2005: 297), but it tends to reinforce existing political inequalities between social groups. As Benjamin Barber argues:

> The age of information can reinforce extant inequalities ... making the resource- and income-poor the information poor as well. The irony is that those who might most benefit from the net's democratic and information potential are least likely to have access to it, the tools to gain access, or the educational background to take advantage of the tools. Those with access, on the other hand, tend to be those already empowered in the system by education, income and literacy. (Barber 1998: 587; see also Norris 2001)

---

[4] Figures from Internet World Stats: www.Internetworldstats.com/stats.htm.
[5] Figures from Internet World Stats: www.Internetworldstats.com/stats4.htm.

That said, the fact that participation is virtual rather than face-to-face may in principle empower engagement by citizens who are often excluded from traditional forms of participation. The next section will focus on one such example, where women who have suffered domestic violence were mobilised to participate in an online discussion forum.

Aside from the effect of the digital divide, we also find that citizens who are attracted to electronic discussions on politics are predominantly those with an extant political interest. For official web-based consultations, there is generally an increase in submissions, but in large part still from organised interests. Most citizens are unaware of (and generally uninterested in) these new opportunities to participate: typically the internet is not viewed as a medium with which to engage in political discussions or other political activities (EOS Gallop Europe 2002). Just as access and proficiency affect engagement in electronic life more generally, patterns of use tend to reinforce existing variations in political engagement. And even amongst those who do engage in political conversation in forums, webchats and blogs, they tend to be attracted to sites that reinforce their already established viewpoints and prejudices. Hence we find a widespread concern that cyberspace reinforces the fragmentation of the public sphere and undermines concern for the public good (Sunstein 2001). Research into online public discussions in chatrooms and Usenet groups suggests that these formats do not encourage considered judgement on the part of participants. For example, Stephen Coleman quotes from a study of political Usenet groups:

> In Usenet political discussions, people talk past one another, when they are not verbally attacking each other. The emphasis is not problem solving, but discussion dominance. Such behaviour does not resemble deliberation and it does not encourage participation, particularly by the less politically interested. (Coleman 2004: 6; see also Sack 2005: 268)

Whilst recognizing the potential limits of these particular forums and groups, Coleman argues that we should not generalise such findings. The design of government-sponsored discussion forums differs substantially, and as such the interactions between citizens are likely to take different forms.

> The environment and structure of communication has a significant effect upon its content; synchronous chatrooms and peer-generated Usenet groups are no more indicative of the scope for online public deliberation than loud, prejudiced and banal political arguments in crowded pubs are indicative of the breadth of offline political discussion. (Coleman 2004: 6)

Scott Wright and John Street concur with this viewpoint, arguing that 'how discussion is organized within the medium of communication helps to determine whether or not the result will be deliberation or cacophony':

> [E]mpirical research into the construction of primarily government-run online discussion forums ... points towards the way in which design is implicated in democratic processes. Put more strongly: the democratic possibilities opened up (or closed off) by websites are not a product of the technology as such, but of the ways in which it is constructed, by the way it is designed. (Wright and Street 2007: 850)

In analysing developments in online forums, Davy Janssen and Raphaël Kies highlight two design characteristics that have significant impact on the form of interaction between citizens and hence the extent to which considered judgement is realised. The first is the 'technical architecture', in particular whether the online discussion space is real-time (chatrooms) or asynchronous (email list; newsgroups; bulletin boards; forums). They argue: 'It is generally recognized that the former are spaces that attract "small talk" and jokes, while the latter constitute a more favourable place for the appearance of some form of rational-critical form of debate' (Janssen and Kies 2004: 4). The second characteristic is the manner in which online discussion spaces are organised. Janssen and Kies offer a non-exhaustive list of variables that are likely to have an effect on deliberative qualities: whether participants are required to identify themselves; limits to openness and freedom of speech; the existence and form of moderation; and the extent to which participants are able to set the agenda for debate (Jansen and Kies 2004: 5). A third factor that they do not explicitly mention, although it is implicit within their discussion of design characteristics, is the quality of the forums created by and for public authorities. Quite simply their design is rarely as attractive and engaging as popular social networking sites: not surprisingly, public authorities lag someway behind in terms of creativity and imagination in this field, which is likely to act as a disincentive to participate, particularly on the part of young people, who often have demanding expectations of websites.

The extent and form of moderation (or facilitation) is a hot topic in the e-democracy world.[6] Most public authority-sponsored discussion forums are moderated to promote more effective dialogue between participants. Within the literature on e-deliberation we find vigorous debate over the extent to which moderation enables (or disables) popular control. While there are concerns (and occasional evidence) that moderators have the

---

[6] The term 'moderation' rather than 'facilitation' tends to be used in e-democracy innovations. Although distinctions can be drawn between the two terms (for example, facilitation is often viewed as being more interventionist), we use the terms interchangeably in this book.

power to censor reasonable contributions, moderation appears particularly necessary in virtual space, where discussions can easily become chaotic (Wright 2006). As Rosa Tsagarousianou argues:

> [T]he perceived impersonal and ephemeral character of CMC [computer-mediated communication] may render users/participants oblivious to the need to maintain some degree of civility ... As both concern over the abuse of public networks and appreciation of the speed and freedom of unmoderated communication seem to be equally significant for network users, the 'moderation versus freedom of speech' dilemma seems to be a central issue in electronic democracy and, as yet, an unresolved one. (Tsagarousianou 1998: 172)

There is evidence that users of some open discussion forums with minimal moderation have been put off by excessive 'flaming' (offensive contributions) by other participants. In an analysis of the City of Santa Monica's Public Electronic Network (PEN), Sharon Docter and William Dutton note that 'users were more concerned about questions of taste, decency, civility, offensive language, personal attacks and threats than any other category of issues ... Concerns over civility ... appear to have been a key factor which prevented more widespread participation in the computer conferences' (Docter and Dutton 1998: 146). Whether we are considering synchronous or asynchronous forms of engagement, moderation can play a crucial function in ensuring the fairness and civility of proceedings, keeping discussions focused and prompting contributions from less confident participants (Wright and Street 2007: 857). The precise form that moderation should take remains an open question: for example, Peter Muhlberger offers evidence that simply providing reminders that participants are citizens at the beginning and during the process is enough to reduce the extent to which participants attempt to manipulate discussions and enhance their sense of community (Muhlberger 2005).

Beyond the form of moderation, there is also contentious debate as to who undertakes the moderation role. This is not always transparent in practice, and again there is little or no comprehensive research in this area (Wright 2006). As with face-to-face innovations, the default position tends to be that moderators should be knowledgeable about the subject under discussion but independent from the political authority sponsoring the engagement. Whether this is the case in practice is another matter. In recognising the importance of public confidence in e-based consultation, Jay Blumer and Coleman offer a challenging proposal for a 'Civic Commons in Cyberspace': an independent, publicly funded agency that would be responsible for 'promoting, publicising, regulating, moderating, summarising, and evaluating' public online discussion and consultation on the activities and proposals of public authorities (Blumler and Coleman 2001: 19).

Its independence from government would enhance the transparency of official consultations and help remove public suspicion of manipulation. Blumler and Coleman argue that such an agency would be designed 'to forge fresh links between communication and politics, and to connect the voice of the people more meaningfully to the daily activities of democratic institutions' (Blumler and Coleman 2001: 16).

Moderation, along with other technical support, adds significant costs to web-based engagement, raising questions about oft-claimed efficiency gains. While emerging evidence suggests that participants are often positive about these new forms of engagement, there are at least three caveats. First, while web-based consultations appear to generate increased submissions, it is not obvious that the level of engagement merits the costs involved, particularly since it is already politically active actors who tend to engage. Second, participants are often disappointed by the lack of direct engagement in discussions by public officials and representatives. The facility is available for them to engage with contributors, but they rarely take the opportunity: it can be a time-consuming and politically risky undertaking. Third, there is some scepticism about the extent to which online contributions actually have any effect on final decision-making (Coleman 2004; Ferguson 2006a; b). The use of ICT means that it is possible to envisage a more open relationship between political representatives and/or public officials and citizens (Coleman 2005), but there is also the danger that as expectations expand, potentially intolerable burdens will be placed on officials – in terms of time, finance and technical support. Just because consultation moves online, it will not escape the suspicion that it is nothing more than a veneer of participation.

Where internet-based engagement may prove more cost-effective and open up new democratic possibilities is in enabling transnational engagement at larger scales of governance. Warren Sacks highlights the existence of what he terms 'very large-scale conversations' (VLSCs) that are 'usually conducted on the Internet through the exchange of email. VLSC facilitates many-to-many exchanges among citizens across international borders' (Sack 2005: 244) through the use of 'Usenet newsgroups and large, electronic mailing lists and weblogs' (246). Because citizens and other actors are not actually required to gather at a single physical location, then in principle their designs know no boundaries. As Latham and Sassen argue: 'what has tended to operate or be nested at local scales can now move to global scales … The new technologies have brought scale to the fore precisely through their destabilizing of existing hierarchies of scale and notions of nested hierarchies' (Latham and Sassen 2005a: 2, 19). There would appear to be relatively few technical problems associated with extending synchronous or asynchronous communication across political boundaries.

However, while VLSCs indicate that more formal transnational engagement could take place, practice exposes another potential barrier to realising inclusiveness beyond the 'digital divide', namely differential language proficiencies. The dominant language on the internet is English, but only 32 per cent of European citizens whose mother tongue is not English believe themselves to be proficient enough to take part in a conversation in that language (Cederman and Kraus 2005: 303). This has implications for the emergence of an inclusive virtual public sphere that cuts across traditional national borders. As Lars-Erik Cederman and Peter Kraus argue in relation to a European demos:

> [L]inguistic barriers in Europe's emerging ensemble of communicative spaces remain fairly high. Moreover, foreign language skills are distributed very unevenly, both socially and geographically, displaying a pattern similar to the use of the Internet. In brief, the linguistically and informationally versatile citizen, who is prepared to get actively involved in European public debates, belongs to the upper strata of society and lives disproportionately in northern or central Europe rather than on the Union's Latin rim. (Cederman and Kraus 2005: 303)

The Futurum discussion forum, established by the European Union to facilitate communication with citizens, attempted to overcome this linguistic barrier by translating its basic webpages into ten languages and allowing citizens to post contributions in any of the EU's official languages. While English remained the predominant language on the forum, a significant minority of threads featured a range of languages (Wodak and Wright 2006: 262). These were not translated unless participants did so themselves (for example, using translation software). Thus those participants who were multilingual or English-speaking were at some advantage.

The question of translation emerged briefly in our discussion of the Europe-wide deliberative poll in Chapter 3, and it is an issue we will reflect on in more detail in the following chapter. While translation software is available for internet users, questions remain about its reliability and usability and the extent to which the nature of translation needs may differ in virtual and face-to-face forms of participation.

Restricted discussion forums: the example of Womenspeak

One of the criticisms of government-sponsored webforums is that the lack of political interest amongst the population and the digital divide combine in such a way that it is the already politically interested and knowledgeable who tend to engage. As such, the properties of the internet do not obviously lend themselves to the design of a participation strategy to engage the politically marginalised. Bucking this trend, the Hansard Society organised Womenspeak in March 2000 to enable survivors of domestic violence to give evidence to the All-Party Domestic Violence Group (APDVG) – Members of Parliament in the UK with a particular interest in domestic violence. Around 200 women registered on a secure, moderated website and were able to exchange experiences with each other and respond to questions and contributions from MPs (Coleman 2004; Moran 2002). Using similar technology, the Hansard Society also developed the innovative HeadsUp resource for young people, which (among other activities) again provides a secure online forum for MPs to consult with young people (Electoral Commission 2004; Smith 2005: 100–2).[7]

The designers of Womenspeak recognised that for reasons of security women who suffered domestic violence would not be willing to attend public meetings. Four elements of the Hansard Society's approach enabled these women to participate in a virtual dialogue on a sensitive area of public policy. First, the organisers worked with a reputable organisation, Women's Aid, to approach potential participants. Second, the discussion forum was secure – it was accessible only to those women who had registered, the relevant parliamentarians and the organisers. Participants were given pseudonyms to ensure privacy. As Margaret Moran, an MP involved in the consultation, notes: 'The anonymity offered by the technology enabled women to tell their stories, often for the first time, without fear of identification and to receive support and advice without fear of reprisal' (Moran 2002). The technology ensured that a silent minority were confident enough to 'talk freely and give honest and personal evidence about their experiences' (IPPR 2004: 33). Third, technical support was provided to the significant number of participants who had no access to or familiarity with the internet: 'Fifty-two per cent of participants had no knowledge of using the Internet before they took part' (Coleman 2004: 7). Women's refuges were able to provide access to participants without computers, and the moderator had experience of working in this sensitive area and so could provide both technical and emotional support. And finally, the asynchronous nature of the discussion forum allowed women time to reflect on existing contributions before posting their own comments at convenient times.

The secure nature of the site and moderation by a project coordinator with experience of working with survivors of domestic violence helped to cultivate an environment where participants were more comfortable

---

[7] www.headsup.org.uk.

about offering testimony and considerations of how policy might be improved. For the majority of women who participated (58 per cent) it was the first time they had been in contact with an MP and '94 per cent of the Womenspeak participants ... had no organisational affiliation related to the subject of the consultation' (Coleman 2004: 8–9). Unlike traditional consultations that tend to attract 'activists', organisers had successfully managed to involve women who would not normally engage. And unlike the experience of most discussion forums, organisers were active in challenging and overcoming the digital divide associated with access, proficiency and use.

Although the discussion forum was designed to have an agenda-setting role – to raise parliamentarians' awareness of issues related to domestic violence – it shared the weakness with other forms of consultation that there was no formal relationship with decision-making. And as with many other consultation exercises (online or offline), participants were generally far from impressed by the seriousness with which the MPs took the process. According to the post-consultation questionnaire, '68 per cent of Womenspeak participants stated that they did not consider that the MPs who took part were interested in what they had to say, and almost four out of ten (39 per cent) were not satisfied with the contributions from MPs' (Coleman 2004: 11). While the parliamentarians participating in Womenspeak 'expressed enthusiasm about its expansive, deliberative nature of collecting evidence' (Coleman 2004: 12), many found it difficult to find time to read all the contributions and engage in the online discussions, reminding us that as with its face-to-face equivalents, ICT-based engagement places burdens on sponsoring institutions and officials.

Whilst most of the women were disappointed by the extent to which they believed their testimonies actually informed parliamentarians, the site acted as a significant support network for participants: 'participants measured success more in terms of group networking than of political interaction' (Coleman 2004: 10). And even though the women were critical of the engagement of parliamentarians, the post-consultation survey suggests that participants generally found it a rewarding experience and would be willing to engage in similar exercises in the future. What Womenspeak indicates is that if carefully designed, internet-based modes of engagement could be integrated into participation strategies to enable the involvement of politically marginalised groups.

Online deliberative polling

In Chapter 3, we introduced the work of James S. Fishkin and his colleagues, who have designed, promoted, organised and analysed deliberative polls. More recently they have begun experimenting with migrating their design online. This appears to be the first example of an online mini-public where participants are recruited by random selection. Online deliberative polling (ODP) exploits the real-time (synchronous), interactive function of the internet so that citizens who are geographically dispersed can deliberate with one another at the same time, in the same virtual space, thus removing some of the difficulties and restrictions associated with bringing large numbers of citizens together at a single physical location (Ackerman and Fishkin 2004: 115). As with the traditional approach to deliberative polling, ODP draws together a large random sample of citizens to deliberate on a particular policy issue. The first ODP in January 2003 was on foreign affairs and involved 280 citizens (Luskin *et al.* 2006); the most recent was in the run-up to the 2004 presidential election as part of *PBS Deliberation Day* (Iyengar *et al.* 2005). Having completed a pre-deliberation survey, participants are assigned to small groups which deliberate for between one and two hours per week over a period of around a month. Participants are then surveyed again. Small-group discussions are led by trained moderators, and the software allows for discussions that are voice- rather than text-based. Participants are able to raise questions which are put to a panel of competing experts. Responses are posted on the ODP website before the next session. As with its offline cousin, at the end of the process, participants are once again surveyed in order to ascertain changes in knowledge and opinions.

We have already discussed the extent to which a random sample realises inclusiveness in Chapter 3 (a theme we will return to in the next chapter). Organisers of ODPs did not simply want to sample existing internet users, so had to respond to the fact that their random sample would include a significant proportion of citizens who did not have internet access and/ or proficiency in electronic forms of communication. In other words, organisers had to consider issues of both presence and voice. For the first ODP, organisers provided offline respondents with personal computers (Luskin *et al.* 2006: 9). In the second, ODP participants were offered a free web TV service (Iyengar *et al.* 2005: 5). Respondents already online were given a cash honorarium.

Organisers of ODPs are also aware of the way in which ICT proficiency can affect the level of engagement by participants and so opted for a moderated, voice-based technology, providing microphones to participants.

> The discussions were voice- rather than text-based. The Lotus Sametime software permitted the moderator to regulate the order of speaking, thus precluding simultaneous comments by different participants. In most instances, participants formed a 'speaking queue', and the microphone was passed accordingly. When the discussion faltered, the moderator would

pose questions or otherwise attempt to stimulate contributions. As in other DPs, the moderators also attempted to prevent anyone from dominating the discussion (Iyengar *et al.* 2005: 8)

Importantly there is evidence that the effects of the ODP were similar to those of the more traditional deliberative poll: participants gained in knowledge and their policy preferences shifted by the end of the process. The results from the foreign policy ODP indicate that knowledge and preferences moved in the same direction as for participants in an offline version that was run for comparative purposes. However, it may be significant that 'changes from online deliberation were less pronounced than in the face-to-face version' (Ackerman and Fishkin 2004: 117; for more detail, see Luskin *et al.* 2006: 17–23). As Robert Luskin and his colleagues note:

> The samples were different. The moderators were largely different. The content and tenor of the small group discussions were different. The expert panelists were different, as were the questions they fielded and answers they gave. Unsurprisingly, therefore, there were statistically significant differences in the magnitude of the policy attitude change on eight of the nine indices. Yet the broad pattern of change was strikingly similar. (Luskin *et al.* 2006: 17)

Ackerman and Fishkin argue that 'these parallel results suggest that online deliberations, if they continue longer, might someday produce even bigger changes than those resulting from the face-to-face process' (Ackerman and Fishkin 2004: 117; see also Luskin *et al.* 2006: 28). But the reverse may also be true: face-to-face engagement may simply have a greater transformative potential than ICT-mediated deliberations. At present, the lack of evidence about the differential impact of online and offline engagement means that we are not in a position to resolve this question.

The organisers of ODPs are obviously concerned about the potential effects of different modes of engagement: as Luskin and his colleagues argue, 'voice- rather than text-based' discussion was chosen 'both to avoid daunting the less literate and to allow more of the affective bonding and mutual understanding characteristic of face-to-face deliberations' (Luskin *et al.* 2006: 9). But even if voice-based discussion is used, how significant is the 'absence of the paralinguistic and other nonverbal communication in face-to-face interactions' (Iyengar *et al.* 2005: 8)? Does computer-mediated engagement affect the extent to which mutual understanding and empathy are realised? Similarly, does the difference in the timeframe for offline and online deliberative polls make a difference? The traditional deliberative poll involves citizens coming together for a weekend and spending a few hours in small-group discussions. In the offline version this discussion is spread over a number of weeks. There is thus a difference in intensity. And there are other differences: participants in the offline version also engage with each other informally during breaks in proceedings; in the online version, participants are able to have discussions with non-participants between online discussions and have more processing time (or time to forget!). Again, the impact of these different elements of online and off-line engagement has yet to be investigated. That said, the evidence that is available from the two online experiments suggests that creating the opportunity for deliberation between participants does affect the nature of judgements: post-deliberation preferences are different from pre-delibera-tion or 'raw' preferences.

The organisers of ODPs suggest that there are a number of efficiency savings to be had by taking the innovation online. First, costs are reduced, although they remain expensive affairs. The costs associated with tradi-tional deliberative polls are extremely high – prohibitive for many public authorities. As Luskin and colleagues note:

> Physically assembling a random sample for a weekend at a single site is both cost and labor intensive. The expenses, mounting into six, sometimes seven figures for national samples, include transportation, hotel accommodations, meals, and honoraria for participating. Online deliberations, by contrast, do not require participants to leave their homes. Those initially lacking online access must be given computers, but a representative sample can still be recruited for a tiny fraction of the cost of transporting participants to a single location and lodging and feeding them there. This advantage, moreover, is likely to increase, as the proportion of the population already online and thus not needing to be given computers increases. (Luskin *et al.* 2006: 6–7)

Second, attracting potential participants to spend a weekend away from home is often difficult, given people's commitments and obligations. In comparison, in the online version, participants are typically required to participate for one or two hours a week and may be able to choose their discussion group to fit in with their own schedule. Third, the lower logis-tical and preparation costs of ODP create 'the possibility of deliberating about real-world events and decisions in something much closer to real time'. Luskin and his colleagues also note a fourth advantage of ODPs which reflects their interest in the design as a social scientific experiment as much as a democratic innovation: they argue that it is much easier with the online version to investigate the effects of participation, because it is possible to automatically record participants' contributions, their use of materials, etc. (Luskin *et al.* 2006: 7). Finally, ODP has a potential scale advantage over its face-to-face counterpart: there are not too many add-itional costs or difficulties involved in generating transnational samples, although the challenge of language proficiency and translation again emerges.

ICT and direct legislation

In our analysis of direct legislation in Chapter 4, we indicated that experimentation with electronic voting has begun. According to Ian Budge (1996), advances in new media technology means that a practical barrier to legislative decisions being taken by direct and binding popular votes has been overcome. Direct democracy can be realised on a large scale, because the technology is now widely available that would allow citizens to make policy and legislative decisions in the comfort of their own homes. However, given the current digital divide, without active provision of technology and requisite training, a significant sector of society would remain marginalised. While many public authorities are experimenting with public kiosks with internet access, a question mark remains as to whether citizens will be motivated to use these facilities to engage in political activities.

Proponents of remote electronic voting (e-voting) suggest that it may prove popular with young people, although empirical evidence for the effect of e-voting is 'scarce and generally inconclusive' (Kersting *et al.* 2004: 278). At most, Pippa Norris suggests, it 'would probably have a modest impact upon the younger generation', and survey evidence from the US 'strongly suggests that e-voting would be used most heavily primarily by people who are already most likely to participate, thereby still failing to reach the apathetic and disengaged' (Norris 2004: 221–2). Technology can increase the convenience of voting; but inconvenience is not the major reason why people (including the young) do not vote (Pratchett 2002: 8).

More extensive use of ICT in direct legislation also brings with it increased security risks. The reliability and robustness of the internet is vulnerable to insider fraud and external attacks and can reduce public confidence in the process. The cost associated with necessary security measures means that the hope that e-voting would reduce the financial burden of organising votes appears to be misplaced (Kersting *et al.* 2004: 278). There are also potential impacts on secrecy. Compared to the privacy of the voting booth, voting at home or work is 'uncontrolled': as such, social pressure and even intimidation and coercion can affect citizens' decisions (Kersting *et al.* 2004: 285).

While most discussion of the use of ICT in direct legislation tends to focus on e-voting, it is equally plausible, if security concerns can be overcome, that petitions for direct legislation could be collected online. There are already examples of the use of electronic petitions in a number of legislatures, although independent from direct legislation. Arguably most prominent is the process used by the Scottish Parliament.[8] The Public Petitions

---

[8] http://epetitions.scottish.parliament.uk/.

Committee website hosts a valid petition for an agreed period of time during which petitioners have the opportunity to attract wider public interest and gather more names in support of their petition. Each e-petition also has a dedicated discussion forum where the petition and related issues can be discussed and debated. After this process ends, the petition is formally submitted for consideration by the Committee. The Estonian government launched a similar electronic portal known as TOM (which translates as 'Today I Decide') in 2001 which allows 'citizens to propose, discuss and refine issues for government attention, before submitting them for a formal response by the relevant agency which has to be made within an agreed timescale' (Pratchett 2007: 10). The timescales in Estonia are remarkably short – citizens have only fourteen days to propose and refine their petitions, and the relevant agency has one month to publish its response – but this has not deterred around 1,645 petitions in the first four years of its operation. For the initiative or popular referendum, a certain number of signatures would trigger the next stage of the direct legislation process, namely a public debate and direct voting. The migration of the petitioning process online may alleviate some of the problems associated with traditional forms of direct legislation discussed in Chapter 4. For example, the use of the internet may make it easier for grassroots groups and even individual citizens to launch propositions and gain the requisite number of signatures. The capacity to link the petition process to webforums also increases the opportunity to structure deliberation into the process.

E-democracy – realising the goods of democratic institutions?

This analysis of ICT-enabled designs indicates that the promise of e-democracy has yet to be fulfilled. As Lawrence Pratchett rightly argues: 'Despite the hopes and rhetoric of many e-democracy champions ... there is little evidence that contemporary initiatives are galvanising public engagement and revolutionising political participation' (Pratchett 2007: 1). Interesting experiments are only beginning to emerge, and 'our understanding of digital formations is nascent' (Latham and Sassen 2005a: 9). Muhlberger represents the views of many analysts of new technology when he states:

> [I]nformation technology stands at the cusp of a potentially revolutionary application permitting large numbers of citizens to easily learn about, deliberate, and act on political and social issues. A major obstacle to this is that very little is known about the best ways to employ such technologies for political discussion as well as the social factors that promote political discussion. (Muhlberger 2005: 2–3)

The sheer variety of designs means that it is difficult to make generalisations about the extent to which ICT enables the realisation of goods of democratic institutions. While the experience of internet discussion forums (independent and government-sponsored) raises the spectre of the digital divide and the danger of attracting only politically interested, technologically savvy individuals, the actual practice of 21st Century Town Meetings, Womenspeak and ODP offer different ways that technology can be utilised to counter these tendencies and enhance aspects of inclusiveness. The various designs indicate that while there is some potential to enhance the realisation of inclusiveness, transparency, efficiency and transferability, democratic and institutional gains cannot be taken for granted.

There are two areas where our analysis is particularly guarded. First, it is striking that ICT has not led to the emergence of new and interesting mechanisms for realising popular control, ICT-enabled direct legislation aside. Much of what we have discussed in this chapter is innovative forms of consultation that add little to our understanding of how citizens can be further integrated into the political decision-making process. Second, our knowledge of ICT-enabled engagement is most clearly nascent in relation to the realisation of considered judgement. To what extent do virtual many-to-many deliberations differ from their face-to-face counterparts, and under what conditions can mutual understanding and empathy be promoted in virtual space? Here the role played by moderators/facilitators in quite different designs clearly needs more detailed and systematic attention than has been offered to date. ICT provides for easier access to information and opportunities to learn about different viewpoints. The extent to which this translates into the realisation of considered judgement remains an open question.

6

Realising the goods of democratic institutions

Having analysed an array of democratic innovations, we are in a far better position to discern the extent to which citizen participation in political decision-making can be institutionalised effectively. This chapter aims to draw out lessons learnt from the analysis of specific innovations in order to gain an understanding of the relationship between institutional design and the realisation of goods of democratic institutions. Initially we will compare and contrast the manner in which different design characteristics affect the realisation of each of the six goods that make up our analytical framework, namely inclusiveness, popular control, considered judgement, transparency, efficiency and transferability. This is a useful comparative exercise that provides evidence that many of the challenges laid down by sceptics and critics of citizen participation can be met if careful attention is given to institutional design. The analysis is limited, however, in the sense that it focuses only on the realisation of each good in isolation. Thus, the second part of the chapter will analyse the degree to which the legitimacy of each democratic innovation rests – at least in part – on the way in which it realises a compelling *combination* of goods. It would be unrealistic to expect any single design to fully realise all six goods in our analytical framework. Each innovation (or type of innovation) realises and prioritises these goods in different ways: legitimacy is tied to these different relative weightings. The chapter will conclude with an exploration of institutional complementarity: the advantages that might be gained through combining innovations to realise increasingly compelling combinations of goods, thus potentially increasing the legitimacy of citizen participation in political decision-making.

Inclusiveness

If democratic innovations simply replicate and reinforce the differential rates of participation witnessed in most other forms of political participation, then their legitimacy will be cast into doubt. After all, one of the attractions of democratic innovations is their potential to tackle the 'unresolved dilemma' of unequal participation (Lijphart 1997). In evaluating democratic innovations we have been sensitive to the way in which two aspects of inclusiveness are realised: presence and voice. Presence turns our consideration primarily to the mode of selection of citizens; voice to the extent to which citizens are able to contribute to proceedings. While all democratic theories build on an affirmation of political equality, difference democrats are noticeably vociferous in their commitment to ensuring both presence and voice for those citizens traditionally marginalised in the political process. It is well known that membership of particular social groups raises the odds of suffering some form of oppression or deprivation and that these citizens are less likely to be present within the decision-making bodies that have the power to effect change. Difference theorists argue that unless modes of engagement are carefully designed, there is a real danger that the needs and rights of politically marginalised social groups will be further neglected (Gutmann 1996b; Phillips 1995; Taylor 1994; Young 1990). As such, 'a democratic public should provide mechanisms for the effective recognition and representation of the diverse voices and perspectives of those of its constituent groups that are oppressed or disadvantaged' (Young 1990: 184). The extent to which democratic innovations have embedded such 'specific mechanisms' and structural incentives to motivate both presence and voice amongst traditionally marginalised social groups is thus central to our consideration of inclusiveness.

Given the range of innovations we have studied, we are well placed to investigate whether a relationship exists between the type of selection mechanism and the extent to which presence is realised. This involves considering not only who participates, but also who has the right to participate: the constituency of the innovation. While a number of theorists, such as Robert Goodin, contend that democratic institutions ought to embed the 'all-affected principle' in constituting the relevant demos (Goodin 2007), this principle is rarely realised in the actual practice of innovations. In most innovations we have analysed, the right to participate is typically delimited by the political boundaries of the public authority organising or sponsoring the innovation, a boundary rarely coterminous with all those potentially affected by the issue under consideration. A common form of political exclusion continues to pervade much democratic practice. Such exclusion is not necessarily inherent within the design principles of innovations, rather the manner in which they are enacted by sponsoring authorities. The structure of participatory budgeting (PB) as practised in Porto Alegre, for example, gives the right to participate to any adult living within the city: all residents (i.e. not just legally defined citizens) can participate in the regional popular assemblies. In comparison, direct legislation and mini-publics are often more restrictive. In the former, who has the right to vote differs across polities, but rarely coincides with all those who are resident. In the latter, much depends on the way that citizens are selected: databases such as telephone directories or voting registers are not comprehensive. Open internet-based discussion forums offer one example of where the impact of traditional political boundaries can be ameliorated (although they suffer from the impact of the digital divide). Even if the desire is present to extend participation rights (or the right to be selected to participate), there are often significant practical barriers to engaging all those potentially affected by a decision.

Beyond the constituency problem, experience from established democratic institutions suggests that differential rates of participation across social groups are reinforced when institutions are open to all to participate. Where there is an equal right to participate, such formal equality does not necessarily equate to substantive equality of presence. This is certainly the case for direct legislation, where participation tends to replicate the unequal turnout at general (and other) elections: income, wealth and education remain crucial variables in predicting participation. Similarly, we have witnessed the emergence of a digital divide in open forms of ICT-enabled engagement. It is citizens with disposable income and higher levels of education who are more likely to have access to, and competence and confidence in using, new technologies and who are typically more motivated to participate in explicitly political online discussion forums.

But this is not a general rule. For example, 21st Century Town Meetings employ targeted outreach amongst more politically disengaged social groups. Being invited to participate has a motivating effect, and participants tend to better reflect the socio-demographics of the population. However, even with specific mobilisation strategies, organisers still report problems with attracting young people and members of minority ethnic groups in significant numbers. Womenspeak offers an example of how careful institutional design motivated participation by citizens from one of the most vulnerable social groups, namely women who have suffered domestic violence. Understandably the innovation was open only to this particular sub-group of women, and potential participants were initially approached by a trusted intermediary organisation. Once committed, the women were given access to a secure internet discussion forum that ensured anonymity and were provided with computer access and technical support if they had little or no technical experience. The carefully designed incentive structure of Womenspeak overcame the understandable reluctance of these women to engage in the political process.

Of all the open innovations we have investigated in this book, arguably participatory budgeting (PB) as practised in Porto Alegre is the most impressive in terms of the mix of institutional incentives for motivating participation amongst politically marginalised social groups. The annual open popular assemblies that are the building block of the budgeting process engage significant numbers of citizens, with particularly high levels of participation by citizens from poor neighbourhoods; significantly above their proportion in the city's population. This has been achieved by fashioning incentives that appeal particularly to the interests of this social group. Turnout at popular assemblies dictates the number of delegates for the regional budget forums where decisions about local investment priorities are discussed: there is an incentive for neighbourhoods to mobilise so that their interests are better represented. Additionally, the interests of poorer neighbourhoods are advantaged by the distribution rules established by the council of the participatory budget (COP), which tend to emphasise principles of social justice. The administration also employs community activists to develop local civic infrastructure in more deprived areas and less mobilised neighbourhoods are often motivated to engage in greater numbers when they witness investment in similar neighbourhoods (the demonstration effect). The clever design of PB motivates a section of the community to participate that is traditionally one of the hardest to mobilise. A significant limitation, though, is that it has been much less successful in engaging citizens from poorer communities in the more strategic thematic strand of the process which prioritises investment in city-wide policy areas, such as environment, social services, transportation, and so forth. On issues where there is no perceived direct and immediate pay-off for neighbourhoods, motivation to participate decreases. The thematic strand replicates familiar differential patterns of political participation. Ensuring more inclusive engagement on more abstract policy issues may require a different form of participation. What becomes clear then from an analysis of PB and other designs is that there is no simple relationship between open innovations and a reinforcement of differential rates of engagement across social groups. The structure of incentives has a substantial effect on the extent to which inclusiveness as presence can be realised.

Many innovations utilise a selection mechanism of some sort that limits the number of participants. This may be for pragmatic reasons – to ensure that the number of participants is manageable – and/or an attempt to ensure a diverse set of participants. If participation is not open to all citizens, the default selection device tends to be selection through election. There is a strong perception within contemporary democratic thought and practice that elections are the only fair and democratic mode of selection. At least in formal terms, elections realise equality in the sense that all citizens have the right to stand as a candidate. But our experience of competitive elections in advanced industrial democracies (and other political systems) is that they perpetuate a political class that is socially differentiated from the general population. For critics, elections simply reinforce a difference and distance between the subjectivity, motives and intentions of citizens and their elected representatives who make decisions in their name (Barber 1984; Offe and Preuss 1991; Phillips 1995).

PB is the only innovation we have studied that uses elections to select citizens, in this case for regional budget forums and the COP. In comparison to the elected legislature in Porto Alegre, these bodies have been more successful in engaging women, the poor, the less well-educated and citizens from minority ethnic communities. However, if compared to the socio-demographics of citizens attending the assemblies, where the economically impoverished tend to be highly visible, then it is apparent that familiar distinctions emerge in the two representative bodies, with income, gender, age and associational membership as significant variables. There is some disagreement amongst analysts as to whether the main variable driving this tendency is availability of time or whether it indicates entrenched discriminatory attitudes and practices (for example, towards the role of women). Two aspects of the design of these representative bodies alleviate the worst oligarchical tendencies of elections: not only are terms short – one year – but elected councillors on arguably the most powerful body, the COP, are limited to two consecutive terms and are subject to immediate recall, ensuring turnover. Beyond Porto Alegre we can find examples of PB where there are quotas for women and other politically marginalised social groups to ensure a more inclusive form of representation.

The failure of most institutions that embed either open access or competitive elections to realise equality of presence across social groups has led to experimentation with an alternative selection mechanism: random selection. Sortition (as it is also known) has strong historical democratic credentials when compared to competitive elections (Goodwin 2005; Manin 1997), although its use is rare in contemporary polities. Sampling techniques can be employed to ensure that randomly selected citizens reflect salient characteristics in the broader population, be it age, gender, ethnicity, and so on. If a citizen chooses not to accept the invitation to participate, then another citizen with similar socio-demographic characteristics is selected – again at random. Once citizens agree to participate in a mini-public, they rarely drop out of the process: the invitation to participate is an important motivating factor. The advantage of sampling techniques is that quotas can be used to ensure a more significant presence for smaller and more politically marginalised social groups. Equally, it is possible to run mini-publics that select only citizens from particular politically marginalised groups. For example, in the 1990s, the UK government sponsored a women-only jury.

In achieving a high degree of inclusiveness, sortition challenges established democratic expectations and conventions. For example, there are no direct lines of accountability between selected citizens and the wider population, and rather than an equal right to participate, sortition entails an equal probability of being selected to participate. While these limitations raise concerns, random sampling can ensure the selection of a more diverse body of citizens, most of whom would not normally put themselves forward to participate. For the realisation of equality of presence across social groups, sortition has a distinct advantage over other modes of selection.

There is a final selection mechanism that has not been institutionalised in any of the innovations we have discussed in this book, namely appointment. Appointment remains a highly controversial selection mechanism for democrats, as the selection criteria and process is typically controlled by the sponsoring public authority. In other words, the decision on who can and cannot participate lies with public officials. A rare example of the use of appointment to select citizens is the Birmingham Race Action Partnership (BRAP) in the UK. The architects of BRAP argue vociferously that the valorisation of elections as the democratic mode of selection tends to undermine the arguably more primary democratic desire for a diverse body of participants. Appointment through interviews can ensure a more diverse group of highly motivated citizens who otherwise would have been unlikely to put themselves forward (Smith and Stephenson 2005). Appointment generates a challenging tension for democratic theorists: a selection mechanism that has non-democratic characteristics (i.e. elite control over the selection process), but can lead to an inclusive and motivated body of citizens. For this reason alone it is worthy of further consideration by democratic theorists and practitioners.

Turning our attention to inclusiveness understood as equality of voice, the variety of innovations offers a range of lessons. Direct legislation remains the only one of the innovations that guarantees equality of voice for all participants in terms of contribution to decision-making – each citizen who participates has equal influence on the final decision. It is clear, however, that any inequality of presence directly translates into an inequality of voice. Differential rates of turnout imply differential impact on decisions across social groups, although the introduction of a requirement for concurrent majorities across groups could mitigate the effects of this trend to some degree. The other mode of voice in popular referendum and initiative is the opportunity to place an issue on the ballot. Again, in principle any citizen can raise a petition, but money proves to be the most basic requirement, given the high number of signatures needed for quali-fication. Apart from rare examples of community-based organisations that manage to mobilise large number of volunteers, propositions that have qualified for the ballot are typically those where professional petition circulators have been employed.

Direct legislation remains unusual compared to the other innovations discussed in this book, because there is no formal process of engage-ment between citizens. Where citizens engage directly with one another, we find that differences in political skills and confidence can have a pro-found effect on voice. Evidence from PB indicates that the most significant variable affecting voice is years of experience in the budgetary process. In other innovations that are one-off events, this has the implication that those citizens who already have relevant skills and confidence will tend to dominate. Again, this tends to privilege the more educated and financially advantaged.

What can be done to better enable equality of voice? Our analysis indi-cates the significance of at least two institutional characteristics. First, the presence of a critical mass or threshold number of citizens from a politi-cally marginalised social group can be crucial in cultivating confidence to contribute to discussions. It also improves the chances that the diver-sity *within* social groups is better represented in deliberations. In PB, the incentive structure encourages the participation of significant numbers of citizens from poorer communities in Porto Alegre, whose voices would likely otherwise be lost. The use of quotas allows mini-publics to ensure that relevant socio-economic characteristics are over-sampled where this is desirable. In the case of Womenspeak, the discussion forum was open only to a particular marginalised social group in order to increase partici-pants' confidence to contribute.

Second, the practice of various types of innovation suggests that effec-tive facilitation or moderation can be crucial to ensuring that marginal-ised voices are heard. Unmoderated internet discussion forums provide clear evidence of what can happen without some level of intervention from a third party or some reminder to participants of their status as citizens: there is little defence against 'flaming'. Insensitive and offensive contri-butions act as a disincentive to participate for most citizens, particularly those from marginalised social groups, who can often be the focus of obscene and offensive contributions. A minimal facilitation/moderation role, then, is to promote and at times even enforce basic procedural rules so that, for example, civility is cultivated in interactions between citizens.

A more interventionist form of facilitation is practised in certain designs, in particular mini-publics, to ensure that proceedings are not dominated by the politically skilled and charismatic. If innovations have been successful in attracting an inclusive group of citizens, then there will be many for whom political participation is a novel experience, and who therefore lack political skills, experience and confidence. There will always be differences between citizens, but effective facilitation is crucial if distinctions between citizens are not to have a material effect on the equality of voice. Our analysis of mini-publics and certain e-democracy innovations indicates the fine line between effective intervention and forms of facilitation that are either too overbearing or too light. In the first instance, third parties can suppress the dynamism of dialogue; in the second, confident citizens dominate. Effective facilitation can be an essential basis for cultivating democratic virtues such as mutual respect and reciprocity amongst citizens who find themselves in unfamiliar environments and unfamiliar company. Arguably the function and requisite capacities of third party intervention in democratic practice is one that is under-appreciated and under-theorised within democratic thought and one worthy of more systematic reflection.[1]

Popular control

The ambition to realise popular control is arguably the most significant means of differentiating democratic innovations from traditional models of consultation. The consistent failure of familiar forms of consultation to materially affect political decision-making generates disillusionment amongst citizens, practitioners and democratic theorists. To what extent does the design of the different innovations alleviate the suspicion that participation has at best little effect on the decision-making process and at worst is no more than a mode of manipulation and co-option by political elites to legitimise decisions made elsewhere?

In our analytical framework, we offered a stylised stages approach to the decision-making process as a way of understanding how citizens may exert power at different points in the process, namely problem definition, option analysis, option selection and implementation. Our evidence indicates that the record of democratic innovations is mixed. In formal terms, some of the designs we have reviewed in this book do not really take us much beyond consultation. For example, only on rare occasions have mini-publics – for example BCCA – had a formal role in the decision-making

---

[1] John Forester (1999) has made a significant contribution to this task in relation to participatory planning.

process, and many of the e-democracy designs – e.g. Womenspeak and online discussion forums – do not radically alter the division of political labour between citizens and public authorities, and the role they play in the decision-making process is rather opaque. But even where innovations have formal powers, citizens may be unable to exercise fully that power in practice.

All forms of direct legislation empower citizens to make the final decision (option selection), and it is for this reason (combined with the *formal* realisation of political equality) that it is the favoured innovation of direct democrats. In initiative and popular referendum, the power to put forward propositions (problem definition) and make final decisions rests with citizens. Citizens make their decisions in private (in the voting booth), free from direct social pressures. In practice, though, we find that the influence of political and economic elites cannot be discounted, particularly when we consider the financial investment that is needed to successfully launch a proposition and the capacity of such elites to influence public debate (option analysis) – an issue we will return to in the next section.

The Citizens' Assembly model can be seen as a step forward compared to other mini-publics since it has been formally institutionalised into the decision-making process. The Assemblies in both British Columbia and Ontario were empowered to recommend an alternative electoral system for their provinces without direct interference by political elites in their deliberations: the recommendation lay with the randomly selected citizen body. As such, citizens exerted control over the analysis of options, making a recommendation to the wider public. It would be churlish not to recognise this as a significant degree of agenda-setting power, but it is limited in at least two senses. First, in both cases the government established the terms of engagement for the Assembly: while the BCCA was empowered to select an alternative electoral system, citizens were not (for example) permitted to suggest a change to the number of elected representatives. This is similar to most other mini-publics, with the exception of consensus conferences, where organisers involve participants in sessions before the event to select relevant issues and experts – citizens exert some influence on the problem definition stage. Second, while the Assemblies could recommend a new electoral system, they did not have direct effect: the final decision on whether to institutionalise a new electoral system was not left in the hands of the Assembly. But neither did it revert to the government: in both British Columbia and Ontario the Assembly's choice of electoral system was put direct to the entire citizenry in the form of a binding referendum.

When we turn to PB, understanding the extent to which popular control is realised is complicated by a number of factors. First, different types of decisions are made in different forums: in neighbourhood and regional popular assemblies, regional budget forums and the COP. Citizens in popular assemblies and the elected delegates in budget forums have significant agenda-setting power in that they are able to define the problems facing their neighbourhoods and propose local investment priorities with little interference from public officials. The COP, constituted by a majority of elected citizens, has significant agenda-setting and decision-making powers: it sets the rules for the following year's budget, confirms the distribution of resources across the city according to the rules established by the previous year's COP and oversees the distribution of resources and work programmes of the municipal authority and its agencies: an unusual power over the implementation process. At a formal level, citizens on the COP have overwhelming voting power, but according to analysts of the budgetary process, they often find themselves reliant on officials from the executive for information and technical advice and overwhelmed with the details of government proposals. Such tensions also emerge in the operation of the thematic element of the budgetary process which deals with city-wide policy considerations – citizens are again reliant on the administration for technical support and guidance. According to Rebecca Abers's analysis, PB suggests that an important distinction should be drawn between participatory bodies that analyse 'top–down proposals' and those that involve a 'bottom–up priority formulation process'. She argues that top–down forms of governance are more likely to have a demobilising effect on citizens: 'In Porto Alegre, participants were much more likely to mobilise passionately against a government veto of their own proposals than to reject government-defined proposals' (Abers 2000: 211). While these insights raise important questions for the design of participatory forms of governance, we again need to be careful not to generalise: evidence from mini-publics suggests that citizens can be empowered to engage critically with proposals from public authorities. Much depends on the institutional context.

In formal terms, the powers of PB are limited because veto power rests with both the mayor and the elected legislature. Because the process is not codified, the devolution of power is at the mayor's discretion. And the structure of checks and balances in Brazilian municipalities means that any budget generated by the executive arm of government has to be agreed by the city's elected legislature. However, the widespread public support for PB across social classes means that these rights of veto have never been exercised. The perceived democratic legitimacy of the budgetary process means that it exceeds its formal status in relation to popular control.

It is difficult to draw general conclusions about the extent to which popular control is realised from such a diversity of designs. There is clearly an important distinction to be made between those innovations where citizens are able to exercise some degree of power independently of public authorities and those where citizens collaborate directly with public officials. Innovations in the former category, for example mini-publics and direct legislation, provide a 'protected space' for citizens to act without direct interference from public authorities. In both cases questions can be raised about the extent to which public authorities are able to influence the terms of reference and conduct of these innovations, but it would be a mistake to neglect the significant opportunity that is opened up for citizens to realise popular control over aspects of the decision-making process.

In the second category of innovation, citizens exercise power in collaboration with public officials. The attractiveness of collaboration (or co-governance) can mask severe imbalances of power: in this kind of shared space citizens are typically at a disadvantage, given the political experience and bureaucratic support enjoyed by public officials. In the COP in Porto Alegre, training and logistical support has been provided to citizens. Yet typically they still remain at a disadvantage to more experienced officials in terms of both the time they can give to the process and their technical knowledge and political capabilities. It may well be that the powers of such a collaborative forum to affect different aspects of the decision-making process are significant, but the extent to which participating citizens are able to influence the exercise of these powers remains open to question. Similar disparities in the citizen–public official interface have been noted in studies of other collaborative structures, for example the board of the Birmingham Race Action Partnership mentioned earlier, where appointed citizens engage directly with officials from the city's major public, private and voluntary sector bodies (Smith and Stephenson 2005).

We also need to consider the question popular control over *what*? Criticism of institutionalised forms of participation is justified if democratic innovations are simply mobilising citizens to engage in decision-making about trivial public matters. This criticism does not appear to have much weight in relation to the innovations we have discussed. PB affects the distribution of a significant proportion of Porto Alegre's capital budget; the BCCA made constitutional recommendations about the province's electoral system; direct legislation has been used to challenge constitutional arrangements, tax regimes, membership of international organisations, state funding of parties, and so on; and a 21st Century Town Meeting was able to have a material impact on the future use of the World Trade Center site following the terrorist attack. These are far from immaterial issues. What all these examples indicate is that for citizens to realise a degree of popular control over a significant policy or constitutional issue it requires extant political authorities to cede authority, whether for pragmatic or enlightened reasons. A readiness to cede or share agenda-setting or decision-making power with citizens thus remains a limiting factor for the institutionalisation of democratic innovations. Relatedly, we must also recognise Ricardo Blaug's challenge that democratic innovations may lack critical democratic import. As Yannis Popadopoulos and Philippe Warin recognise there is a difficult balance to be struck between public authorities enabling participation and subverting (intentionally or not) popular control: 'As necessary as state support may be for consolidating participatory devices and making them effective ... it is nevertheless not sufficient and can even reduce their critical impact' (Popadopoulos and Warin 2007: 596).

Considered judgement

To respond to the objections of sceptics who believe that citizens lack the capacity to make sound political judgements and will instead project raw or unreflective preferences, evidence is needed that the design of innovations can encourage and cultivate informed and public-spirited dispositions. The challenge to democratic innovations to cultivate considered judgement is twofold. First, citizens need to be well informed on the technical aspects of the issues under consideration. And beyond good technical knowledge, considered judgement requires that citizens are not limited by their own private interests, but reflect on the views of other citizens, who may have vastly different social perspectives; in other words, cultivate 'enlarged mentality'.

Our analysis of the different innovations indicates yet again that context is highly significant in the realisation of considered judgement. Institutional design can have a profound effect in at least two ways. First, the extent to which innovations place cognitive demands on participants varies, both in terms of the complexity of the issue they are dealing with and the number of citizens involved in coming to judgements. Second, institutional characteristics affect the degree to which citizens are motivated to distance themselves from private conditions and circumstances that limit and inhibit the exercise of judgement. Arguably the innovation where citizens are least prepared to make considered judgements is direct legislation. Much of the information citizens receive about propositions is highly partisan in nature, and evidence suggests that only a minority have reasonably detailed knowledge of the issues under consideration. A significant number of citizens make up for this lack of knowledge through the use of heuristics to guide their judgements: they are influenced, for example, by the public positions of trusted individuals or organisations. But even if lack of knowledge can potentially be overcome, critics contend that direct legislation lacks a motivational structure that orientates citizens towards the appreciation and consideration of the perspectives of other citizens. Beyond often highly partisan public debates, there is no formal process whereby citizens are encouraged to develop their awareness of the ways in which their decisions may affect the conditions and circumstances of others.

In comparison, mini-publics do not expect all citizens to come to judgements, but rather create a protected space for a limited number of participants in which balanced information is offered and discussion and debate between citizens from quite different social groups is promoted. First, careful consideration is given to selecting witnesses who will provide a balance of competing expert and lay knowledge on the issue at hand. Here, the design of the Citizens' Assemblies in British Columbia, Ontario and the Netherlands has particular advantages over other, shorter mini-publics: in recognition of the difficulty of the charge facing participants, they engage in substantial learning and deliberation phases. They are also exposed to the views of the wider public and interest groups through a consultation phase. Second, sampling techniques can ensure that participants reflect a variety of salient socio-demographic characteristics, so that in the process of coming to judgements, citizens come face-to-face with other citizens with quite different social backgrounds and life experiences. The failure of the BCCA to ensure the presence of a critical mass of citizens from minority ethnic communities (the two Aboriginal citizens added at the last minute aside) may have had an effect on the decision, as their particular perspectives were never fully articulated. Third, facilitators play a crucial role in cultivating mutual respect and reciprocity amongst the diverse body of citizens, ensuring that citizens hear the voices of all participants during their deliberations. Thus, mini-publics offer some succour to deliberative democrats who wish to emphasise the importance of free and fair discussion and reason-giving in the cultivation of considered judgement.

However, the practice of mini-publics may also indicate potential limiting conditions for advocates of deliberative democracy. Compare, for example, the highly partisan debates in the unguarded public sphere of direct legislation with the facilitated debates of the BCCA, which took place over a number of months; or discussions in unmediated, large-scale internet discussions with the carefully facilitated interactions of online deliberative polling. A highly structured and protected space may well be the most conducive environment to promote citizen engagement in a form that is an approximation of democratic deliberation and thus cultivates mutual understanding and considered judgement. If this is an accurate diagnosis, then it calls into question the idea that a form of deliberative democracy that *directly* engages citizens can be institutionalised on a large scale. That said, evidence from British Columbia suggests that under the right conditions, mini-publics can be linked to more informal, less structured deliberations of the broader public as a heuristic: the judgements of those citizens who were aware of the BCCA were influenced by its representative qualities and/or its expertise in the province-wide referendum. We will return to this point later in the chapter.

The structure of PB also provides insights into how institutional design can affect the nature of judgements. Here the ingenious separation of tasks into different spaces in the budgeting process has significant effect. While the initial motivation to participate in the popular assemblies may well be competitive in the sense that citizens are attempting to influence the distribution of resources in the interests of their own neighbourhoods, accounts of the practice of PB's representative bodies suggest that more public-spirited judgements often emerge. Delegates on the regional budget forums come face-to-face with delegates from other neighbourhoods and are able to learn about their needs and expectations. There is evidence that at times the competitive logic has been tempered, as delegates develop regional priority lists that recognise not just levels of mobilisation in the popular assemblies, but also the relative needs of neighbourhoods. The structure and tasks of the COP also have an effect on participants' judgements. All regions of the city have an equal number of councillors, and their deliberations are primarily focused on the rules that govern the budgetary process, particularly the criteria that will guide the following year's resource allocation. The remit and structure of the COP orientate participants to considerations of social justice. These conditions orientate participants away from a simple representation of their own regions' interests and towards the consideration of fair and just distributional rules and procedures.

However, we also need to recall our earlier concerns regarding the citizen–public official interface in the COP. On occasion, citizens engaged in collaborative decision-making may not be in a position to make sound judgements on government proposals: they are often overwhelmed by technical details and professional language. It is difficult to determine whether this represents a problem of competence or whether the institutional setting is putting too much pressure on citizens. Participants in different types of mini-public have discussed highly technical and scientific policy issues and the evidence strongly suggests that citizens can make well-reasoned judgements. Observers may disagree with the substantive nature of judgements made in these forums – for example, the choice of a particular electoral system in British Columbia – but accept that decisions are well considered. Since there is no single 'right answer' for the types of political issues dealt with by mini-publics, the emergence of well-reasoned judgements that participants are able to account for and the wider public understand is all that can be expected. This, then, suggests that it is the *conditions* under which citizens are required to make judgements that have a substantial effect: in other words the nature of the citizen–public official interface may be the cause of problems in bodies such as the COP. Citizens are expected to engage directly with public officials, but without their years of experience and level of bureaucratic support. To be effective in such environments, citizens are required to quickly master and interpret the findings of detailed official reports and engage in often technical debates with officials versed in abstract professional languages. Should we be surprised that under these conditions citizens are not always able to cultivate considered judgement? This failure appears to be more a matter of the institutional context in which citizens find themselves than a generic lack of intellectual or imaginative capacity.

Transparency

The good of transparency turns our attention to two characteristics of institutions. First, internal transparency: the extent to which participants are made aware of the conditions under which they are participating. And second, external transparency or publicity: the extent to which the non-participating public are aware of how the innovation functions, its role in the decision-making process and how participants came to their judgements.

For those designs that are not much more than innovative forms of consultation – for example, Womenspeak – it is not surprising to find expressions of disappointment when participants realise that their contributions are unlikely to affect political decisions. This is also a weakness of many mini-publics: critics argue that the lack of clarity about their role in the decision-making process allows public authorities to ignore or cherry-pick recommendations. Where the terms of reference of an innovation are not clearly laid out, sceptics and critics of citizen participation are right to raise the spectre of co-option (an issue we touched on in our discussion of popular control): a belief that citizens are engaged by public authorities simply to justify decisions made elsewhere. It is significant, however, that in the three innovations that we have given particular attention to in this book – PB, the BCCA and direct legislation – the role of citizens in the decision-making process is highly formalised, and participants generally understand how the innovation operates and its relationship with official decision-making procedures. PB provides one of the most sophisticated approaches to internal transparency, with formalised mechanisms for public officials and budget delegates and councillors to account for their actions, particularly in the popular assemblies, and a computerised information management system that provides details of the nature and progress of work contracts.

A more complex picture emerges when we turn to external transparency or publicity. Publicity becomes a crucial consideration if an innovation and its outputs are to be deemed legitimate and trustworthy. While critics of direct legislation explicitly question the impact of money and the misrepresentation of information on the fairness of public debates that precede voting, it is the gap between participants and the wider population in those innovations that engage a more limited number of citizens that can cause problems.

Although PB engages an impressive number of citizens and its selective bodies are open to observers, the majority of the population are not involved in the process. Community organisations play an important role as information conduits to those not directly engaged, and there is a broad understanding of how the budget process works across the population, even if the details of the complex process are generally poorly understood. There is strong support for the process, even amongst the middle class, who tend not to directly benefit in terms of resource distribution, based on an acceptance that PB is a fair and open method of budgetary allocation, particularly when compared to earlier corrupt modes of clientalism.

Publicity has arguably been one of the weaknesses of mini-publics and emerging e-democracy innovations. While participating citizens may be aware of the conditions under which they participate, the same cannot be said for the broader public, who are often not aware of the innovation's role in the decision-making process, or even its very existence! Many mini-publics end with the publication of a report of the citizens' reasoning and recommendations – a necessary condition for realising publicity – but these often languish on an official's shelf or the dark recesses of a public authority's website. Even the Citizens' Assemblies were unable to buck this trend fully. They may represent a novel democratic approach to dealing with a highly salient political issue, but even though their recommendations were placed on province-wide ballots and publicity leaflets sent to every household, the level of awareness of their existence and activities was remarkably low. In British Columbia, the majority of voters became aware of the BCCA only when they read their ballot paper. The importance of publicity – and the failure of the government (whether consciously or not) to properly fund the referendum campaign – cannot be overstated: those citizens who were aware of the BCCA were more likely to vote for its recommendations. There is emerging evidence that mini-publics can have a significant effect on the judgements of the broader population.

The BCCA is thus one example amongst many where serious attention has been paid to realising internal transparency but where the realisation of publicity has been less well served. Part of the blame clearly rests with sponsors and organisers of innovations, who often do not place as much importance on publicity as other aspects of institutional design. However, the news media are also complicit. Reviewing a range of democratic experiments, Papadopoulos and Warin are 'struck by the media's silence concerning these devices ... and the lack of questioning on such limited media coverage' (Popadopoulos and Warin 2007: 598). The current media climate, where news values tend to cultivate an oversimplification of political issues and an attraction to conflict, is fairly inhospitable to reporting on what are often quite complex forms of engagement (Parkinson 2006). The problems associated with realising publicity and the ways that these might be remedied lack consistent analysis in the literature on citizen participation. If such deficiencies in publicity are not attended to, the legitimacy of democratic innovations will, justifiably, be questioned.

Efficiency

Democratic innovations place demands on citizens and public authorities. The extent of these demands differs widely depending on the design of the innovation. It is difficult to sustain high levels of engagement amongst citizens who have other interests and demands on their time, although our analysis indicates that under certain conditions it is possible to institutionalise impressive levels of citizen engagement. This is generally reliant upon significant financial and bureaucratic support – and at times, institutional restructuring – on the part of public authorities.

While PB requires ongoing commitments from citizens and public officials – it is an annual cycle of participation – in Porto Alegre it cleverly embeds a division of labour such that a relatively small group of citizens are actually involved in the most intense aspects of engagement as a budget delegate or councillor. PB aims to involve significant numbers of citizens in neighbourhood and annual regional popular assemblies, which it achieves because citizens perceive a direct relationship between their participation and budget investments. Beyond these assemblies, attention turns to the activities of the elected delegates and councillors. In this way, the budgetary process appears to have created a sustainable division of political labour, attracting large numbers *and* enabling detailed and ongoing discussions, decisions and scrutiny by selected citizens. While the original mode of area-based engagement has continued to motivate involvement, citizens have been less inclined to engage with the less immediate and more technical city-wide thematic forums. The incentive structure for these broader policy issues is clearly not as attractive to most of the citizen body: they do not perceive a direct effect between their participation and investment decisions. This indicates that broad policy issues may be most effectively and efficiently dealt with through other forms of engagement, with a completely different incentive structure – mini-publics, for example. As for the costs to the administration, to effectively embed PB, the executive in Porto Alegre had to be willing to undertake significant bureaucratic restructuring to support citizen engagement and ensure that investments are delivered. Most significantly this involved the creation of a planning office to coordinate the process and provide technical support and a new community development department charged with building civic infrastructure and facilitating budget forums. Bureaucratic reorganisation of public authorities may well be necessary for effective participatory governance to be institutionalised. In the case of Porto Alegre and other Brazilian municipalities the high costs of administrative reorganisation and continued promotion of PB are typically viewed as worth paying, given the unattractive alternative of clientalism that it replaced. In more well-established democracies, this calculation may well be different.

Mini-publics also require financial commitments if they are to be effective. Depending on the details of the design, there can be significant costs associated with sampling, mobilisation, accommodation, attraction of experts, facilitation, and so on. But, when well organised, evidence suggests that participants are highly motivated and gain much from the experience of engagement. Mini-publics offer a rare type of input into the decision-making process: a forum in which politically contentious issues (for example, electoral reform) can be dealt with in a considered manner. There is some evidence from British Columbia that as the wider population becomes aware of the existence and activities of mini-publics, they have confidence in the capacities of their fellow citizens to make sound decisions. If this finding holds across other examples, then the rationale for embedding mini-publics will increase.

In terms of sheer numbers, direct legislation achieves the most impressive levels of engagement, and, compared to other innovations, makes the fewest demands on citizens in terms of time (unless citizens are trying to qualify a proposition). But even with the low costs associated with voting on propositions, direct legislation has a relatively poor record in reversing differential turnout across social groups. In any calculation of the costs and benefits of direct legislation, its effects on the way in which other institutions operate, for example, political parties, courts, and so forth, will need to be considered and will depend on the form that direct democracy takes. Public authorities are required to undertake additional functions in relation to organising and regulating the process, but also in terms of implementation of decisions. We have noted that there are some concerns that decisions are not always effectively implemented by resistant bureaucracies.

The uneven relationship between low costs of participation to citizens and inclusiveness is also found in many internet-based discussion forums, which tend to attract the already politically interested and engaged unless institutional incentives are carefully designed, as in the example of Womenspeak. Targeted mobilisation strategies, technical support for those with little or no experience of ICT and attentive moderation dramatically increase costs. The rhetoric around computer-mediated communication has often been one of mass engagement at low cost. Compared to its highly expensive offline variant, online deliberative polling is one example where there are potential cost savings, since participants (citizens, moderators and experts) do not have to be brought to a single geographical location, with the associated travel and subsistence costs. But there are still significant technical and facilitation costs involved. As with other forms of engagement, there is an important balance to be struck, and innovations will fail if they place unacceptable burdens on citizens and public officials.

There is no clear formula that can guide us as to how far fiscal and bureaucratic investment in innovations and supporting institutions will overcome the barriers associated with the economy of time. Much depends on the structure of incentives that each innovation embodies. Citizens are willing to accept high demands on their time and energy under certain circumstances. Also important in any calculation is the attractiveness of alternative political scenarios where participation is not an established part of the decision-making process. The failure to embed participation effectively may have its own associated costs: for example, producing ineffective policy that fails to respond to the interests and perspective of citizens and/or is perceived to lack legitimacy. Calculations of efficiency are (unfortunately) not clear-cut.

Transferability

What is particularly striking about the innovations we have discussed is the range of different political contexts in which they have been used and the impressive range of issues that have been tackled. Whereas many critics and sceptics contend that participation can only be effective (if at all) at the local level, many of these innovations indicate how participation can be institutionalised on larger scales and for complex political problems.

Innovations appear to travel reasonably well between polities, although forms of engagement have been promoted under the label 'PB', 'citizens' juries', and so forth in cases where the actual institutional design does not merit that designation. Here we find that organisers or sponsors have either purposely used these labels to pass off poor imitations (often to save money but gain kudos) or have simply failed to understand the centrality of certain aspects of the institutional design. There are plenty of examples of 'citizens' juries' which have been facilitated by a public authority itself rather than by an independent organisation and where citizens have not been selected randomly. A number of 'participatory budgets' are little more than consultation exercises with organised interests that exert little or no real influence over the distribution of resources. Either way, adequate policy transfer has not occurred, which can have a negative effect on the use of the design elsewhere. There is a danger that these designs will lose their legitimacy if poor imitations trade under their name, And for the political scientist, it makes comparative assessment difficult.

We have plenty of evidence that mini-publics and direct legislation can be implemented in a variety of different democratic polities. Policy entre-preneurs including thinktanks (in particular, the IPPR, the King's Fund and the LGMB in the UK) and academics such as James Fishkin have been active in promoting mini-publics. The work of Fishkin and his colleagues suggests that mini-publics are not limited to advanced industrial democ-racies, but can be effective in non-democratic states such as China (Fishkin *et al.* 2006). The impact of institutionalising direct legislation is arguably more significant on the other institutions of the polity, but much rests on the particular form of direct legislation and how it is embedded: the diffe-rence between Swiss and Californian structures and political culture is instructive. Particular care is needed in polities with entrenched minorities that might continually suffer defeat (Allen 2004). The rules of the process and the extent of constitutional protection are crucial.

The experience of PB indicates the role that transnational organisations such as the World Bank and other UN agencies can play in promoting policy transfer. Evidence suggests that PB can be embedded in quite dif-ferent political systems, although there are important caveats. Certain political, fiscal and social conditions may need to be in place for PB to work effectively. First, a degree of fiscal autonomy for the polity in ques-tion: the devolution of authority over significant resources to city mayors in Brazil provided an important condition for the success of the design. In polities where public authorities do not enjoy such fiscal independence, it is difficult to imagine how such a budgeting process could work. Second, significant numbers of citizens are mobilised in Porto Alegre around basic infrastructure investment decisions in their own neighbourhoods. When more strategic policy issues are the focus (in the thematic element of the budgetary process), participation is much reduced and is dominated by the middle-class and organised groups. Where basic infrastructure is in place – as it is in most advanced industrial democracies – the incentive structure is radically altered, arguably making it more difficult to motivate participation from within politically marginalised communities. This is perhaps why many PBs engage organised groups rather than reaching out to ordinary citizens, particularly the poor. Third, the competitive aspect of PB that sees investment decisions in neighbourhoods affected in part by levels of mobilisation may be unacceptable in some regimes. PB is a rare example of an innovation that materially rewards participation: equating investment to participation can be controversial.

Most of the innovations we have discussed in the book have been developed to engage citizens in the political decision-making processes of public authorities at state or sub-state level. They offer strong evidence to respond to critics and sceptics who argue that participation can be effective only on the most local level. While these are, and will continue to be, significant locations of political power, there are limitations. First, we are witnessing the emergence of new forms of governance at these levels: increasingly, multi-sector arrangements are taking responsibility for policy-making and the provision of goods and services. New and more complex governing codes are emerging, and lines of accountability are becoming blurred (Stoker 1998). But both democratic theory and the actual practice of democratic innovations tend to remain state-focused. There are very few examples of institutionalised forms of citizen participation in the decision-making processes of these emerging forms of network governance and little relevant analysis within democratic theory. On the (rare) occasions where democratic engagement is considered, the tendency is to assume that the involvement of voluntary or community organisations can act as a proxy for direct citizen engagement. A rare example where citizen participation has been taken seriously is the Birmingham Race Action Partnership (BRAP), mentioned briefly earlier in this chapter. Appointed community advocates engage with local organisations in issue forums and networks and also sit on the BRAP board with representatives of major public, private and voluntary organisations in the city. The experience of participating on the BRAP board bears more than a passing resemblance to problems associated with the COP in Porto Alegre: even with ongoing support, community advocates found themselves at a distinct disadvantage when engaging with decision-makers from the city's major institutions who were experienced in partnership working and had extensive bureaucratic support (Smith and Stephenson 2005). As the examples in this book highlight, the challenge to design democratic innovations that engage a single public authority is formidable; designing devices that enable citizen participation in the decision-making of new forms of multi-sector governance will demand even more creativity and imagination. But, as governing codes change, so must our thinking about institutional design and democratic theory.

Second, we have limited evidence of effective transnational engagement. Does this mean that citizen participation is not possible at this level? Some designs such as PB will be difficult to institutionalise effectively at such a scale. The operation of a participatory budget across the state of Rio Grande do Sul involves compromising elements of the classic Porto Alegre design, which arguably lessens its democratic purchase. But other designs, such as mini-publics and direct legislation, may well be effective on larger scales, and information and communication technology (ICT) holds much promise for engaging citizens across space and time in ways that were previously inconceivable. There are at least two limiting factors for transnational engagement, beyond the issue of new modes of multi-sector governance discussed above. The first is financial: transnational engagement will be expensive, particularly if it requires citizens to congregate in the same physical space. This is where e-democracy innovations may have an advantage if their potential can be fully realised, although they are far from cost-free enterprises. The second is linguistic: to date almost all innovations have used a single language as the medium of communication. In most cases this is the particular polity's official language, while cross-national internet discussion forums have tended to expect contributions in English. Thus, innovations that cross linguistic communities typically embed a mode of exclusion that marginalises citizens who are not competent in the requisite language. To what extent can multilingualism be designed into democratic innovations in order to remove or at least reduce this mode of exclusion? Will Kymlicka offers a sustained challenge to such an ambition:

> Put simply, democratic politics is the politics of the vernacular. The average citizen only feels comfortable debating political issues in their own tongue. As a general rule, it is only elites who have fluency with more than one language, and who have the continual opportunity to maintain and develop these language skills, and who feel comfortable debating political issues in another tongue within multilingual settings. Moreover, political communication has a large ritualistic component, and these ritualised forms of communication are typically language-specific. Even if one understands a foreign language in the technical sense, without knowledge of these ritualistic elements one may be unable to understand political debates. For these and other reasons, we can expect – as a general rule – that the more political debate is conducted in the vernacular, the more participatory it will be. (Kymlicka 1999: 121)

Given the growing linguistic diversity within advanced industrial democracies, let alone in latent transnational polities, Kymlicka's analysis appears to be a counsel of despair for multilingual democratic practice.

While we cannot realistically expect all citizens to reach the level of linguistic competence to be comfortable debating in multilingual settings, there are other answers to Kymlicka's challenge (Archibugi 2005). For example, direct legislation can cut across linguistic communities by ensuring that official information is published in more than one language. However, this does nothing to alter the likelihood that informal public debates surrounding direct legislation will take place in the vernacular of each political community, mediated by elites with linguistic capabilities.

In those innovations that involve direct interaction between citizens – for example, mini-publics – we have two choices. The first is to select for linguistic competence in the specific language to be used. It is an empirical question as to the extent to which such a selection criteria would skew participation across different social groups and cleavages and whether these distinctions would be politically relevant in transnational engagement. If the participation of particular social groups is deemed a priority, then a language with which these groups are comfortable could be selected as the official language of engagement – for example, operating in the language of the most oppressed rather than the dominant social group.

A second and obvious answer is concurrent translation. After all, missing from Kymlicka's account of the politics of the vernacular is a recognition that members of the political elite do not always have the necessary linguistic capacity to debate in multilingual settings and yet are able to interact effectively through the use of translators. Employing translators, or translation software for ICT-enabled engagement, potentially overcomes linguistic barriers. Kymlicka is surely right to argue that the majority of citizens are most comfortable debating political issues in their mother tongue, but this does *not* entail that they are not willing and able to engage in democratic innovations that cut across linguistic groups.

There are though two potential constraints to multilingual innovations. The first is cost. Translation is expensive and hence adds to the burden on public authorities. The second relates to the extent to which engagement that relies on translation can realise democratic virtues such as mutual understanding. As we have already seen, Kymlicka argues that 'political communication has a large ritualistic component, and these ritualised forms of communication are typically language-specific. Even if one understands a foreign language in the technical sense, without knowledge of these ritualistic elements one may be unable to understand political debates' (Kymlicka 1999: 121). This is reminiscent of the question that was left open in the last chapter, namely whether there is a difference between internet-based and face-to-face deliberation because of the absence of 'paralinguistic and other nonverbal communication' in the former (Iyengar *et al.* 2005: 8). Translation is a different kind of mediation, and experience amongst political elites and in other settings (e.g. international academic and business symposiums) suggests that employing translators need not be a barrier to effective engagement. To begin to understand any effect, we will need to build evidence from actual practice. Fortunately experiments are beginning to take shape that will offer some much-needed evidence, for example, the pan-European deliberative poll, 'Tomorrow's Europe', held in October 2007 and mentioned in Chapter 3. Early evidence from this experiment suggests that transnational and translingual engagement – the poll involved randomly selected citizens from twenty-seven countries, with translation into twenty-two languages – need not be a significant practical barrier to citizen participation.

If democratic innovations can be embedded at different levels – from local through to transnational – then they could play an important role in cultivating or reinforcing a sense of belonging to an existing or emerging polity. This is particularly the case where an actual or potential polity cuts across linguistic and other cultural communities. This is a direct challenge to the strong current within contemporary political theory that follows Kymlicka (amongst others) in arguing that a 'shared history, religion, ethnicity, mother tongue, culture or conception of the good' is the only basis for a sustainable political community that realises democratic values (Mason 2000: 127). Andrew Mason develops an alternative position under which culturally diverse polities might flourish. He argues that 'the citizen of a state might in principle have a sense of belonging to a polity without thinking that there is any real sense in which they belong *together*' in the deeper senses emphasised by Kymlicka and others (Mason 2000: 127). If it is possible to cultivate an 'inclusive political community' on such a foundation, then democratic innovations could play a significant role, in particular because they can explicitly engage citizens in a process of developing and affirming the conditions under which they cooperate *as citizens* (Mason 2000: 138).

The legitimacy of innovations

So far in this chapter, we have considered the ways in which different design characteristics affect the realisation of each of the six goods of our analytical framework. In these terms, the actual practice of innovations indicates a capacity to respond (to varying degrees) to the challenges laid down by critics and sceptics of citizen participation. So, for example, the design of mini-publics can cultivate considered judgement; direct legislation can embed popular control; and so forth. However, these considerations relate to the realisation of *individual* goods. As we argued in Chapter 1, the legitimacy of innovations rests on the manner in which they realise a *combination* of these goods: the way that goods are weighted in relation to each other. While the democratic legitimacy of innovations will rest to a significant extent on the manner in which the four democratic goods – inclusiveness, popular control, considered judgement and transparency – are realised, the goods of efficiency and transferability are significant when we consider innovations' practical import. The combination and weighting of goods arguably has an effect on both the type of issues that an innovation is legitimately designed to deal with and at what point innovations are legitimately embedded in the political decision-making process.

The design of direct legislation places most weight on the realisation of inclusiveness and popular control. The manner in which these two goods are realised through a ballot and (in the case of initiative and popular referendum) petitioning process that is at least formally open to all citizens makes it most appropriate for dealing with significant political and constitutional issues that can be presented in a yes/no format. In practice the realisation of both inclusiveness and popular control is somewhat undermined by differential turnout and the impact that financial resources can have on the petition process, the public debate and thus the final result. The capacity of direct legislation to deal with complex issues is highly constrained by the structure of propositions. Multi-choice ballots, including preferendums, offer one way of extending options, but the options remain limited and there is no flexibility to generate genuinely creative solutions beyond the choices offered. While the design affords popular control over problem definition and option selection, there is no scope to analyse options and generate creative solutions beyond the options offered on the ballot, and there is the danger of implementation deficit. Direct legislation is typically used for issues that are considered to affect the whole of a political community. As such, many critics point to the negative effect that this can have on minority communities, who may be the victims of discriminatory propositions. We have noted two methods of reducing this discriminatory potential. The first is providing constitutional protection to minorities that limits the types of issues that can be proposed. The second is giving veto powers to minorities, such that concurrent majorities are required across affected social groups for a measure to pass. The relative simplicity of direct legislation means that, in principle, transparency should be fairly easy to realise, although in practice the misrepresentation of propositions and information has negative effects.

A very different combination and weighting of goods is expressed by mini-publics, where particular emphasis is placed on realising inclusiveness – although in a completely different manner from direct legislation – and on the cultivation of considered judgement. Typically, mini-publics receive a charge from a sponsoring authority, which means they have little influence on problem definition. The selection mechanism also tends to limit the extent to which mini-publics are viewed as a legitimate body to make final political decisions, and they have no role in implementation. The strength of mini-publics thus lies at the option analysis stage, in the evaluation and prioritisation of different policy options. The space that is created to enable deliberation between citizens means that mini-publics are particularly appropriate for dealing with complex policy problems: for example, consensus conferences indicate the extent to which citizens are willing and able to deal with challenging scientific and technical considerations. Where citizens are involved in generating recommendations (i.e. not deliberative polling), the opportunity exists to engage in problem solving. The development of creative solutions moves us beyond the either/or of direct legislation. The use of sampling techniques also means that mini-publics can be highly sensitive in selecting participants from particular social groups. If a policy is likely to disproportionately affect a particular group in society, participants can be selected to ensure a critical mass of citizens or even a complete panel from that demographic. Mini-publics can be sensitive to difference across social groups in a way that is difficult to achieve in other designs. Where the practice of mini-publics requires particular attention is in relation to publicity, otherwise the gap between the preferences of citizens involved in mini-publics and the raw, often unreflective preferences of public opinion can lead to legitimacy problems.

The third form of innovation represented by PB again offers a completely different combination and weighting of goods. Arguably, the institutional design as embedded in Porto Alegre expresses all four democratic goods, with different weight placed on these goods in the different bodies of the budgeting process. The institutional rules promote a form of inclusiveness that emphasises the engagement of the traditionally politically marginalised; popular control is realised to an impressive extent over all four stages of the decision-making process; considered judgement is cultivated particularly in the deliberation over distribution rules; and, importantly, transparency is promoted in a city where clientalism and corruption once dominated. Citizens define the nature of the problems that need to be dealt with, as well as potential investment solutions in their own neighbourhood and regional popular assemblies and in the regional budget forums. These budget forums evaluate and prioritise the various options proposed by neighbourhoods, and the COP makes decisions on the distribution of resources across regions and other areas of investment. Unlike the other designs discussed in this book, delegates and councillors in the budget forums and COP also play a role in overseeing the implementation of investments by public agencies, and significant numbers of citizens in the popular assemblies hold elected citizens and public officials accountable for their actions. PB, as the name suggests, tends to focus on the distribution of resources across the polity. Evidence from Porto Alegre suggests that it is most effective as a mode of engagement when it focuses on the distribution of resources directly to neighbourhoods and regions of the city where the impact of investment is demonstrable. Here, significant numbers of citizens from poor neighbourhoods are motivated to participate. However, as we have already indicated, there may be limits to the reach of PB. While it has proved a particularly compelling mechanism (even to the middle-class, who tend not to be recipients of investments) to revitalise a previously unaccountable and corrupt allocation of resources across a large urban area, much of its legitimacy may be tied to these particular conditions. The design may not be appropriate beyond allocating investment in basic infrastructure. There has been much less success in Porto Alegre in engaging an inclusive cadre of citizens in more complex, strategic-level investment decisions that do not have an obvious demonstration effect for their neighbourhoods (for example, city-wide investments in environmental improvement, health and education policy, and so on). The appropriateness of the design for advanced industrial democracies needs to be considered, given that much of this basic infrastructure is in place.

Given the variety and early stage of development of e-democracy innovations it is difficult to draw conclusions about the weighting of goods. There is certainly potential for internet-based discussion forums to define problems and to analyse options and perhaps even to act as a mechanism for the overseeing of implementation. The legitimacy of actual decision-making would rest very much on the capacity of such forums to engage an inclusive range of participants and to ensure fairness and equality in interactions. The potential is present for interesting designs to emerge that challenge the way we traditionally consider the institutionalisation of citizen participation.

This brief survey of the effect of different combinations and weightings of goods indicates the extent to which design characteristics affect the legitimate reach of democratic innovations, be it in terms of the appropriateness of issues or the stage at which the innovation is embedded within the decision-making process. The manner in which innovations realise very different combinations and weightings also highlights the extent to which it is near meaningless to make generalised statements about the legitimacy of citizen participation per se. Institutional design matters.

Institutional complementarities

Each design has its strengths and weaknesses in the manner in which goods are realised and weighted. By recognising the potential institutional complementarities of innovations, it is possible to conceive of reinforcing these strengths and diminishing weaknesses. In this vein Michael Saward advocates sequencing innovations. Using the language of democratic principles rather than goods, he suggests that:

> [T]he single most important question when thinking through the new possibilities for democracy is this: *which devices, singly and in combination, enact desired interpretations of democratic principles within and across the different stages of the decision-making process?* (Saward 2003b: 168)

By sequencing innovations, 'devices favoured by advocates of particular "models" of democracy may be combined in new ways to enact new styles of democracy' (Saward 2003b: 169). The combination of democratic innovations is compelling, since it can realise goods in ways that are not possible when individual innovations are used in isolation. In Saward's language, sequencing a series of devices can 'enact and define' democratic principles 'in ways which offer a cumulatively richer evocation of those principles' (Saward 2003b: 170).

Saward's work is an important contribution to an emerging literature on institutional complementarity: the potential of combining democratic devices (we will use the term 'combine' rather than 'sequence', because different innovations may be organised at the same time and not just consecutively as 'sequence' suggests). The idea of institutional complementarity has been picked up and developed enthusiastically within the ever-expanding literature on deliberative democracy (see, for example, Carson and Hartz-Karp 2005; Goodin 2005; Mansbridge 1999; Parkinson 2006). A precursor to such work is the agenda of strong democracy offered by Benjamin Barber, who aims to institutionalise 'strong democratic talk' in an expansive range of institutions, including what we would term democratic innovations (Barber 1984: 261–311). More recently, Robert Goodin offers an analysis of the different 'moments' within representative democracies (caucus room, parliamentary debate, election campaign and post-election arguing and bargaining):

> [W]hile we cannot seriously expect all the deliberative virtues to be constantly on display at every step of the decision process in a representative democracy, we can realistically expect that different deliberative virtues might be on display at different steps in the process … Different ways of arranging our political affairs have different implications for the sequencing of deliberative virtues. (Goodin 2005: 193)

Similarly, John Parkinson offers one model of what he terms 'a legitimate deliberative democracy' in which different actors and institutions (activist networks, experts, bureaucracy, micro-techniques, media, elected assembly and direct techniques) play significant roles in enhancing deliberation at different stages of the decision-making process (Parkinson 2006: 166–73).

These are imaginative attempts to understand the way in which democratic deliberation can be cultivated at different points and by different actors in the political process. Our approach to understanding institutional complementarities is slightly different. First, it is not explicitly deliberative in its ambition, although combining innovations may well have the effect of increasing the deliberative quality of citizen participation. Our aim is to understand how institutional combinations might enhance the realisation of goods of democratic institutions. Second, Barber, Goodin and Parkinson offer elaborate attempts to consider the complementarities of a variety of different types of institutions of advanced industrial democracies. Whilst recognising the importance of the broader institutional architecture, our approach is less ambitious: to consider the effects of combinations of democratic innovations.

We are not simply left in a position of having to imaginatively project institutional complementarities, since we have come across examples already in this book. PB is actually a combination of at least three different types of democratic device operating at different levels: popular assemblies open to all citizens; regional budget forums where delegates are elected according to the numbers that turn out in the popular assemblies; and the COP, where each region has two elected councillors. We have noted how each of these bodies embeds particular institutional characteristics and realises democratic goods in different ways. When combined they generate the combination of goods that we associate with PB as a process. Other examples of PB are often democratically less compelling than the original Porto Alegre design because they combine different types of devices (for example, institutions engaging only accredited organised interests) that realise a less attractive mix of democratic (and other) goods.

We can also imagine ways that limitations of PB might be lessened by drawing lessons from the practice of other innovations. For example, Marion Gret and Yves Sintomer appear to argue that if the budgetary process is to be successfully scaled up, then we should consider random selection for positions on the COP (Gret and Sintomer 2005: 126–7). In other words, this element of PB would take the form of a mini-public. This modification would ensure that councillors were drawn from across social groups, unlike present practice, which has a tendency to reinforce traditional differentials in participation. Mini-publics might also offer a more inclusive mechanism for engaging citizens in the more strategic, thematic elements of PB. A different combination of institutional incentives would emerge by altering the design characteristics of component bodies, in this case the method of selection for the COP or thematic budget forums. But modifications can have unintended ramifications: for example, in potentially enhancing inclusiveness, the perceived accountability of the COP may be diminished, thus having an adverse effect on the overall legitimacy of the process. Institutional design inevitably involves some level of compromise between goods.

The institutional arrangements put in place to make decisions about a new electoral system in British Columbia and then Ontario are also an example of an interesting combination of innovations. Two innovations – a mini-public and a constitutional referendum – were run in series, creating an overall design that overcame limitations in each individual design and realised a richer combination of goods than either of the innovations in isolation. A similar pattern was witnessed in Australia, with a deliberative poll preceding the constitutional referendum (Warhurst and Mackerras 2002), although this sequence was less formalised.[2] Mini-publics are strong on realising a form of inclusiveness through the use of random sampling techniques and engendering democratic deliberation between participants such that they are in a position to make considered judgements. However, the nature of the selection method raises concerns about extending decision-making powers to mini-publics, since random selection undermines our established conceptions of political accountability. A constitutional referendum, on the other hand, offers a mode of popular control where all citizens are accorded equal rights to participate in ratification, but the associated public debate rarely strays beyond the highly partisan. In principle, then, these two innovations are highly complementary. In the sequence adopted in British Columbia and Ontario, all citizens were formally in a position to consider the deliberations and recommendations of the Citizens' Assembly when casting their ballots. The judgements of the Assembly can be considered a heuristic for the broader citizen body: an indication of how they might have made judgements *if* they had been party to intense and informed deliberations.

In practice, however, we have noted that there were a number of limitations to this particular combination of innovations. First, the lack of a significant publicity campaign in British Columbia meant that many citizens were unaware of the BCCA's work. Second, no remedial strategies were put in place to overcome the consistent problem that referendums fail to achieve an inclusive turnout: the voice of marginalised groups in the final decision remains less audible. In principle these two deficiencies could be remedied to a certain extent: the practice of this sequence could be improved.

While the British Columbia and Ontario experiments are highly imaginative, additional elements could be added that would potentially

---

[2] Barber suggests a different combination, with direct legislation requiring a mandatory tie-in with neighbourhood meetings and virtual town meetings (Barber 1984: 284–6).

increase the realisation of democratic goods – in particular, other aspects of popular control. First, a petitioning process could be introduced at the beginning of the process. Rather than the government having agenda-setting power over when and on what issues a combination of mini-public/ referendum is to be used, the power would rest with the public. The process would be a combination of citizen initiative and/or popular referendum with one or more well-resourced mini-publics. It is possible that a mini-public, initiated by a successful petitioning process, could have a role in not only offering a considered recommendation to the wider public, but also in shaping the way that a petition is then presented on a ballot and/ or in recommending particular forms of participation in the run-up to any vote. Second, introducing a two-stage ratification process – a second ballot would be held after a short period of time to confirm or reject the result of the first ballot – would provide the opportunity for citizens to further reflect on their preferences, thus potentially enhancing the real-isation of considered judgement. While we are still left to consider how to overcome unequal participation in petitioning and voting, such combin-ations embody demands of direct *and* deliberative democrats: embedding agenda setting and decision-making *and* democratic deliberation. We can combine democratic innovations in ways that are productive from both theoretical perspectives. Democratic goods can be realised in com-pelling combinations that embody the ambitions of different theories of democracy.

The structure of PB reminds us that we should not only consider the combination of democratic devices in series (sequencing is the most com-mon mode of conceptualising complementarities), but also in parallel: the budget forums and the COP meet during the same time period. The work of Peter Dienel also offers a precedent for parallel complementarity: he often replicated a number of planning cells and then collated the results in the final citizens' report. For example, in 2001–2, eighteen planning cells were convened in five different locations to deliberate on issues relating to consumer protection in Bavaria, thus increasing the number of par-ticipants in the process to 425 (Hendriks 2005: 84–5). It is also possible to imagine a combination of innovations, such as the petition-mini-pub-lic-ballot(s) process, where one or more mini-publics are run alongside a more open form of participation, potentially with some degree of inter-action. Here the possibility of integrating e-democracy innovations is highly promising. It is not difficult to imagine large-scale internet discus-sion forums established in parallel with a mini-public such as the Citizens' Assembly which, minimally, could provide an opportunity for interested citizens to follow and discuss the Assembly's proceedings and, maximally, allow them to interact with the Assembly through a submissions process or the direct participation of Assembly members in the internet forum. While e-democracy innovations remain at an early stage of development, the potential for combining them with face-to-face innovations such as mini-publics is worthy of investigation.

These various suggestions of institutional complementarities are indicative: there are numerous variations for combining democratic innovations in series and/or parallel that may realise compelling combinations of goods.

Conclusion

Drawing together the evidence from earlier chapters, it is not unreasonable to argue that with careful consideration, imagination and political will, enhancing citizen participation in political decision-making is feasible and can realise significant goods that we associate with democratic institutions. Many of the challenges of critics and sceptics of citizen participation can be met if careful consideration is given to institutional design. No design is perfect: it is difficult to imagine any innovation or combination of innovations that can fully realise all six goods that form the basis of our analytical framework, not least because there are different ways that goods can be realised. But given that our contemporary polities often fail to effectively realise democratic goods such as inclusiveness, popular control, considered judgement and transparency, the kinds of institutions that we have analysed in this book offer promising ways of enhancing contemporary democratic practice through citizen participation in political decision-making.

Conclusion

The preceding chapters have evaluated the extent to which different innovations (and, latterly, combinations of innovations) realise the six goods of democratic institutions that we selected as the basis of our analytical framework in Chapter 1. These concluding remarks provide an occasion for reflection on the effectiveness of this approach to analysing citizen participation in political decision-making. The methodological aim has been to proffer a theoretically informed analytical framework that allows us to undertake meaningful comparative studies of democratic innovations. In so doing, the approach bridges the unfortunate 'disciplinary divorce within the academic study of politics, between normative theory and empirical political analysis' (Beetham 1999: 29). The analysis can be understood as a contribution to what might be termed an *institutional* theory of democracy, since the method generates an appreciation of the democratic and practical qualities of actually existing institutional designs.

Why is such an institutional theory important? First, it articulates feasibility constraints on democratic theory per se. Much political theory operates at a highly abstract level, engaged in debates about the proper principles and ideals that should ground our understanding of democracy. However, if little or no attention is given to the institutional expression of these principles, then theory is in a weak position to guide our political judgements and actions. As Ian Shapiro argues, 'speculation about what ought to be is likely to be more useful when informed by relevant knowledge of what is feasible' (Shapiro 2003: 2). A similar point is made by Joseph Carens in relation to theories of justice when he writes: 'if someone puts forward a principle of distribution but cannot describe, even in theory, how to arrange social institutions to implement that principle in a stable and effective way, then we are bound to ask whether the principle can really be regarded as an ideal for human societies' (Carens 1985: 64).[1] An institutional theory of democracy is thus an alternative approach to a deductive form of analysis that we earlier argued tends to dominate the literature, where institutions are evaluated according to a predetermined theory of democracy. In evaluating designs, we do not have to commit ourselves to one particular democratic theory or model of democracy, thus side-stepping endless, and at times unproductive, theoretical debates about the proper principles and ideals (and particular meaning of those principles and ideals) that should ground our analysis. The intention has been to generate a framework that speaks to quite different theoretical traditions, in the sense that some or all of the goods of the analytical framework would be recognised as important to all (or at least most) democratic theorists. It is difficult to conceive a democratic theory that did not have something to say about the democratic goods of inclusiveness, popular control, considered judgement and transparency. Also crucial to the analysis has been the inclusion of two more practically orientated goods of institutions – efficiency and transferability – within the analytical framework that force us to confront feasibility constraints. This is an explicit recognition that democratic theory often gets carried away with itself, overlooking or ignoring the very real limitations that exist for the institutionalisation of democratic participation, both in terms of the varying locations of political power and the demands placed on citizens and public authorities.

A second argument for an institutional theory of democracy comes from the other direction: too often political science fails to provide an account of why political institutions matter. Political scientists have developed ever more sophisticated techniques for investigating political institutions and behaviours, but often have little to say about their desirability. Again, Shapiro argues that 'explanatory theory too easily becomes banal and method-driven when isolated from the pressing normative concerns that have fuelled worldwide interest in democracy in recent decades' (Shapiro 2003: 2). In bridging the gap between political theory and political science, an institutional theory of democracy provides resources for answering the age-old question 'What should be done?'.

A particular value of this approach to the analysis of democratic innovations is its reflective capacity: not only as a guide to action, but also because we are then in an excellent position to interrogate the commitments and evaluative claims of democratic theorists. Such an interrogation has been

---

[1] See Mason (2004) for a discussion of the arguments about theories of justice and feasibility constraints which offers a stout defence of more abstract theorising.

an implicit element of the analysis of different innovations throughout the book. Focusing on the way that designs realise particular combinations of goods forces us to recognise and consider the trade-offs that occur in actual institutions, but which can often be ignored (or not understood) at a more abstract, theoretical level of analysis. To sketch out the way that this analysis prompts reflection on democratic theory, let us briefly consider the case of deliberative democracy, currently the dominant mode of theorising in contemporary democratic theory. In Chapter 1 we offered James Bohman's summary of this theoretical enterprise: 'Deliberative democracy, broadly defined, is … any one of a family of views according to which the public deliberation of free and equal citizens is the core of legitimate political decision making and self-government' (Bohman 1998: 401). It is striking that such a definition assumes that all four democratic goods are realised: inclusiveness, popular control, considered judgement and transparency. One obvious way, then, that the study of innovations enables an interrogation of the evaluative commitments of deliberative democrats is that it provides evidence that institutional design involves compromises in realising each of these goods fully (let alone the practical goods of efficiency and transferability). The ideal theoretical world clashes with the trade-offs implicit in institutional design. Realistically, it is difficult to conceive of any institution that will realise effectively the six goods that we isolated in our analytical framework. Theorists would thus do well to reflect on the way that trade-offs between goods occur such that they can better inform the difficult design choices that must be made in practice.

A number of influential theorists of deliberative democracy – for example, Jürgen Habermas and John Dryzek – have recognised the potential tension between democratic deliberation and decision-making: their theories explicitly separate these two democratic moments. Habermas locates will-formation in the informal public sphere, while decision-making takes place in the institutions of government (Habermas 1996; Squires 2002). Dryzek's reinterpretation of deliberative democracy similarly locates authentic deliberation in the networks of civil society, often orientated in opposition to the practices of the state (Dryzek 2000). This separation is enacted on the ground that decision-making constrains deliberation in at least two ways. First, decision implies an end point to the openness and ongoing nature of deliberation (Mansbridge 1996: 47). We witness tensions between the desire to realise considered judgement and efficiency in decision-making (Chambers 2001: 241). Second, there are concerns that decision-making powers will alter or even undermine the dynamics of deliberation: rather than an orientation towards mutuality and reciprocity as required for considered judgement, participants will make instrumental calculations in relation to the forthcoming decision. As we discussed in Chapter 4, this is one element of the critique of direct legislation offered by deliberative democrats: its majoritarian structure is seen to discourage mutuality and reciprocity.

Rather than simply embrace this separation, democratic innovations (and combinations of innovations) indicate how deliberation (as realised through a combination of inclusiveness, considered judgement and publicity) might be embedded in participatory institutions that have significant decision-making powers (realise popular control). There are lessons to be drawn, for example, from the way that the different structures and tasks of the bodies that constitute participatory budgeting (PB) enable significant levels of both democratic deliberation and popular control. The analysis in this book suggests that a more sophisticated theoretical account of the relationship between deliberation and decision-making is needed, beyond a zero-sum perspective.

The creative combination of innovations adopted in British Columbia and Ontario that linked a Citizens' Assembly with a binding referendum provides another occasion in which citizen deliberation and decision-making are both realised to an impressive extent. This sequence has the additional value of providing an empirical case with which to interrogate the evaluative claims of theorists such as Michael Saward, who (as we noted in Chapter 1) has argued that the apparently antagonistic models of deliberative and direct democracy can be combined productively to overcome their individual weaknesses: deliberation in a mini-public prior to the direct decision-making of a referendum creates a more legitimate democratic process where all citizens (not just those in the mini-public) are encouraged to reflect on their preferences before making political choices (Saward 2001). Evidence from British Columbia and Ontario offers insights into the effectiveness of connections between the deliberations of a mini-public and the public ratification process of a referendum. This forces theorists to confront a number of issues, including, for example, the degree to which we can realistically expect such an arrangement to realise publicity effectively in contemporary polities and the extent to which a mini-public can be a legitimate 'deliberative heuristic' for the broader population in lieu of large-scale democratic deliberation.

A further theme that emerges from the evaluation of innovations is the need for more careful consideration of the facilitation of democratic deliberation. Deliberative democratic theory is full of statements about the general facilitating conditions – in particular, the rights, principles and dispositions – necessary for the emergence and sustenance of public deliberation between free and equal citizens. However, our analysis of mini-publics, PB and internet discussion forums, in particular, highlights the fundamental role that *active* facilitation plays in realising such rights, principles and dispositions. Citizens do not necessarily come fully formed in a deliberative sense: facilitators continually shape and reshape the conditions for deliberation. This is perhaps most striking in the regional budget forums of PB, where facilitators play a role in motivating delegates to not only consider their own neighbourhood's interests, but to develop more solidaristic judgements about the needs of other neighbourhoods, the region and (in the COP) the city itself. Analysis of the practice of facilitation can help in better understanding the way in which often explicitly self-interested motivations are at times transformed into a more public-spirited orientation. The practice of mini-publics and online forums can offer fruitful comparisons of the effect of different modes of facilitation under quite different institutional conditions. Such theoretical elaboration is strangely absent from the literature.

This brief discussion of the tension between deliberation and decision and the role of facilitation is simply indicative of the value for theorists of analysing empirical cases in terms of the extent to which they realise goods of democratic institutions. While we focused here on deliberative democracy, we could equally have interrogated widely held commitments and evaluative claims in other democratic theories. The promise of an institutional approach is a more nuanced account of how goods are realised in practice *and* more nuanced developments in democratic theory.

One criticism of this approach to analysing democratic institutions might be that it speaks primarily to instrumental theories of participation (Parry 1972: 19–26) that tend to dominate democratic theory at this particular juncture. In particular, citizen participation is of value because the realisation of compelling goods of democratic institutions increases the legitimacy of the political decision-making process. The analysis elucidates the conditions under which compelling combinations of goods – and, hence, legitimacy – are realised. This contribution to instrumental theories of participation does not mean that this approach has no value in considering intrinsic theories of participation that recognise the beneficial effects of participation for citizens, such as cultivating political efficacy, as a way of citizens coming to an understanding of their interests or as a mode of moral and political education (Parry 1972: 26–31). Participatory democrats, in particular, extol the virtues of the intrinsic properties of participation, although it is often an (at least) implicit element of most other democratic theories. Can an institutional approach speak to this important aspect of democratic thought?

The answer is a qualified yes. Institutions are not simply structures through which democratic goods are realised (although this remains important for instrumental theories of participation), but are also the medium through which democratic agency is expressed. Institutional design is integral to the form that democratic agency can take. While the approach we have adopted towards the analysis of innovations does not provide a systematic assessment of the extent to which citizens experience the value of participation, the realisation of the four democratic goods in the analytical framework – inclusiveness, popular control, considered judgement and transparency – is arguably a necessary condition for democratic agency within the formal political process. Similarly, the institutional goods of efficiency and transferability indicate the extent to which citizens are willing to bear the costs of participation in different political contexts. Institutions within which a compelling combination of these goods are realised are likely to create conditions that foster and cultivate the moral and political education, reflexivity and empowerment that are fundamental to participatory theories of democracy (Warren 1996). Certainly these goods resonate with the theoretical ambitions of writers such as Carole Pateman (1970), who is interested in institutions that embody political equality and provide occasion for citizens to gain and practise democratic skills and capacities by taking control of political decision-making.

This discussion takes us back to Ricardo Blaug's distinction between incumbent and critical democracy that we raised in the Introduction to the book when defining the reach of democratic innovations (as opposed to other forms of democratic engagement and activity). On his reading of democratic practice, democratic innovations would be one version of incumbent democracy – a method of managing and ordering citizen participation – as compared to critical democracy, which seeks 'to resist such management and to empower excluded voices in such a way as to challenge existing institutions' (Blaug 2002: 107). We questioned whether such a stark distinction was helpful in distinguishing forms of democratic participation, and evidence from our analysis of innovations suggests that there are institutional contexts that explicitly empower excluded voices and enable citizens to challenge the practices of more established institutions. Blaug's distinction suggests that any form of institutionalisation is disempowering in a democratic sense; but our analysis provides evidence to suggest that democratic innovations can at times be constitutive of the realisation of the kind of democratic agency that he wishes to celebrate. A simple distinction between institutionalised and non-institutionalised forms of participation is not helpful. Both institutionalised and non-institutionalised participation can express, and equally deny, democratic agency.

The particular combination of goods that make up the analytical framework is then both theoretically and practically compelling, in the sense that inclusiveness, popular control, considered judgement and transparency are implicit within the very idea of democratic participation, and efficiency and transferability embody practical considerations of feasibility. The focus on these goods also provides the occasion to engage fully with the arguments of critics and sceptics of enhanced citizen participation in political decision-making. Too often theorists ignore these uncomfortable challenges, to the detriment of both democratic theory and practice. The analysis of innovations generates evidence that while these various critical and sceptical voices remain significant, in certain institutional contexts it is possible to mitigate, and at times overcome, problems related to differential rates of participation, political competence, co-option and manipulation, the economy of time and the limits imposed by scale. A virtue of the broad analytical framework is that it can provide evidence as to the weight and significance of these quite different challenges.

The analysis suggests that the analytical framework offers an effective means of connecting theoretical and empirical studies of democratic innovations. The framework has enabled us to generate useful comparative data on very different modes of citizen participation and insights into how design features of democratic innovations affect the realisation of goods of democratic institutions and, therefore, democratic agency. And it is important to recognise that the method is not limited to the study of democratic innovations. After all, the framework is constituted by goods of democratic *institutions*. Hence the framework could as easily be applied to any other form of political institution or practice. This approach is therefore offered as a first step in the development of an institutional theory of democracy which incorporates both theoretical and empirical accounts of the practice of democratic institutions.

The aim of this book has been twofold. First, it aims to offer an effective method for analysing democratic innovations, one that provides for comparative analysis across very different designs and which could be extended to analysing any other type of democratic institution. In this sense it is a contribution to the methodological development of democratic theory. Second, the book can be seen as a contribution to the crucial exercise of imagining the potential future direction of advanced industrial democracies. In the book's Introduction we cited Russell Dalton's argument that it is essential that democratic reform 'move beyond the traditional forms of representative democracy ... to provide new opportunities for citizen input and control' (Dalton 2004: 204). Representative democracy as it exists now is not the end point of democratic development – for some, our current representative structures do not necessarily warrant the description 'democratic' and 'cannot be all for which we can reasonably hope' (Dunn 2005: 185). Democratic innovations offer practical examples that force us to consider how we are governed and how we might better institutionalise the democratic ideal. On one level, then, this book is a comparative analysis of democratic innovations; on another level it is a contribution to the imaginative and practical task of exploring what democracy might mean and become.

References

Abers, Rebecca Neaera 1998. 'Learning Democratic Practice: Distributing Government Resources through Popular Participation in Porto Alegre, Brazil', in Mike Douglass and John Friedmann (eds.) *Cities for Citizens*. Chichester and New York: Wiley, 39–65.

    2000. *Inventing Local Democracy: Grassroots Politics in Brazil*. Boulder and London: Lynne Rienner.

    2003. 'Reflections on What Makes Empowered Participatory Governance Happen', in Archon Fung and Erik Olin Wright (eds.) *Deepening Democracy: Institutional Innovations in Empowered Participatory Governance*. London: Verso, 200–7.

Abramson, Jeffrey 1994. *We, The Jury*. New York: Basic Books.

Ackerman, Bruce and James S. Fishkin 2004. *Deliberation Day*. New Haven: Yale University Press.

Agriculture and Environment Biotechnology Commission 2002. 'A Debate about the Issue of Possible Commercialisation of GM Crops in the UK (Letter to the Secretary of State for the Environment, Food and Rural Affairs)', 26 April.

Allegretti, Giovanni and Carsten Herzberg 2004. *Participatory Budgets in Europe: Between Efficiency and Growing Local Democracy*. Amsterdam: Transnational Institute and the Centre for Democratic Policy-Making.

Allen, Danielle S. 2004. *Talking to Strangers: Anxieties of Citizenship since Brown v. Board of Education*. University of Chicago Press.

Arblaster, Anthony 1994. *Democracy*. Milton Keynes: Open University Press.

Archibugi, Daniele 2005. 'The Language of Democracy: Vernacular or Esparanto? A Comparison between the Multiculturalist and Cosmopolitan Perspectives', *Political Studies* **53**: 537–555.

Arendt, Hannah 1968. *Between Past and Future*. New York: Viking Press.

    1982. *Lectures on Kant's Political Philosophy*. University of Chicago Press.

Audit Commission 1999. *Listen Up! Effective Community Consultation*. London: Audit Commission.

Bachrach, Peter 1967. *The Theory of Democratic Elitism*. Boston: Little and Brown.

Baiocchi, Gianpaolo 2003a. 'Participation, Activism and Politics: The Porto Alegre Experiment', in Archon Fung and Erik Olin Wright (eds.) *Deepening Democracy: Institutional Innovations in Empowered Participatory Governance*. London: Verso, 45–76.

(ed.) 2003b. *Radicals in Power: The Workers' Party (PT) and Experiments in Urban Democracy in Brazil*. London: Zed Books.

2005. *Militants and Citizens: The Politics of Participatory Democracy in Porto Alegre*. Stanford University Press.

Barber, Benjamin 1984. *Strong Democracy: Participatory Politics for a New Age*. Berkeley: California University Press.

1998. 'Three Scenarios for the Future of Technology and Strong Democracy', *Political Quarterly* **113**: 573–89.

Barnett, Anthony and Peter Carty 1998. *The Athenian Option: Radical Reform for the House of Lords*. London: Demos.

Bartels, Larry M. 1996. 'Uninformed Votes: Information Effects in Presidential Elections', *Amercian Journal of Political Science* **194**: 194–230.

Beetham, David 1992. 'Liberal Democracy and the Limits of Democratisation', *Political Studies Special Issue (Prospects for Democracy)* **40**: 40–53.

1999. *Democracy and Human Rights*. Cambridge: Polity.

Benhabib, Seyla (ed.) 1996. *Democracy and Difference*. Princeton University Press.

Bennett, Fran 2004. *From Input to Influence: Participatory Approaches to Research and Inquiry into Poverty*. Birmingham: Joseph Rowntree Foundation.

Blais, André, R. Kenneth Carty and Patrick Fournier 2008. 'Do Citizen Assemblies Make Reasoned Choices?', in Mark E. Warren and Hilary Pearse (eds.) *Designing Deliberative Democracy: The British Columbia Citizens' Assembly*. Cambridge University Press, 127–44.

Blaug, Ricardo 2002. 'Engineering Democracy', *Political Studies* **50**: 102–16.

Blumler, Jay G. and Stephen Coleman 2001. *Realising Democracy Online: A Civic Commons in Cyberspace*. London: IPPR.

Bohman, James 1998. 'The Coming of Age of Deliberative Democracy', *Journal of Political Philosophy* **6**: 400–25.

Bookchin, Murray 1992. *Urbanisation without Cities: The Rise and Decline of Citizenship*. Montreal: Black Rose Books.

Bowler, Shaun and Todd Donovan 1988. *Demanding Choices: Opinion, Voting, and Direct Democracy*. Ann Arbor: University of Michigan Press.

2001. 'Popular Control of Referendum Agendas: Implications for Democratic Outcomes and Minority Rights', in Matthew Mendelsohn and Andrew Parkin (eds.) *Referendum Democracy: Citizens, Elites, and Deliberation in Referendum Campaigns*. Basingstoke: Palgrave, 125–46.

2002. 'Democracy, Institutions and Attitudes about Citizen Influence on Government', *British Journal of Political Science* **32**: 371–90.

Brighouse, Harry and Erik Olin Wright 2006. 'A Proposal to Transform the House of Lords into a Citizens' Assembly, www.ssc.wisc.edu/~wright/Published%20 writing/Democratizing-House-of-Lords.pdf.

Brown, Mark B. 2006. 'Survey Article: Citizens Panels and the Concept of Representation', *Journal of Political Philosophy* **14**: 203–25.

Bryan, Frank 2004. *Real Democracy: The New England Town Meeting and How It Works.* University of Chicago Press.

1999. 'Direct Democracy and Civic Competence: The Case of Town Meeting', in Stephen L. Elkin and Karol Edward Soltan (eds.) *Citizen Competence and Democratic Institutions.* Pennsylvania State University Press, 195–224.

Budge, Ian 1996. *The New Challenge of Direct Democracy.* Cambridge: Polity.

2001. 'Political Parties in Direct Democracy', in Matthew Mendelson and Andrew Parkin (eds.) *Referendum Democracy: Citizens, Elites and Deliberation in Referendum Campaigns.* Basingstoke, Palgrave, 67–87.

Burnheim, John 1985. *Is Democracy Possible?* Cambridge: Polity.

Butler, David and Austin Ranney (eds.) 1994a. *Referendums around the World: The Growing Use of Direct Democracy.* Washington: AEI Press.

1994b. 'Theory', in David Butler and Austin Ranney (eds.) *Referendums around the World: The Growing Use of Direct Democracy.* Washington: AEI Press, 11–23.

Cabannes, Yves 2004. 'Participatory Budgeting: A Significant Contribution to Participatory Democracy', *Environment and Urbanization* **16**: 27–46.

Cabinet Office 2001. 'Government Memorandum in Response to the Public Administration Select Committee's Sixth Report on Public Participation: Issues and Innovations', in House of Commons Select Committee on Public Administration, *Public Participation: Issues and Innovations: The Government's Response to the Committee's Sixth Report of Session 2000–01.* London: HMSO.

2004. *Code of Practice on Consultation.* London: Cabinet Office.

Cain, Bruce E., Russell Dalton and Susan E. Scarrow 2003. *Democracy Transformed? Expanding Political Opportunities in Advanced Industrial Democracies.* Oxford University Press.

Carens, Joseph 1985. 'Compensatory Justice and Social Institutions', *Economics and Philosophy* **1**: 39–67.

Carson, Lynn and Janette Hartz-Karp 2005. 'Adapting and Combing Deliberative Designs', in John Gastil and Peter Levine (eds.) *The Deliberative Democracy Handbook: Strategies for Effective Civic Engagement in the 21st Century.* San Francisco: Jossey-Bass, 120–38.

Carty, R. Kenneth, André Blais and Patrick Fournier 2008. 'When Citizens Choose to Reform SMP: The British Columbia Citizens' Assembly on Electoral Reform', in André Blais (ed.) *To Keep or to Change First Past the Post? The Politics of Electoral Reform.* Oxford University Press, 140–62.

Cederman, Lars-Erik and Peter A. Kraus 2005. 'Transnational Communication and the European Demos', in Robert Latham and Saskia Sassen (eds.) *Digital Formations: IT and New Architectures in the Global Realm.* Princeton University Press, 283–311.

Chambers, Simone 2001. 'Constitutional Referendums and Democratic Deliberation', in Matthew Mendelsohn and Andrew Parkin (eds.) *Referendum Democracy: Citizens, Elites, and Deliberation in Referendum Campaigns.* Basingstoke: Palgrave, 231–55.

2004. 'Behind Closed Doors: Publicity, Secrecy, and the Quality of Deliberation', *The Journal of Political Philosophy* **12**: 289–410.

2007. 'Quantity Versus Quality: Dilemmas of Mass Democracy', University of British Columbia, Centre for the Study of Democratic Institutions Working Paper: Citizen Engagement No. 3, http://democracy.ubc.ca/fileadmin/template/main/images/departments/CSDI/working_papers/ChambersCSDIWorkingPaper2007CE3.pdf

Citizens' Assembly on Electoral Reform 2004. *Making Every Vote Count: The Case for Electoral Reform in British Columbia (Technical Report)*. Vancover: Citizens' Assembly on Electoral Reform.

Civic Alliance to Rebuild Downtown New York 2002. *Listening to the City: Report of Proceedings*. New York: Civic Alliance.

Cohen, Joshua 1989. 'Deliberation and Democratic Legitimacy', in Alan Hamlin and Phillip Pettit (eds.) *The Good Polity: Normative Analysis of the State*. Oxford University Press, 17–34.

1996. 'Procedure and Substance in Deliberative Democracy', in Seyla Benhabib (ed.) *Democracy and Difference*. Princeton University Press, 95–119.

Coleman, Stephen 2004. 'Connecting Parliament to the Public via the Internet: Two Case Studies of Online Consultations', *Information, Communication and Society* 7: 1–22.

2005. *Direct Representation: Towards a Conversational Democracy*. London: IPPR.

Commission on Poverty, Participation and Power 2000. *Listen Hear: The Right to Be Heard*. Bristol: Policy Press.

Cooke, Bill and Uma Kothari (eds.) 2001. *Participation: The New Tyranny?* London: Zed Books.

Coote, Anna and Jo Lenaghan 1997. *Citizens' Juries: Theory into Practice*. London: IPPR.

Coote, Anna and Deborah Mattinson 1997. *Twelve Good Neighbours*. London: Fabian Society.

Crawford, Mike, Deborah Rutter and Sarah Thelwall 2003. *User Involvement in Change Management: A Review of the Literature. Report to NHS Service Delivery and Organisation Research and Development*. London: NHS Institute for Health Research.

Cronin, Thomas 1999. *Direct Democracy: The Politics of Initiative, Referendum, and Recall*. Cambridge, MA: Harvard University Press.

Crosby, Ned 1996. *Trustworthy democratic facilitation (manuscript)*. Minneapolis: Jefferson Center.

2007. 'Peter C. Dienel: Eulogy for a Deliberative Democracy Pioneer', *Journal of Public Deliberation* 3, http://services.bepress.com/jpd/vol3/iss1/art7.

Crosby, Ned and Doug Nethercut 2005. 'Citizens' Juries: Creating a Trustworthy Voice of the People', in John Gastil and Peter Levine (eds.) *The Deliberative Democracy Handbook: Strategies for Effective Civic Engagement in the 21st Century*. San Francisco: Jossey-Bass, 111–19.

Cutler, Fred, Richard Johnston, R. Kenneth Carty, André Blais and Patrick Fournier 2008. 'Deliberation, Information and Trust: The BC Citizens' Assembly as Agenda-Setter', in Mark E. Warren and Hilary Pearse (eds.) *Designing Deliberative Democracy: The British Columbia Citizens' Assembly*. Cambridge University Press, 166–91.

Dahl, Robert 1970. *After the Revolution*. New Haven: Yale University Press.

1989. *Democracy and Its Critics*. New Haven: Yale University Press.

1998. *On Democracy*. New Haven: Yale University Press.

Dalton, Russell J. 2004. *Democratic Challenges, Democratic Choices: The Erosion of Political Support in Advanced Industrial Democracies*. Oxford University Press.

Dalton, Russell J., Wilhelm Burklin and Andrew Drummond 2001. 'Public Opinion and Direct Democracy', *Journal of Democracy* 12: 141–53.

Davies, Celia, Margaret Wetherell and Elizabeth Barnett 2006. *Citizens at the Centre: Deliberative Participation in Healthcare Decisions*. Bristol: Polity Press.

Davies, Stella, Susan Elizabeth, Bec Hanley, Bill New and Bob Sang (eds.) 1998. *Ordinary Wisdom: Reflections on an Experiment in Citizenship and Health Care*. London: King's Fund.

de Borda Institute 2006. 'Voting Systems', www.deborda.org/votingsys.shtml.

Dienel, Peter 1996. 'Das "Burgergutachten" und seine Nebenwirkungen', trans. Corrine Wales as 'The "Citizens' Report" and Its Wider Effects', *Forum für Interdisziplinare Forschung* 17: 113–35.

Dienel, Peter and Ortwin Renn 1995. 'Planning Cells: A Gate to "Fractal" Mediation', in Ortwin Renn, Thomas Webler and Peter Wiedemann (eds.) *Fairness and Competence in Citizen Participation: Evaluating Models for Environmental Discourse*. Dordecht: Kluwer, 117–40.

Docter, Sharon and William H. Dutton 1998. 'The First Ammendment Online: Santa Monica's Public Electronic Network', in Roza Tsagarousianou, Damian Tambini and Cathy Bryan (eds.) *Cyberdemocracy: Technologies, Cities and Civic Networks*. London: Routledge, 125–51.

Dolowitz, David P. and David Marsh 2000. 'Learning from Abroad: The Role of Policy Transfer in Contemporary Policy-Making', *Governance* 13: 5–24.

Dryzek, John 2000. *Deliberative Democracy and Beyond*. Oxford University Press.

Dunn, John 2005. *Setting the People Free: The Story of Democracy*. London: Grove Atlantic.

East End Health Action, Greater Easterhouse Community Health Project, NHS Greater Glasgow, and Oxfam 2003. *Have You Been PA'd? Using Participatory Appraisal to Shape Local Services*. Glasgow: Oxfam GB.

Eckersley, Robyn 1992. *Environmentalism and Political Theory: Toward an Ecocentric Approach*. London: University College London Press.

Eisenberg, Avigail 2001. 'The Medium Is the Message: How Referendums Lead Us to Understand Equality', in Matthew Mendelsohn and Andrew Parkin (eds.) *Referendum Democracy: Citizens, Elites, and Deliberation in Referendum Campaigns*. Basingstoke: Palgrave, 147–65.

Electoral Commission 2003. *Compulsory Voting (Factsheet 06–04)*. London: Electoral Commission.

2004. *Hansard Society HeadsUp Internet Forum*. London: Electoral Commission.

Electoral System Civic Forum 2006. *Recommendations*. Amsterdam: Electoral System Civic Forum.

Electoral System Civic Forum Secretariat 2007. *Process Report*. Amsterdam: Electoral System Civic Forum Secretariat.

Elster, Jon 1998. 'Deliberation and Constitution Making', in Jon Elster (ed.) *Deliberative Democracy*. Cambridge University Press, 97–122.

EOS Gallop Europe 2002. *Flash Eurobarometer 135: Internet and the Public at Large*. Brussels: EOS Gallop Europe.

Ferguson, Ross 2006a. *Digital Dialogues: Interim Report, December 2005–August 2006*. London: Hansard Society / Department for Constitutional Affairs.

(ed.) 2006b. *TellParliament.net Interim Evaluation Report 2003–5*. London: Hansard Society.

Fiorino, Daniel J. 1990. 'Citizen Participation and Environmental Risk: A Survey of Institutional Mechanisms', *Science, Technology and Human Values* 15: 226–43.

Fischer, Frank 2000. *Citizens, Experts, and the Environment: The Politics of Local Knowledge*. Durham, NC: Duke University Press.

Fishkin, James S. 1991. *Democracy and Deliberation*. New Haven: Yale University Press.

1997. *The Voice of the People*. Durham, NC: Duke University Press.

2004. '*Online "Deliberative Poll" Gives Picture of Informed Public Opinion in Election'*. Research Paper, Centre for Deliberative Democracy, Stanford University, http://cdd.stanford.edu/research/index.html.

Fishkin, James S. and Cynthia Farrar 2005. 'Deliberative Polling', in John Gastil and Peter Levine (eds.) *The Deliberative Democracy Handbook: Strategies for Effective Civic Engagement in the 21st Century*. San Francisco: Jossey-Bass, 68–79.

Fishkin, James S. and Robert C. Luskin 2000. 'The Quest for Deliberative Democracy', in Michael Saward (ed.) *Democratic Innovation: Deliberation, Representation and Association*. London: Routledge, 17–28.

Fishkin, James S., Baogang He, Robert C. Luskin and Alice Siu 2006. 'Deliberative Democracy in an Unlikely Place: Deliberative Polling in China', Research Paper, Centre for Deliberative Democracy, Stanford University, http://cdd.stanford.edu/research/index.html.

Forester, John 1999. *The Deliberative Practitioner: Encouraging Participatory Planning Processes*. Cambridge, MA: MIT Press.

Freeman, Richard 2006. 'Learning in Public Policy', in Michael Moran, Martin Rein and Robert E. Goodin (eds.) *The Oxford Handbook of Public Policy*. Oxford University Press.

Frey, Bruno S. 1994. 'Direct Democracy: Politico-Economic Lessons from Swiss Experience', *The American Economic Review* 84: 338–42.

Frey, Bruno S. and Alois Stutzer 2006. 'Strengthening the Citizens' Role in International Organizations', *Review of International Organizations* 1: 27–43.

Fung, Archon 2003a. 'Deliberative Democracy, Chicago Style: Grass-Roots Governance in Policing and Public Education', in Archon Fung and Erik Olin Wright (eds.) *Deepening Democracy*. London: Verso, 111–43.

2003b. 'Survey Article: Recipes for Public Spheres: Eight Institutional Design Choices and Their Consequences', *Journal of Political Philosophy* 11: 338–67.

2004. *Empowered Participation: Reinventing Urban Democracy*. Princeton University Press.

2005. 'Varieties of Participation in Democratic Governance', Paper prepared for the Midwest Political Science Association Meeting, Chicago, April 7–10.

2007. 'Democratic Theory and Political Science: A Pragmatic Method of Constructing Engagement', *Amercian Journal of Political Science* 101: 443–58.

Gerber, Elizabeth R. 1999. *The Populist Paradox: Interest Group Influence and the Promise of Direct Legislation*. Princeton University Press.

Gerber, Elizabeth R. and Simon Hug 2001. 'Legislative Responses to Direct Legislation', in Matthew Mendelson and Andrew Parkin (eds.) *Referendum Democracy: Citizens, Elites, and Deliberation in Referendum Campaigns*. Basingstoke: Palgrave, 88–128.

Gibson, Rachel K. and Sarah Miskin 2002. 'Australia Decides? The Role of the Media in Deliberative Polling', in John Warhurst and Malcolm Mackerras (eds.) *Constitutional Politics*. St. Lucia: Queensland Press, 163–76.

Gibson, Rachel K., Andrea Rommele and Stephen J. Ward (eds.) 2004. *Electronic Democracy: Mobilisation, Organisation and Participation via New ICTs*. London: Routledge.

Goldfrank, Benjamin 2003. 'Making Participation Work in Porto Alegre', in Gianpaolo Baiocchi (ed.) *Radicals in Power: The Workers' Party (PT) and Experiments in Urban Democracy in Brazil*. London: Zed Books, 27–52.

Goldfrank, Benjamin and Aaron Schneider 2003. 'Restraining the Revolution or Deepening Democracy? The Workers' Party in Rio Grande do Sul', in Gianpaolo Baiocchi (ed.) *Radicals in Power: The Workers' Party (PT) and Experiments in Urban Democracy in Brazil*. London: Zed Books, 155–75.

Goodin, Robert E. 2005. 'Sequencing Deliberative Moments', *Acta Politica* **40**: 182–96.

　　2007. 'Enfranchising All Affected Interests, and Its Alternatives', *Philosophy and Public Affairs* **35**: 40–68.

Goodin, Robert E. and John S. Dryzek 2006. 'Deliberative Impact: The Macro-Political Uptake of Mini-Publics', *Politics and Society* **34**: 1–26.

Goodwin, Barbara 2005. *Justice by Lottery*. Exeter: Imprint Academic.

Gret, Marion and Yves Sintomer 2005. *The Porto Alegre Experiment: Learning Lessons for Better Democracy*. London: Zed Books.

Guidry, John A. and Pere Petit 2003. 'Faith in What Will Change: The PT Administration in Belém', in Gianpaolo Baiocchi (ed.) *Radicals in Power: The Workers' Party (PT) and Experiments in Urban Democracy in Brazil*. London: Zed Books, 53–78.

Gutmann, Amy 1996a. 'Democracy, Philosophy, and Justification', in Seyla Benhabib (ed.) *Democracy and Difference*. Princeton University Press, 340–7.

　　1996b. 'Responding to Racial Injustice', in K. A. Appiah and Amy Gutmann (eds.) *Color Conscious: The Political Morality of Race*. Princeton University Press, 106–78.

Habermas, Jürgen 1996. *Between Facts and Norms*. Cambridge: Polity.

Hall, Declan and John Stewart 1997. *Citizens' Juries in Local Government: Report from the LGMB on Pilot Projects*. Luton: LGMB.

Hansen, Mogens Herman. 1991. *The Athenian Democracy in the Age of Demosthenes: Structure, Principles, Ideology*. Oxford: Blackwell.

Harvard University Center for Urban Development Studies 2003. *Assessment of Participatory Budgeting in Brazil*. Washington, DC: Inter-American Development Bank.

Held, David 1995. *Democracy and the Global Order*. Cambridge: Polity.

Hendriks, Carolyn M. 2005. *Consensus Conferences and Planning Cells*. San Francisco: Jossey-Bass.

Henn, Matt, Mark Weinstein and Sarah Forrest 2005. 'Uninterested Youth? Young People's Attitudes towards Party Politics in Britain', *Political Studies* 53: 556–78.

Hirschman, Albert O. 1970. *Exit, Voice, and Loyalty: Responses to the Decline in Firms, Organizations and States*. Cambridge, MA: Harvard University Press.

House of Commons Select Committee on Public Administration 2001. *Sixth Report on Public Participation: Issues and Innovations*. London: HMSO.

Hughes, Colin 1994. 'Australia and New Zealand', in David Butler and Austin Ranney (eds.) *Referendums around the World: The Growing Use of Direct Democracy*. Washington, DC: AEI Press, 154–73.

IPPR 2004. *Lonely Citizens: Report of the Working Party on Active Citizenship*. London: IPPR.

Iyengar, Shanto, Robert C. Luskin and James S. Fishkin 2005. 'Deliberative Preferences in the Presidential Nomination Campaign: Evidence from an Online Deliberative Poll', paper available from The Center for Deliberative Democracy, Stanford University, http://cdd.stanford.edu/research/index.html.

Jacobs, Lawrence R., Theodore Marmor and Jonathan Oberlander 1998. *The Political Paradox of Rationing: The Case of the Oregon Health Plan*. Cambridge, MA: John F. Kennedy School of Government, Harvard University.

James, Michael Rabinder 2008. 'Descriptive Representation in Citizen Assemblies', in Mark E. Warren and Hilary Pearse (eds.) *Designing Deliberative Democracy: The British Columbia Citizens' Assembly*. Cambridge University Press, 106–26.

Janssen, Davy and Raphaël Kies 2004. 'Online Forums and Deliberative Democracy: Hypotheses, Variables and Methodologies', paper prepared for the Conference on 'Empirical Approaches to Deliberative Politics', European University Institute, Florence, 22–23 May.

Jenkins, Richard and Matthew Mendelsohn 2001. 'The News Media and Referendums', in Matthew Mendelsohn and Andrew Parkin (eds.) *Referendum Democracy: Citizens, Elites, and Deliberation in Referendum Campaigns*. Basingstoke: Palgrave, 211–30.

Jensen, Jakob Linaa 2003. 'Minnesota E-Democracy Survey Report', www.e-democracy.org/research/edemsurvey2002-jakobjensen.pdf.

John, Peter 1998. *Analysing Public Policy*. London: Pinter.

Jonsen, Albert R. and Stephen Toulmin 1998. *The Abuse of Casuistry: A History of Moral Reasoning*. Berkeley: University of California Press.

Joss, Simon 1998. 'Danish Consensus Conferences as a Model of Participatory Technology Assessment: An Impact Study of Consensus Conferences on Danish Parliament and Danish Public Debate', *Science and Public Policy* 25: 2–22.

Joss, Simon and John Durant (eds.) 1995. *Public Participation in Science: The Role of Consensus Conferences in Europe*. London: Science Museum.

Kamarck, Elaine Ciulla and Joseph S. Nye Jr. (eds.) 2002. *Governance.com: Democracy in the Information Age*. Washington, DC: Brookings Institution Press.

Kersting, Norbert and Harold Baldersheim (eds.) 2004. *Electronic Voting and Democracy*. Basingstoke: Palgrave.

Kersting, Norbert, Ronald Leenes and Jorgen Svensson 2004. 'Conclusions: Adopting Electronic Voting – Context Matters', in Norbert Kersting and Harold Baldersheim (eds.) *Electronic Voting and Democracy*. Basingstoke: Palgrave, 276–305.

Klüver, Lars 1995. 'Consensus Conferences at the Danish Board of Technology', in Simon Joss and John Durant (eds.) *Public Participation in Science: The Role of Consensus Conferences in Europe*. London: Science Museum, 41–52.

Kobach, Kris W. 1993. *The Referendum: Direct Democracy in Switzerland*. Aldershot: Dartmouth.

1994. 'Switzerland', in David Butler and Austin Ranney (eds.) *Referendums around the World*. Washington, DC: AEI Press, 98–153.

Kriesi, Hanspeter 2002. 'Individual Opinion Formation in a Direct Democratic Campaign', *British Journal of Political Science* 32: 171–91.

Kuper, Richard 1997. 'Deliberating Waste: The Hertfordshire Citizens' Jury', *Local Environment* 2: 139–53.

Kymlicka, Will 1999. 'Citizenship in an Era of Globalisation', in Ian Shapiro and Casiano Hacker-Cordon (eds.) *Democracy's Edges*. Cambridge University Press.

Lang, Amy 2007. 'But Is It for Real? The British Columbia Citizens' Assembly as a Model of State-Sponsored Citizen Empowerment', *Politics and Society* 35: 35–69.

2008. 'The Agenda Problem in Participatory Governance: Evidence from the BC Citizens' Assembly', in Mark E. Warren and Hilary Pearse (eds.) *Designing Deliberative Democracy: The British Columbia Citizens' Assembly*. Cambridge University Press, 85–105.

Latham, Robert and Saskia Sassen 2005a. 'Digital Formations: Constructing an Object of Study', in Robert Latham and Saskia Sassen (eds.) *Digital Formations: IT and New Architectures in the Global Realm*. Princeton University Press, 1–36.

(eds.) 2005b. *Digital Formations: IT and New Architectures in the Global Realm*. Princeton University Press.

Lijphart, Arend 1997. 'Unequal Participation: Democracy's Unresolved Dilemma', *American Political Science Review* 91: 1–14.

Linder, Wolf 1994. *Swiss Democracy*. New York: St. Martin's Press.

Lowndes, Vivien, Lawrence Pratchett and Gerry Stoker 2001. 'Trends in Public Participation: Part 2 – Citizens' Perspectives', *Public Administration* 79: 445–55.

Lukensmeyer, Carolyn J. and Steve Brigham 2002. 'Taking Democracy to Scale: Creating a Town Hall Meeting for the Twenty-First Century', *National Civic Review* 91: 351–66.

Lukensmeyer, Carolyn J., Joe Goldman and Steven Brigham 2005. 'A Town Meeting for the Twenty-First Century', in John Gastil and Peter Levine (eds.) *The Deliberative Democracy Handbook: Strategies for Effective Civic Engagement in the 21st Century*. San Francisco: Jossey-Bass, 154–63.

Lupia, Arthur 1994. 'Shortcuts versus Encyclopedias: Information and Voting Behavior in California Insurance Reform Elections', *Amercian Political Science Review* 88: 63–76.

Lupia, Arthur and Richard Johnston 2001. 'Are Voters to Blame? Voter Competence and Elite Maneuvers in Referendums', in Matthew Mendelsohn and Andrew Parkin (eds.) *Referendum Democracy: Citizens, Elites and Deliberation in Referendum Campaigns*. Basingstoke: Palgrave, 191–210.

Lupia, Arthur and John G. Matsusaka 2004. 'Direct Democracy: New Approaches to Old Questions', *Annual Review of Political Science* 7: 463–82.

Luskin, Robert C., James S. Fishkin and Shanto Iyengar 2006. 'Considered Opinions on U.S. Foreign Policy: Face-to-Face versus Online Deliberative Polling', paper available from The Center for Deliberative Democracy, Stanford University, http://cdd.stanford.edu/research/index.html.

Luskin, Robert C., James S. Fishkin and Roger Jowell 2002. 'Considered Opinions: Deliberative Polling in Britain', *British Journal of Political Science* 32: 455–87.

Macedo, Stephen 1999. *Deliberative Politics*. Oxford University Press.

MacPherson, C. B. 1977. *The Life and Times of Liberal Democracy*. Oxford University Press.

Magleby, David B. 1984. *Direct Legislation: Voting on Ballot Propositions in the United States*. Baltimore: Johns Hopkins University Press.

1994. 'Direct Legislation in the American States', in David Butler and Austin Ranney (eds.) *Referendums around the World: The Growing Use of Direct Democracy*. Washington, DC: AEI Press, 218–57.

Manin, Bernard 1997. *The Principles of Representative Government*. Cambridge University Press.

Mansbridge, Jane 1980. *Beyond Adversarial Democracy*. University of Chicago Press.

1996. 'Using Power/Fighting Power', in Seyla Benhabib (ed.) *Democracy and Difference*. Princeton University Press, 46–66.

1999. 'Everyday Talk in the Deliberative System', in Stephen Macedo (ed.) *Deliberative Politics: Essays on Democracy and Disagreement*. Oxford University Press, 211–39.

Mason, Andrew 2000. *Community, Solidarity and Belonging*. Cambridge University Press.

2004. 'Just Constraints', *British Journal of Political Science* 34: 251–68.

McIver, Shirley 1997. *An Evaluation of the King's Fund Citizens' Juries Programme*. Birmingham: Health Services Management Centre.

Mendelsohn, Matthew and Andrew Parkin 2001. 'Introduction: Referendum Democracy', in Matthew Mendelsohn and Andrew Parkin (eds.) *Referendum Democracy: Citizens, Elites and Deliberation in Referendum Campaigns*. Basingstoke: Palgrave, 1–22.

Merkle, Daniel M. 1996. 'The National Issues Convention Deliberative Poll', *Public Opinion Quarterly* 60: 588–619.

Miller, David 1992. 'Deliberative Democracy and Social Choice', *Political Studies (Special Issue: Prospects for Democracy)* 40: 54–67.

Moran, Margaret 2002. *Womenspeak: E-Democracy or He Democracy?* London: Fawcett Society (Occasional Paper).

Muhlberger, Peter 2005. 'The Virtual Agora Project: A Research Design for Studying Democratic Deliberation', *Journal of Public Deliberation* 1: Article 5, http://services.bepress.com/jpd/vol1/iss1/art5.

Nagel, Jack 1992. 'Combining Deliberation and Fair Representation in Community Health Decisions', *University of Pennsylvania Law Review* 140: 1965–85.

Newman, Janet, Marian Barnes, Helen Sullivan and Andrew Knops 2004. 'Public Participation and Collaborative Governance', *Journal of Social Policy* 33: 203–23.

Norris, Pippa 2001. *Digital Divide: Civic Engagement, Information Poverty, and the Internet Worldwide.* Cambridge University Press.

  2004. 'Will New Technology Boost Turnout?', in Norbert Kersting and Harold Baldersheim (eds.) *Electronic Voting and Democracy.* Basingstoke: Palgrave, 193–225.

Norton, Andy, Bella Bird, Karen Brock, Margaret Kakande and Carrie Turk 2001. *A Rough Guide to PPAs. Participatory Poverty Assessment: An Introduction to Theory and Practice.* London: Overseas Development Institute.

Nylen, William R. 2003. 'An Enduring Legacy? Popular Participation in the Aftermath of the Participatory Budgets of João Monlevade and Betim', in Gianpaolo Baiocchi (ed.) *Radicals in Power: The Workers' Party (PT) and Experiments in Urban Democracy in Brazil.* London: Zed Books, 91–112.

Offe, Claus and Ulrich K. Preuss 1991. 'Democratic Institutions and Moral Resources', in David Held (ed.) *Political Theory Today.* Cambridge: Polity, 143–71.

Ontario Citizens' Assembly on Electoral Reform 2007. *One Ballot, Two Votes: A New Way to Vote in Ontario.* Toronto: Ontario Citizens' Assembly on Electoral Reform.

Ontario Citizens' Assembly Secretariat 2007. *Democracy at Work: The Ontario Citizens' Assembly on Electoral Reform.* Toronto: Ontario Citizens' Assembly on Electoral Reform.

Oregon Health Decisions 1990. *Health Care in Common: Report on the Oregon Health Decisions Community Meeting Process.* Tualatin, OR: Oregon Health Decisions.

Palmer, Jane (ed.) 1999. *UK National Consensus Conference on Radioactive Waste: Final Report* Cambridge: UKCEED.

Parkinson, John 2001. 'Deliberative Democracy and Referendums', in Keith Dowding, James Hughes and Helen Margetts (eds.) *Challenges to Democracy.* Basingstoke: Palgrave, 131–52.

  2006. *Deliberating in the Real World: Problems of Legitimacy in Deliberative Democracy.* Oxford University Press.

Parliamentary Office of Science and Technology 2001. *Open Channels: Public Dialogue in Science and Technology.* London: POST.

Parry, Geraint 1972. 'Introduction', in Geraint Parry (ed.) *Participation in Politics.* Manchester University Press, 3–38.

Parsons, Wayne 1996. *Public Policy.* Aldershot: Edward Elgar.

Pateman, Carole 1970. *Participation and Democratic Theory.* Cambridge University Press.

Pattie, Charles, Patrick Seyd and Paul Whiteley 2005. *Citizenship in Britain: Values, Participation and Democracy.* Cambridge University Press.

Pharr, Susan and Robert D. Putnam (eds.) 1999. *Disaffected Democracies.* Princeton University Press.

Phillips, Anne 1991. *Engendering Democracy.* Cambridge: Polity.

  1995. *The Politics of Presence.* Oxford University Press.

Pitkin, Hannah 1967. *The Concept of Representation.* Berkeley: University of California Press.

Popadopoulos, Yannis and Philippe Warin 2007. 'Major Findings and Paths for Research: A Concluding Note', *European Journal of Political Research* **46**: 591–605.

Popkin, Samuel 1991. *The Reasoning Voter: Communication and Persuasion in Presidential Elections*. University of Chicago Press.

Posner, Richard A. 2003. *Law, Pragmatism, and Democracy*. Cambridge, MA: Harvard University Press.

Pratchett, Lawrence 2002. *The Implementation of Electronic Voting in the UK*. London: Local Government Association.

2006. *Understanding E-democracy Developments in Europe*. Strasbourg: Council of Europe.

2007. 'Local Democracy in Europe: Democratic X-Ray as the Basis for Comparative Analysis', *mimeo*.

Price, David 2000. 'Choices Without Reasons: Citizens' Juries and Policy Evaluation', *Journal of Medical Ethics* **26**: 272–6.

Price, Vincent and Peter Neijens 1998. 'Deliberative Polls: Toward Improved Measures of "Informed" Public Opinion', *International Journal of Public Opinion Research* **10**: 145–76.

Qvortrup, Matt 2005. *A Comparative Study of Referendums: Government by the People*. Manchester University Press.

Ratner, R. S. 2008. 'Communicative Rationality in the Citizens' Assembly and Referendum Processes', in Mark E. Warren and Hilary Pearse (eds.) *Designing Deliberative Democracy: The British Columbia Citizens' Assembly*. Cambridge University Press, 145–65.

Reeve, Andrew and Alan Ware 1992. *Electoral Systems*. London: Routledge.

Revill, Jo (2007). '"Sham" Citizens' Juries Face Controls', *The Observer*, 30 September.

Rihoux, Benoît and Wolfgang Rüdig 2006. 'Analyzing Greens in Power: Setting the Agenda', *European Journal of Political Research* **45**: S1–S33.

Royal Commission on Environmental Pollution 1998. *Setting Environmental Standards (Twenty-first Report)*. London: HMSO.

Sack, Warren 2005. 'Discourse Architecture and Very Large-Scale Conversation', in Robert Latham and Saskia Sassen (eds.) *Digital Formations: IT and New Architectures in the Global Realm*. Princeton University Press, 242–82.

Sanders, Lynn 1996. 'Against Deliberation', *Political Theory* **25**: 347–76.

Sang, Bob and Stella Davies 1998. 'Facilitating a Citizens' Jury: Working with "Perfect Strangers"', in Stella Davies, Susan Elizabeth, Bec Hanley, Bill New and Bob Sang (eds.) *Ordinary Wisdom; Reflections on an Experiment in Citizenship and Health Care*. London: King's Fund, 35–64.

Santos, Boaventura de Sousa 1998. 'Participatory Budgeting in Porto Alegre: Toward a Redistributive Democracy', *Politics and Society* **26**: 461–510.

Sartori, Giovanni 1987. *The Theory of Democracy Revisited*. Chatham House.

Saward, Michael 1998. *Terms of Democracy*. Cambridge: Polity.

2000. 'Direct and Deliberative Democracy', paper presented at the Copenhagen ECPR Joint Sessions. Copenhagen, 14–19 April.

2001. 'Making Democratic Connections: Political Equality, Deliberation and Direct Democracy', *Acta Politica* **36**: 361–79.

2003a. *Democracy*. Cambridge: Polity.

2003b. 'Enacting Democracy', *Political Studies* **51**: 161–79.

Saxonhouse, Arlene W. 1993. 'Athenian Democracy: Modern Mythmakers and Ancient Theorists', *PS: Political Science and Politics* **26**: 486–90.

Schlosberg, David, Stuart W. Shulman and Stephen Zavestoski 2006. 'Virtual Environmental Citizenship: Web-Based Public Participation in Rulemaking in the United States', in Andrew Dobson and Derek Bell (eds.) *Environmental Citizenship*. Cambridge, MA: MIT Press, 209–36.

Schneider, Aaron and Ben Goldfrank 2000. 'Budgets and Ballots in Brazil: Participatory Budgeting from the City to the State', *IDS Working Paper 149*. Brighton: Institute of Development Studies.

Schumpeter, Joseph 1976. *Capitalism, Socialism and Democracy*. London: Allen and Unwin.

Shapiro, Ian 2003. *The State of Democratic Theory*. Princeton University Press.

Silva, Marchelo Kunrath 2003. 'Participation by Design: The Experiences of Alvorada and Gravataí, Rio Grande do Sul, Brazil', in Gianpaolo Baiocchi (ed.) *Radicals in Power: The Workers' Party (PT) and Experiments in Urban Democracy in Brazil*. London: Zed Books, 113–30.

Sirianni, Carmen and Lewis Friedland 2001. *Civic Innovation in America: Community Empowerment, Public Policy, and the Movement for Civic Renewal*. Berkeley: University of California Press.

Smith, Daniel A. 1998. *Tax Crusaders and the Politics of Direct Democracy*. New York: Routledge.

Smith, Graham 2003. *Deliberative Democracy and the Environment*. London: Routledge.

2005. *Beyond the Ballot: 57 Democratic Innovations from around the World*. London: Power Inquiry. www.soton.ac.uk/ccd/events/SuppMat/Beyond%20the%20Ballot. pdf.

Smith, Graham and Susan Stephenson 2005. 'The Theory and Practice of Group Representation: Reflections on the Governance of Race Equality in Birmingham', *Public Administration* **83**: 323–43.

Smith, Graham and Corrine Wales 1999. 'The Theory and Practice of Citizens' Juries', *Policy and Politics* **27**: 295–308.

2000. 'Citizens' Juries and Deliberative Democracy', *Political Studies* **48**: 51–65.

Sniderman, Paul M., Richard A. Brody and Phillip E. Tetlock 1991. *Reasoning and Choice: Explorations in Political Psychology*. Cambridge University Press.

Somin, Ilya 1999. 'Voter Ignorance and the Democratic Ideal', *Critical Review*, **12**: 413–58.

Squires, Judith 2002. 'Deliberation and Decision-Making: Discontinuity in the Two-Track Model', in Maurizio Passarin D'Entreves (ed.) *Democracy as Public Deliberation: New Perspectives*. Manchester University Press, 133–56.

Stewart, John, Elizabeth Kendall and Anna Coote 1994. *Citizens' Juries*. London: IPPR.

Stoker, Gerry 1998. 'Governance as Theory: Five Propositions', *International Social Science Journal* **155**: 17–28.

Sturgis, Patrick, Caroline Roberts and Nick Allum 2005. 'A Different Take on the Deliberative Poll: Information, Deliberation and Attitude Constraint', *Public Opinion Quarterly* **69**: 30–65.

Sunstein, Cass R. 2000. 'Deliberative Trouble? Why Groups Go to Extremes', *Yale Law Journal* **110**: 71–119.

2001. *Republic.com*. Princeton University Press.

Talpin, Julien 2007. 'Who Governs in Participatory Budgeting Institutions? A Comparative Study of the Decision-Making Processes in Three European Cases of Participatory Budgeting', paper prepared for the CINEFOGO Conference 'Citizen Participation in Decision-Making', University of the West of England, Bristol, UK, 14–15 February.

Taylor, Charles 1994. 'The Politics of Recognition', in Amy Gutmann (ed.) *Multiculturalism*. Princeton University Press, 25–74.

Thompson, Dennis 2008. 'Who Should Govern Who Governs? The Role of Citizens in Reforming the Electoral System', in Mark E. Warren and Hilary Pearse (eds.) *Designing Deliberative Democracy: The British Columbia Citizens' Assembly*. Cambridge University Press, 20–49.

Thompson, Simon and Paul Hoggett 2001. 'The Emotional Dynamics of Deliberative Democracy', *Policy and Politics* **29**: 351–64.

Tomorrow's Europe 2007. 'EU Citizens Accept Need for Pension Reform, Resist Enlargement: First EU-Wide Deliberative Poll Reveals Citizens' Considered Preferences', press release. Paris: Notre Europe. http://cdd.stanford.edu/polls/eu/2007/eu-dpoll-pressrelease.pdf.

Traugott, Michael W. 2003. 'Can We Trust the Polls? It All Depends', *The Brookings Review* **21**: 8–11.

Trechsel, Alexander H., Raphaël Kies, Fernando Mendez and Philippe C. Schmitter 2003. *Evaluation of the Use of New Technologies in Order to Facilitate Democracy in Europe: E-democratising the Parliaments and Parties of Europe*. Florence: European University.

Tsagarousianou, Roza 1998. 'Electronic Democracy and the Public Sphere: Opportunities and Challenges', in Roza Tsagarousianou, Damian Tambini and Cathy Bryan (eds.) *Cyberdemocracy: Technologies, Cities and Civic Networks*. London: Routledge, 41–59.

Tsagarousianou, Roza, Damian Tambini and Cathy Bryan (eds.) 1998. *Cyberdemocracy: Technologies, Cities and Civic Networks*. London: Routledge.

Uhr, John 2002. 'Rewriting the Referendum Rules', in John Warhurst and Malcolm Mackerras (eds.) *Constitutional Politics*. St Lucia: University of Queensland Press, 177–200.

Verba, Sidney, Norman H. Nie and Jae-On Kim 1978. *Participation and Political Equality*. Cambridge University Press.

Wagle, Swarnim and Parmesh Shah 2003. *Case Study 2 – Porto Alegre, Brazil: Participatory Approaches in Budgeting and Public Expenditure Management (Note No. 71)*. Washington, DC: Social Development Publications, World Bank.

Warhurst, John and Malcolm Mackerras (eds.) 2002. *Constitutional Politics*. St Lucia: University of Queensland Press.

Warren, Mark E. 1996. 'What Should We Expect from More Democracy? Radically Democratic Responses to Politics', *Political Theory* **24**: 241–70.

(ed.) 1999. *Democracy and Trust*. Cambridge University Press.

2001. *Democracy and Association*. Princeton University Press.

2008. 'Citizen Representatives', in Mark E. Warren and Hilary Pearse (eds.) *Designing Deliberative Democracy: The British Columbia Citizens' Assembly*. Cambridge University Press, 50–69.

Warren, Mark E. and Hilary Pearse (eds.) 2008a. *Designing Deliberative Democracy: The British Columbia Citizens' Assembly*. Cambridge University Press.

2008b. 'Introduction', in Mark E. Warren and Hilary Pearse (eds.) *Designing Deliberative Democracy: The British Columbia Citizens' Assembly*. Cambridge University Press, 1–19.

Watson, Tom and Mark Tami 2001. *Making Voting Compulsory*. London: Fabian Society.

Wodak, Ruth and Scott Wright 2006. 'The European Union in Cyberspace: Multilingual Democratic Participation in a Virtual Public Sphere', *Journal of Language and Politics* **5**: 251–75.

World Bank 1996. *The World Bank Participation Sourcebook*. Washington, DC: World Bank.

Wright, Scott 2006. 'Government-Run Online Discussion Fora: Moderation, Censorship and the Shadow of Control', *British Journal of Politics and International Relations* **8**: 550–68.

Wright, Scott and John Street 2007. 'Democracy, Deliberation and Design: The Case of Online Discussion Forums', *New Media and Society* **9**: 849–69.

Young, Iris Marion 1990. *Justice and the Politics of Difference*. Princeton University Press.

2000. *Inclusion and Democracy*. Oxford University Press.

Zimmerman, Joseph F. 1999. *The New England Town Meeting: Democracy in Action*. Westport: Praeger.

Index